Mute Phone Calls

Mute
Phone Calls

and Other Stories

BY

RUTH ZERNOVA

Translated by Ann Harleman,
Martha Kitchen, and Helen Reeve

Selected, Edited, and with an

Introduction by Helen Reeve

RUTGERS UNIVERSITY PRESS

New Brunswick, New Jersey

Library of Congress Cataloging-in-Publication Data

Zernova, Ruf´ Aleksandrovna.
    Mute phone calls and other stories / by Ruth Zernova; translated
by Ann Harleman, Martha Kitchen, and Helen Reeve; selected, edited
and with introduction by Helen Reeve.
        p.   cm.
    Translated from Russian.
    ISBN 0-8135-1735-4 (cloth)—ISBN 0-8135-1736-2 (pbk.)
    1. Zernova, Ruf´ Aleksandrovna—Translations into English.
I. Reeve, Helen. II. Title.
PG3490.E7A26 1991
891.73´44—dc20   91-4786
                                                                   CIP

British Cataloging-in-Publication information available

Contents

Preface and Acknowledgments

The idea for a collection of stories by Ruth Zernova grew out of my continuing delight with her writing and the realization that English-speaking readers have been denied the pleasure of knowing her stories. The American and English publishing markets of the last several decades have insisted on a specific kind of Russian fiction by a particular kind of Soviet writer—the political writer protesting against censorship, against ideology, against outright repression. It is true that most of such literature could be printed only outside the Soviet Union, but our interest in it reflected a definite Cold War attitude. If we consider Soviet literature in its widest sense, we can see that the English-speaking reader has been shortchanged.

The academic world has been much more hospitable than the commercial to a richer variety of Russian fiction. My first translation of a Zernova story, "A Long, Long Summer," was for a course on Women in Literature in which students read fiction from several countries. We did not deal in political questions, rather we explored new theories in criticism and whether women writers have a different focus or specific stylistic characteristics. Zernova's story, where a cloudless summer sky serves as a backdrop for fairly sharp moral and political insights, surprised us all—particularly because it sustains a powerful sense of calm, of serene happiness. For the following course, I translated "Mute Phone Calls," darker in mood and color than "A Long, Long Summer," yet lively, with an upbeat (but *not* happy) ending. My students were fascinated by the honesty, the ease, the seriousness, and the clarity of her stories, by her world, which they had not seen before.

Eventually I translated four more Zernova stories and succeeded in interesting a young colleague, Martha Kitchen, in translating two more—all with the conviction that we were bringing something new to the English-speaking reader. (Zernova's stories had been translated into a number of European languages.) Recently we learned that we were not alone in our endeavor: Ann Harleman was translating Zernova's recent collection *Zhenskie rasskazy* (Women's Stories). We decided to combine our efforts in order to present those stories which most successfully express Zernova's voice and Zernova's world.

All three of us are grateful to the author for having reviewed these translations with us, providing us with references we might have otherwise missed, and offering invaluable advice.

Ann Harleman would like to thank Sam Driver and Catherine Chvany for their very great help with aspects of content and style; the Rockefeller Foundation and the National Endowment for the Humanities for their generous financial support; and the Santa Cruz Translation Institute and the staff of the Villa Serbelloni at Bellagio for providing the ideal working atmosphere.

I thank warmly Heddy Kalikoff, Glenn Young, and Martha Kitchen for their many editorial suggestions at various stages of my work, and particularly for their faith in my project.

Finally, my special gratitude goes to Regula Noetzli for her rare combination of sensitivity, endurance, and professionalism.

Helen Reeve
Connecticut College
June 1991

Mute Phone Calls

Introduction

It is generally held that novels create worlds of their own, but short stories do not. Ruth Zernova's stories challenge this presumption. She projects a very clear sense of a Russian world that is also specifically her own, a world that embraces many elements, the sunny exuberance of the Ukraine, the speech and humor of Odessa, the erudition of the Leningrad intelligentsia, the seasonal changes at a camp in the Altai. She is at home with classical Russian and Western European literature, as well as detective stories and popular magazines. She plays classical piano, but also sings Russian folk songs and popular prison songs. Mainly, she writes; and she tells stories about herself and her world.

Zernova was born in 1919 in Tiraspol, near Odessa, into a family of professionals; her father was a commodities researcher, her mother, a teacher. She remembers a happy childhood, full of fun and play. The children were brought up learning languages; she learned French from a *Mademoiselle* who came to their house three times a week; German from a *Fräulein* who took her and several other boys and girls for long walks during which speaking German was the rule. Naturally, there were years of piano lessons. Her first original writing was at the age of four. She remembers printing carefully in large letters in a fat notebook, "A PLAY, ACT I, SCENE I—IRA, RUNNING IN, SAYS 'LISTEN, LENA' "—which filled the page, and that ended that. When she was eight, she read all of Lermontov's *Hero of Our Time,* with much excitement. At school, where instruction was in both Russian and Ukrainian, she would often be asked to write for festive occasions like International Youth Day.

When she attended high school in Odessa, she thought the large port city very cosmopolitan, full of different nationalities—Russians and Ukrainians, Germans and Italians, Greeks and Frenchmen and Jews. The family lived in a large apartment, spacious at first, which gradually became crowded as they had to accept other tenants and their families. After graduating in 1936, Zernova left for Leningrad to attend the Leningrad Institute of Philosophy, Literature, and History, which admitted only one of every eight applicants. The Institute soon merged with Leningrad University, where she continued to study French, although the most memorable lectures were those of the top scholars of Russian literature. She also studied German with the famous Professor Propp. And it was while studying in Leningrad that she gathered up her courage to call on Anna Akhmatova, who invited her back and asked to hear her poems.

Students lived modestly: six to a room. The food was poor; clothes were simple—dressing up for parties meant adding a collar to the one basic black dress and wearing lots of lipstick and perfume. One fellow student, Levinton, wrote poems to Zernova (bad ones, she says). In her second year, she and other students of French were asked if they would go abroad, and if they could learn Spanish quickly. They were to work as translators for Soviet advisors in the Spanish Civil War. She could not wait to see the big world! And the struggle in Spain was important; she wanted to get to the very front lines. Instead, she was assigned to headquarters and spent eight months in Catalonia, where she was wounded but soon recovered. After the retreat of the Republicans and Communists, she returned via Paris to Leningrad. It was 1939, and the returning university students were no longer allowed to finish their studies but were given immediate work assignments. Zernova joined the office staff of the Ministry of the Navy in Moscow.

During the German invasion she spent a few years in Tashkent, to which many of her family and friends had been evacuated. At first she tried to resume her studies, but decided instead to work for TASS as a translator, typist, and editor for their *slukhachi* for the East, the listeners who monitored broadcasts from Turkey, India, and Persia. It was in Tashkent that she met her future husband Ilya Serman, who had been discharged after being wounded at the front and was now busy finishing his dissertation on *Crime and Punishment*—which she undertook to type. Their daughter Nina was born in Tashkent, in 1944, and their son Mark in Leningrad, in 1946.

Zernova finished Leningrad University in 1947. She began writing articles and reviews for *Zvezda* [Star], and took the job of translating from French the early nineteenth-century works of Charles Nodier. She was thought of as a writer, and she and her husband enjoyed the friendship of many literary people. These active, productive years ended abruptly with their arrests in 1949 and exile to separate camps. The children, Mark two and Nina four, stayed behind, separated not only from their parents but from each other, staying with different relatives until 1954 when Ruth and Ilya were finally released.

In camp, Ruth wrote her first story, "Tonechka," in pencil, in a notebook sent her from home. It is a love story in the form of a whispered conversation between the young Tonechka and another, older prisoner as they marched to work under convoy. Upon Zernova's return to Leningrad, the story was widely read in manuscript, and was immediately noticed. Critic and writer Pavel Gromov declared it "a lovely story"; he took it to the famous Vera Panova, novelist and short story writer, who was gathering material for an anthology of short stories. She liked "Tonechka" very much and asked to see another story by Zernova. The young writer immediately wrote "Kuzka's Mother" and happily submitted it to Panova. But in the autumn of 1956 with the invasion of Hungary the political winds changed again. Panova's anthology was cancelled and withdrawn from publication, and she was openly criticized at a Writers' Union meeting. "Tonechka" and "Kuzka's Mother" were returned to Zernova ("Tonechka" to be published eight years later, and "Kuzka's Mother" twenty-five years later, in the United States).

Like Panova and others, Ruth also kept writing for journals, brief pieces dealing with moral issues for the popular magazine *Yunost* [Youth]. But fiction engaged her much more. Another prestigious magazine, *Ogonyok* [The Flame], published her next short story, "Scorpion Berries." This story received huge acclaim, and won for Zernova the *Ogonyok* fiction prize. (It is interesting that our journals and publishers did not pick it up—was it too mild politically? or too regional in its setting?) Many Soviet readers identifying with the characters wrote to her asking her about the story. "Scorpion Berries" also stirred up many writers and critics. Some declared she was born to be famous, others praised the bright, Ukrainian spirit, the bold colors, and southern exuberance of the story, still others wondered how she could be so forgiving (toward Nazi sympathizers). Certain critics praised "Scorpion Berries" for standing out against the dominant Soviet fiction, which was controlled in emotion and well-crafted in design but too cold at heart. Aleksandr A. Bek, the Stalin prize laureate, called it "marvelous."

Panova was more cautious; she did not like it as well as "Tonechka." She considered "Scorpion Berries" too boisterous, free, or even lush. That year Panova held her usual writing seminar "for the young writers from the northwest," where Zernova worked alongside Sergei Tkhorzhevsky, Yeligy Stavsky, Rid Grachev, and two other writers. They all respected Panova deeply as an accomplished, experienced, and talented writer and teacher who commanded unquestioning respect. In the case of "Scorpion Berries," however, they differed with her, as did the general reader. It was published separately, and then in anthologies; it was reviewed in the major magazines. Her subsequent stories were quickly published in the leading magazines *Ogonyok* and *Novy Mir*. Zernova soon joined the Writers' Union.

After the publication of the anthology *Scorpion Berries* in 1961, other collections followed: *Light and Shadow* (1963); *Bacalao* (1963); *The Sunny Side* (1968); *A Long, Long Summer* (1968); *Stories about Anton* (1968); and (not the present collection, despite the title) *Mute Phone Calls* (1974). She was also invited by Mosfilm to write screenplays.

In the mid-seventies, the political climate changed again, but this time Zernova and Serman emigrated to Israel, where she continued to write. Her stories and essays began appearing in *Russkaya mysl* [Russian Thought] and *Ekho* [Echo] in Paris and *Vremya i my* [Our Time and We] in Israel, and in *Novy amerikanets* [The New American] and *Novoe russkoye slovo* [The New Russian Word] in New York. She has also published a translation of a large biography of Golda Meier, another collection of all (but one) new stories, *Women's Stories* (1981), and a collection of essays, *It Was In Our Times* (1988). *Novy zhurnal* in New York may soon publish some of her stories, and a collection of stories,

Israel and Its Surroundings, has just been published by Alia in Jerusalem.

This collection, *Mute Phone Calls and Other Stories,* Zernova's first book in English, spans three decades of her writing career, from "Kuzka's Mother" to "Umbria's Tender Haze." Yet the focus of the collection is not on the author's development as a writer, but on the distinct world and voice she creates as a woman writer, different from writers and poets closest to her, like Vera Panova and Frida Vigdorova, or at some distance, Anna Akhmatova, Olga Berggolts, and Margarita Aliger. Her prose ranges more freely, in language, from vernacular and regional to richly descriptive and poetic, and in narrative technique, from relying on the slightest thread of a story to knitting together an intricately contrasting setting using flashbacks and inner dialogues. She is less bound or motivated by her Soviet setting—whether Socialist realism and ideology or prison experiences—than her contemporaries. She seems less concerned with crafting a story than letting it grow (novel-like) and catching a multitude of bright unexpected moments in snatches of conversations or unfinished thoughts. The reader soon learns to listen to the silences as part of the music.

Zernova's work recalls Boris Eikhenbaum's idea that it is a woman's task to preserve memory and to pass it on, to forge a link between generations. Although she accomplishes far more in her writing than that, she invariably brings her characters (and her readers) to confront the past, present, and future. The narrator of "A Long, Long Summer," a writer herself, observes the little preschoolers in the summer camp beyond her fence with affection and joy, through which she makes us sense her pain of never having seen her own children at that age (she was in the Gulag then). Her pain is never described directly but emerges here and there, in her mention of how only little Alyosha is still wearing sandals when it turns cold, or how deeply Tanechka misses grown-up Shurik. The contrast of what is seen and said about the gaily playing children, and what is created in the tension of the unstated reality of the daily life (divorces, uncomprehending teachers, camp memories) emerges through the interplay among the many figures. The setting suggests Russia in a few strokes— the picket fence, the summer porch with the typewriter, the candy in the little brown bag, a Turgenev-like sense of summer lightness.

"Witches" anchors itself more narrowly in women talk: memory, gossip, beliefs, fears, witchcraft—a strong world of imaginings that, on the other hand, in "Umbria's Tender Haze" turns into a poetic world of colors, sounds, and premonitions of religious and artistic experience. Between these stories lie some that relive camp and war experiences ("Bacalao," "The Bronze Bull," "Kuzka's Mother") or growing political persecution ("Elizabeth Arden"), but always out of a woman's sense of love, or friendship, or instinct of family loyalty ("Scorpion Berries"). In no way heroic or exceptional, and often even lost and despairing, the women in these stories emerge capable of reclaiming their lives, lives of inner experience, lives that bring with them the past, "the sweetness of remembering."

Helen Reeve
Connecticut College
1991

A Long, Long Summer

in memory of Frida Vigdorova

"AND we thought you were bad guys."

That is just how he said it, without hesitating or even pausing slightly to prepare us for it.

That evening I caught my husband studying his face in the mirror.

"So you want to figure out why we look like bad guys to them," I guessed.

"Ridiculous," said he. "They're only playing."

This is their third day here. They came from Leningrad to live in the country, on the other side of the rather low, sparse picket fence that separates the two properties. On their first day, dizzy from the sun, the air, the tall grass, they ran about the place, yelled victory, climbed in their toy houses and darted out again, rode the wooden horses, and drove along the paths in a small open wagon that by evening had only three wheels. In their white linen hats they all look alike, just like ants. And, like ants, they are busy doing things we don't understand.

The sound of a tambourine opens their day. An elderly teacher with a patient, worn-out face strikes the tambourine and calls: "The middle group—this way!"

Somewhere over there other tambourines and voices can be heard: "Little ones—to me! Seniors—over here, please!" We watch the middle group since they bustle around right under our porch windows. We're beginning to recognize some of them: the tanned boy—when did he manage to get a tan?—such narrow eyes—he is the one who made faces during the first exercise session. We name him Timur. And the well-grown snub-nosed strong fellow— that's Hefty. And the girl with the "sorceress" hairdo—long blond braids down her shoulders, blond bangs to the bridge of her nose. We watch these three. My painter friend told me some time ago that she enjoys children in the abstract, "aesthetically": their proportions, their movements. But to spend a whole day among little children—no, thanks!

3

I still think that, maybe, I would. Perhaps because my life turned out so that I didn't see my children when they were that age. Circumstances separated us from them when the older girl was four, and the younger boy two; and then I saw them again as schoolchildren. Their childhood wasn't granted me; perhaps that is why other children fascinate me so. These, the middle ones.

We fascinate them. On the second day, they discovered us, looking inquisitively at our house through the fence. We opened a window on our porch—Timur and Hefty ran up a bit closer, and behind them, tentatively, the Sorceress. They whispered something to each other and cast sidelong glances at us. But they couldn't decide to start talking to us. That was the second day.

On the third day, under our window, I find a purple segment from a toy pyramid. I walk over to the fence and ask:

"Who lost this?"

Timur approaches, and behind him, slightly pigeon-toed, Hefty.

"Must've been Olenka," says Timur, with a shy, but cunning smile. "She's little, she's always leaving things around the place. I'll give it back to her!"

The Sorceress comes running, skipping—but stops short, stays further back.

"What's that tapping in your place?" asks Hefty.

"When you're sitting at your table something keeps tapping. We can hear it."

"That's my typewriter."

"Can we see it?"

"Maybe."

"And we thought you were bad guys," says Timur.

That is how we got to know each other.

And now our peace is gone.

In the morning, before the tambourine, we hear a shout:

"Their window's open!"

Like sparrows they rush to the fence.

"How many rooms've you got?"

"How big's your family?"

"Where are you going?"

"When are you coming back?"

And when I get up—everybody shouts: "Don't shut your window!"

4

They bring their friends to the fence: this is Olenka, she is little, she was crying yesterday. Did you hear her? And this is Stepan.

Timur turns out to be Alyosha, Hefty—Kostya, and the Sorceress—Tanya Serova. Besides her, there are two more Tanyas in their group. And yes, of course, there are several Natashas, two Iras, and two Andreys.

But Stepans—just one.

Stepan has an angel's face and a perfectly round mouth. He doesn't talk to us. He throws braided tufts of grass into our garden and then falls flat, deftly, like a real grenadier. Obviously, they have a television in their house.

Tanya Serova says:

"I've got three daddies; and a little Igoryochek."

"And I've got a dog Kazbek," says Alyosha. "A real hunting dog. He happens to live in Estonia too. In the fall we'll go there again. You know, they've got everything in Estonia, chickens, and dairy stuff, and everything. . . ."

"I'm going on a trip next fall too!" shouts Tanya Serova. "And I've got dogs! Two! Three! And cats, they walk . . . they walk up and down the stairs . . . where we live . . . where we're going to live."

Three dogs—I can understand that. But three daddies? Why such a multitude?

It is evening. They have all had dinner and gone to bed. All is quiet. Only—for the last time today—Olenka is crying again.

When Olenka cries the whole kindergarten comes running. Olenka's crying is a spectacle. She sobs loudly, with feeling, roars like a lion, or lets out a long sustained shriek like a ship's siren. Her tears don't shed, but drop like peas on her chest and in her lap. . . . For a moment she'll stop crying and look around to see if her audience is assembled—and then she'll turn it on all over again.

Olenka isn't in any program. She is not quite three, and is two or three years younger than our "middle" group. She lives here with her mother who works either as a nurse or a cook. During quiet hours she sometimes goes walking around the huge garden quite alone, softly, as if she were listening for something; or she might be making mudpies in the sandbox all by herself. She likes to cry when she's surrounded by others, but she prefers to play alone.

Our middle ones, though, are a gregarious bunch. They always share their games. In the morning, they come running to the fence and call to me:

"We dreamed of parents' day!"

Can it really be that they dream the same dreams?

"When are your kids going to be here?"

"My daughter isn't coming, she's practice-teaching. But my son will."

"When's he coming? Today?"

"As soon's he's done with exams."

"What grade's he in?"

"He's not in a grade, he's in college."

"What if he comes today?"

"He might."

"What's his name?"

"Shurik."

"I've got a Shurik too," says Kostya. "He lives on our block. He's a driver."

"My brother's name is Shurik," says pretty Inga.

And Tanya Serova:

"I'll go meet your Shurik. I'll go out to the road and meet him."

"You're not supposed to go on the road!" says Kostya.

"But I'll go with somebody else."

"And now we'll all go to the clearing—you stay—and we'll go berry picking."

For some reason, Alyosha is quiet. He stares me down with his black eyes, smiling awkwardly, and keeps silent. His teeth are black too—his loving parents, I bet, keep feeding him candy. Finally he asks:

"Is it true that Stepanka came right up under your window?"

"That was yesterday," says Tanya Serova.

Actually, it happened this morning. Their nap divides their day in half, all that happened in the morning is called "yesterday." After all, so much has happened since this morning, and then there was naptime. . . .

Stepan is an enterprising fellow. Not one of the other children thought that you could simply climb over the fence, not even

Alyosha. But Stepan figured it out. Suddenly his white hat popped up right under my window. He asked if he could play with my typewriter, got 'no' for an answer, and dashed off. And now, it looks like Alyosha too is trying to think of a way of getting into our garden. He and Stepan are friends. Both get into things, both get punished, both get it constantly from the teacher: "Stepan—you again? Alyosha—you again?"

"And whose bike is that?" asks Kostya. "I saw it in your room. Whose bike is it, huh?"

"That's Shurik's."

"Your Shurik knows how to ride it?"

"Yes, he does."

"Is he gonna give us a ride?"

"I bet he will."

"When? Wish he'd get here soon."

Suddenly he is here! Huge, with black eyebrows, wonderful. Exams are over—passed well or not, who knows—but they are over. No field work required this year. What's more, he's done his farming stint. Two months' freedom ahead of him, two whole months of complete freedom.

"It is quiet here, like in a railroad station," says he. "You sure picked out a good vacation spot."

He gulps down his dinner quickly, and part of ours as well. Then he takes his bicycle out and begins pumping up the tires. I open the porch window and see the whole middle group at the fence in prayerful silence, watching a man's beautiful work. Only Kostya notices me, winks, and calls out: "We're just watching!"

Shurik straightens up and notices them.

"Hi!" says he. "I'm going to the store. Can I get anybody anything?"

They feel awkward. What could they want? But Stepan, pulling himself up by his elbows, dangles on the fence easily, like a marionette, and says quite seriously:

"You gonna give me a ride on your bike?"

"Sure!" promises Shurik. "You bet I will! And I'll give you one too," says he to Vova who has a constant cold. "And you."

"Me too?" asks Tanya Serova, trying to push her face between the slats.

"Sure."

And he's off.

From this moment on we cease to exist in our own right. We are Shurik's mommy and daddy, that is our station in life.

At eight in the morning, before the tambourine, behind the fence we hear, drawn out and piercing:

"Shuuu-rik!"

The "rik" sounds short and sharp.

They watch out for him, and rush to the fence as soon as he appears, then run out onto the street to take a closer look. Stepan once brought him two cookies "Sadko"—probably out of a package from home. Alyosha conducts long intellectual discussions with him.

"But d'you know why our blood doesn't spill out? It's all in little pellets, and these pellets run after each other, 'round and 'round."

"And do you know how to say 'table' in German? Der Tisch!"

"And do you know where palm trees grow out in the open? In Sukhumi."

"How do you know that?" asks Shurik, deafened by this stream of information.

"My Granma tells me. She works in the school."

It is clear that the most devoted person is Tanya Serova. She is first to rush out from the bedroom shouting:

"Shuu-rik!"

"Tanya, he's still asleep. He went to bed late."

Shurik now sleeps at least twelve hours. He's exhausted from his studies.

"Wake him up. We want to see him. 'Cause we like him a lot."

As soon as he appears she is glued to the fence and doesn't budge. She makes faces, astounding faces, as she tells her no less astounding stories.

"Before, we lived with daddy Vasya. That's when I was real real little. And then we moved and lived with daddy Tolya. And now we're gonna move again, to a separate place, three rooms, and everyone will have his own room, and we'll be there by ourselves with daddy Oleg. I've got three daddies. And Grampa got buried in a ditch, when there was war. And I cried and cried."

"When was that? During the war?"

"Sure!" she agrees, doesn't hesitate for a moment. She goes on: "And I also have a little Igoryochek, he's in the nursery."

"What a liar she is!" Shurik says to me afterwards in respectful astonishment. "You never know with her: is she making it up, or lying? After all, there's a basic difference between the two."

Why do they like him so much? Because he rides a bicycle? He hasn't given them a single ride yet. He says to me: "I've got to get permission from the teacher, but I don't feel like asking her. She might think I'm coming on to her." So I say to him:

"The very idea! The teacher is much older than you are. She wouldn't be interested in you."

"I don't mean that one. There's another one, with a braid, in a blue smock."

True, there is another one. I thought she was with the seniors. But she too appears to work with "our" group. They work in shifts.

"Hey, on the fence, everybody," commands Shurik. "I'll take a picture of you."

He picks them up, one by one, and sets them on the fence. Here are both Natashas, and Vova with his cold, and Andryusha, and pretty Inga. And in the middle—our favorites: Alyosha, Kostya, Tanya Serova, and Stepan.

"And then we'll get the pictures, right, Shurik? You'll give us the pictures?"

"Of course!" says Shurik. "Tomorrow I'll go into town and have them developed."

I can see it happening. He is getting bored out here in the country.

From our window we can see a dead fir tree. Its branches start out low, as if to ask: Why are you all running around here and not paying attention to me?

Stepan did. As soon as the teacher turned away—Stepan was there: his white hat lay dropped somewhere, his hair tousled at the back of his head, his face concentrated and matter-of-fact. In an instant he was nearly at the top. The teacher barely managed to get him down.

A minute later he was bringing some water over in a wheelbarrow, to make mud pies. And his buddy Alyosha ran behind him honking like a dumptruck.

Am I seeing things, or is it really so? These two never talk to each other; they're always together, next to each other; they are comfortable and intent on playing together, but they have no time to talk. And yet Alyosha enjoys having a conversation.

Stepan is an inventive fellow. The other day it stopped raining. Everybody was delighted to slosh around in the puddles with their rubber boots. But Stepan got a bit of string somewhere, tied it to a stick, and sat at the edge of the puddle: "I'm gonna catch me some fish!" For this inventiveness he catches something else quite often from his teacher.

The teacher—the elderly one, with a lemon sour expression—has started watching our porch too. She and I say hello now, she smiles when she sees us—adding sugar to the lemon. But the second one, the one with the braid, pretends that we don't even exist.

Shurik never managed to meet her. He's apparently fully booked up for the season. One day a "Volga" drives up to our cottage; a girl whom I've disliked for some time gets out, accompanied by an elderly man I've never met. Turns out he's her dad. He drove her to our place although we'd never met him before in our lives.

We are sitting on our porch with him, groping for a topic of conversation. But her dad is only interested in cars, and we can barely tell a Volga from a Moskvich. Finally he launches into a monologue, tells us about the construction of an automobile plant, and the rest of us fall silent with a sigh of relief.

Shurik and his girl, however, have slipped out, and stopped by the fence. On the other side, the little kids have gathered. I can't hear what they are saying, but I notice that Tanya's face shows boredom. Shurik calls over to us:

"We're going to the bay!"

Now the story about the automobile plant comes to a halt. Dad interrupts himself and gets up:

"I guess I'll drive them over, if you don't mind."

"Not at all, by all means, go ahead."

"I like that quay a lot."

Now that could have been our signal to start talking about local road construction, a great conversation might have developed. But he left.

"Come, wash your feet, wash your feet!" shouts one of the

nannies under our window. "Stepan, I'm talking to you! Tanya Serova, how did you get your legs all scratched up? I'll get the doctor to put iodine on them."

Tanya keeps getting scratches on her knees and nettle burns on her hands. She explores for worms and caterpillars, takes flowers apart, digs little holes in the ground, and pries into ant hills. Why do these crawling creatures fascinate her?

It must hurt when they rub the washcloth over her scratches and scabs. But she says nothing. She is afraid of iodine. Perhaps she is proud.

Ten minutes later, just before dinner, I hear bitter, desperate crying. I look out the window—it's Tanya Serova. The proud Tanya Serova is sobbing desolately; her nose is swollen, and she wipes her eyes with her loose hair like Mary Magdalene.

Vova with his cold is trying to stroke her head; but she pushes him away with her elbow and moves off—she is not interested in pity. What happened? Kostya runs after her, talking as he follows her, but she shrugs him off too. No, she doesn't need anybody— nobody can help her now—not even grown-ups. She runs to the deep end of the garden where we cannot see her or her misery.

"They'll cut her belly open!" explains Alyosha, and his face glows with excitement. "The teacher said they'll cut her belly open. 'Cause she ate raw potatoes!"

"They'll cut her belly open!" triumphantly shouts little Andrey. "Yesterday'll be parents' day and they'll cut her belly open."

"Yesterday!" Alyosha mocks. "You mean 'tomorrow.' "

Don't they feel sorry for Tanya? Are they simply cruel, these children? Or does interest in such an unusual event surpass all other emotions—sympathy, pity, compassion? And somewhere deep in the garden proud Tanya cries from terror and contrition, and no one dares console her because she forbids them to see her tears.

After naptime she quietly turns up again by the fence; no one mentions tears or raw potatoes. She says to Shurik:

"My daddy has a car too!"

"Just one?" asks Shurik.

"Two!" answers Tanya without hesitation.

"I thought so," says Shurik approvingly.

I like Tanya Serova very much. And not just "aesthetically"—

although, from that point of view, one could watch her all day with pleasure. I like her proud courage.

It is parents' day. The middle group settles down with all the parents in a special meeting place—under our windows. The parents look their children over, adjust their collars and trousers, hug them—and then feed them, feed them, and feed them. Maybe, deep down, they suspect that they've been starved here? The children don't mind, they oblige for once; they just keep eating. They just had lunch, and they'll soon have supper—the small mouths swallow and swallow as if they were bottomless.

Tanya's daddy and mommy come to visit her. Mommy is young, pretty, fashionably dressed. So, she has managed to run through three husbands? Daddy is very affectionate with Tanya—he must be a good person.

Stepan's mother keeps chasing after her son all over the place. They are very like each other: round faced, an O for a mouth, fair-haired. Neither one can keep still for two seconds.

But Kostya sits quietly by his mother. They talk, slowly, seriously. Kostya's mother is tall, middle-aged, tired. And they eat not cookies or candy but large, matter-of-fact sandwiches.

Alyosha is alone today. No one came to visit him—but he looks the same: interested and happy.

Later he explains to us:

"Anyway, they'll come see me. They'll have to bring me shoes, 'cause I've only got sandals and rubber boots. I think, it's only that daddy's too busy, and mommy doesn't feel well, and Granma can't leave her."

"And where does your daddy work?"

"In the N.I.I. He works lots and lots. Sometimes we wait and wait for him, and he doesn't turn up until the next morning."

And he beams his black-toothed, happy smile.

What can you say to that?

Now the children are called in for their naps. Parents' day is over. The mothers, greedy for more, look longingly after their children. The kids run off cheerfully, not a bit worried. Only Kostya, who starts running off at full speed, suddenly comes back and cries out plaintively:

"Mom! You come too!"

"I can't, sweetie!" says mommy in a low, trembling voice. "You all have to go to bed, and for me it's time to go back to town, on my shift. I can't, my angel!"

She says it in the Moscow way: aingel.

"You always have to go on your shift!" Kostya reproaches her.

After parents' day we got to talking with one of the teachers, the middle-aged one. I asked her about the parents. But she knows very little about them.

"Alyosha isn't mine, and Tanya isn't either. They're from another kindergarten, and they were placed here only for the summer. Alyosha must have a well-educated family . . . he's quite advanced. But lazy and sloppy."

Alyosha—sloppy? He looks so trim in his shirts and little shorts. Well, she must know, she sees a lot more of him. But how is he lazy?

"Of course he's lazy. You take a look at him when the children tidy up. Others do it on their own, look around to see what they can do, but he—never. Wasn't taught to. A very spoiled boy. You've barely changed his clothes, and he's dirty all over again. You may have noticed the two girls I have here, the two Natashas? These are my girls, tidy, modest, good girls."

How can one see in Alyosha—in the happy, inquisitive, and polite Alyosha—only that he is untidy and not used to picking up?

"In general, our children are more modest," she confides in me. "And better disciplined. We're from the Nevsky region, and they're from somewhere on the Vasilievsky Island."

Ours, not ours, I can understand that. It's genuine. She'll always prefer hers over those who come only for the summer. I'm curious, do the new ones notice this?

"I notice you often watch us. Did you see how Alyosha behaves during morning exercises? He makes faces, clowns around. It's because he was badly brought up. He's a very excitable boy. And too stuffed with all kinds of information. Discusses things. Discusses! Is the development of the mind the main point? A child must understand discipline."

"Is Stepan yours?"

"Stepan's mine. True, he too has no discipline. He and Alyosha simply found each other. Alyosha, at least, doesn't break anything. But Stepan is like a fire. In his hands everything catches fire.

13

Take toys, for example. He breaks his own, he breaks somebody else's. . . . Yesterday his mother brought him a dump truck—where's it now? And it probably wasn't easy for her to buy a toy, she's alone now. Her husband died last winter. Fell from the scaffolding at a construction site."

Must be that Stepan has his father's quick manner, his deftness, this—how shall I put it—soldier's quick wit. How ably he threw his grass grenades into our garden. But his father couldn't have been a soldier, he was too young. His grandfather, probably. And Stepan must now grow without a man's watchful eye: he must learn on his own how to hammer nails, how to split and saw wood. . . . Although nowadays, who needs it, sawing wood? They probably live in a new house, with hot water and central heating.

It is hard to be with children. I have enough experience, and I'm old enough—and still I find it very tiring.

When Shurik was in second grade, he asked his father:

"Why aren't men ever teachers in kindergarten? They treat children much better!"

Who gave him such an idea? Was I too stern with him that day, or was he remembering his teacher? She too was middle-aged, she too was often tired.

"Our children probably bother you a lot? Your son encouraged them to do it. We simply don't know how to stop this."

"Don't try to stop it. We're not bothered."

Nowadays when Shurik appears, everybody calls Tanya. She comes running at the call—her hair flying, her white hat slammed down all the way to her nose. How she can see the world from under that hat is a mystery.

"When're you gonna give us a ride on your bike?" she asks. "When're you picking up our pictures?"

All the time—it's "us," "our" . . . Tanya is a great collectivist. But Shurik—he is her recognized prerogative.

"Ah, on my birthday, when I get a lot of candy, I'll treat Shurik!" she declares without addressing anyone in particular.

"And when'll that be?"

But Tanya doesn't know. No one knows his birthday, including the precocious Alyosha.

The girl-I-don't-like comes fairly often; her relatives live not far from us. Shurik takes off with her for days on end. They drop in on us for a short while, and when she is here, nobody calls on Shurik. Why is that?

The kids've gotten quite used to us. Now, when Shurik gets on his bicycle, they shout to him:

"Shurik! Bring us some candy! Some cookies! Doughnuts!"

Stepan intercepts him on the road and says quite business-like:

"Shurik, please bring me some milk chocolates, in a little bag."

Only Alyosha and Stepan use the polite "you" to Shurik.

Shurik, it's true, once brought two hundred grams of Teatralny candy and gave it to Tanya to share with everyone. Many felt shortchanged. Stepan said:

"Give me two!"

Kostya was indignant:

"What a smarty! Others get none, and you get two?"

But in fact, there was enough for everybody. And Shurik's popularity soared.

Summer is in full swing—the raspberries are ripe, the trees are laden with fairly large green apples. Kostya begins a conversation with me.

"Pick some berries for us."

"I can't Kostenka, these berries belong to the landlord."

"How 'bout an apple?"

"They belong to the landlord, too."

"A flower, then, a small one?"

But the flowers are not ours either.

Shurik is about to leave. He is going to hitchhike to visit ancient Russian cities. I'd like to ask him if the girl-I-don't-like is going with him, but I restrain myself. He taught me not to ask questions. Now I ask them of myself. One question in particular, the one that bothered the fifteen-year-old Natasha Rostova:

"What are you like, you men? The way we are? Or not?"

Because, with time I understand my own son less and less. Perhaps because I'd always imagined him as someone so different as he was growing up. How many parents can afford their imaginings? One has to love one's children for what they are, and not for what they might have become.

All this I tell myself quite often.

When they see me, the kids behind the fence ask forlornly:

"And where's Shuu-rik?"

I repeat to each one that he left and that he'll come back soon. But Tanya Serova wishes to know exactly when that'll be. With her sense of tomorrow and yesterday, that's fairly difficult to explain.

"We'll have a nap, and another nap, and another—and then he'll come? Right? On parents' day?"

I myself can't say exactly. Because my son's idea of time is not very different from Tanya's. He can't figure things out in advance. A day is so long, so full—who'd take it into his head to peek into the next one?

But finally he is back. He comes at night when the kindergarten is asleep and dreaming of him. Just yesterday Vova with his cold said to me:

"One boy in our bedroom dreamed about Shurik!"

In the morning I watch how they meet. The entire congregation has gathered at the fence. Tanya thrusts her head through the slats and holds on to Shurik's huge hand. She even pushes her white hat back so as to see better. And says nothing. She is happy.

Moved, Shurik comes in saying:

"We must arrange a farewell party before they go. Let's buy candy, and pastry maybe? And, mainly, some lemonade. And then ask them over. Imagine what a feast that'll be!"

Then he takes out his bicycle and Alyosha calls:

"Shurik! Where're you off to now?"

Answers Tanya:

"He'll be right back. He won't be gone long any more! He'll be here all the time!"

In the evening, as I walk by the kindergarten on my way home, an ambulance passes me going in the other direction.

As always, my heart sinks. Automatically, my mind takes attendance. No, it can't be us. My husband is in town, my daughter is practice-teaching, and I saw Shurik half an hour ago. And here he comes, with the girl-I-don't-like.

"Alyosha fell from the tree," he shouts. "Was he ever crying! He ate the apple I gave him, but kept crying between bites. Don't look so scared, it wasn't that high. He's all right."

"All right? They took him to the hospital. I saw the ambulance."

"No. Why should he go to the hospital? He simply hurt himself. They'll probably just put him in their observation ward."

But they did take him to the hospital. The next day, the kids are eager to tell me the whole story.

"Flat on his back on the rock! He climbed the dead tree, started calling Shurik—and fell. Right onto the rock. They took him to the hospital."

With his back onto a rock—that could be real serious. And tomorrow is parents' day.

"Shurik, let's go visit Alyosha this evening!" I suggest. "He'll be very happy to see you."

"This evening?" repeats Shurik. "Oh, I think that I'll be busy tonight."

"Do you really have such important things to do?"

"Maybe not so important . . ."

And so we are unable to agree. The nurse from the kindergarten is on her way to visit Alyosha. The next day the older teacher tells us:

"Nothing serious. They say everybody there knows him already. Can't lie still for a moment, a real *Vanka-vstanka*. To tell the truth, he's exactly like before . . ."

"But he fell with his back onto a rock . . ."

"Who has seen this rock? There's no rock there at all. I went there especially to see for myself. Ah, today he'll be happy—his grandmother came to visit him today. An educated lady, listened to all we had to say, and then said: 'Don't worry, we know that he gets into mischief!' "

And so I didn't meet Alyosha's grandmother.

But then, I met Tanya's mother. Naturally, our conversation centered around Shurik:

"I thought he was her age. But apparently he's already a college student!"

During the conversation Tanya doesn't look at me, and somehow pretends she's not listening. Something about this conversation disturbs her. Mommy is one thing, and we and Shurik are a different thing, and now that we're all together, we don't add up. Something's new, unusual . . . She is different too. Her hair is braided, the nylon ribbons stick out like propellers. And her white hat's rim is turned up.

"She talks to us about you," I say. "And about little Igor, and about daddy Oleg . . ."

"Oh, she's probably told you about the three daddies?" asks her mother. "She likes to do that. She calls her grandfathers 'daddy.' My husband and me, she used to call us by our first names, she refused to recognize us as her parents. We've finally talked her into calling us mom and dad, but before—she wouldn't do it for anything!"

So here's the solution to the three daddies. And we thought . . .

Somehow I haven't been seeing the girl-I-don't-like lately. Do you suppose that she left to go somewhere else in her car?

It turns out, yes, she is gone. Chauffeured by her dad. And invited Shurik's closest friend to go with them. How about that! Such a thing I wouldn't have expected even from her. I'm openly indignant, and then not so openly, for a long time; and then it occurs to me that I've simply been jealous—not of my son, but for my son. But he's fairly composed. Or maybe he is controlling himself.

Meanwhile, the end of the summer is creeping up on us. Not the fall quite yet, but the end of the summer. If the morning is clear, by midday there is rain. If there is fog in the morning, we can expect a warm day. But instead of warmth, the wind comes rushing in from somewhere—at five meters per second, ten meters per second, fifteen . . . Fifteen winds per second! These winds attack the ill-fated dead tree—and suddenly it breaks with a howling screech.

Yesterday, I saw Stepan stealthily threaten it with his clenched fist—for Alyosha.

The rest of them don't mention Alyosha. Neither Tanya, nor Vova, not even the just Kostya. They're busy with their own things. The fall has supplied them with new games. They now spend much more time in their toy houses, where they play mother-daughter and infirmary.

On duty at the infirmary is usually Vova with the cold—no doubt he has seen a fair number of doctors in his short life. At any rate, he gives injections into the kids' bottoms with such zeal that the older teacher finds it necessary to stop the game. I guess she's right. Then they set up the infirmary game right in the clearing, and this same Vova gets under one blanket with tidy Natasha;

he likes to hug girls. And Kostya tucks Tanya in. The way he does it, you can sense his tender concern.

During the whole summer I never saw war games. How peaceful our time is! Some fifteen years ago boys played only war. Suddenly a war would flair up, spread like an epidemic, to the other groups, even the girls, even the tots. The morning would start with shooting, yelling: You're dead! You're dead! I don't understand very well who fought whom—and Shurik isn't around to explain it to me.

Shurik left again, hitchhiking. He has big plans—he wants to get as far as the Crimea. Maybe the girl and her dad went there?

"So when'll you be back?" I ask.

"End of August, probably. I'll help you move things back into the city."

"But the kids'll get picked up on the twenty-third. We were going to arrange a farewell party for them."

Remembering the party he smiles.

"Main thing—the lemonade!" says he. "When I was little, I liked lemonade best of all."

"So maybe you'll be back by the twenty-third?"

"I'll try," says he without looking at me.

He won't be back, I know.

He leaves without awaiting Alyosha's return, without saying good-bye to anyone, not even Tanya Serova. The pictures remain undeveloped. And, again, the kids call out plaintively:

"And where's Shuu-rik?"

But they no longer expect him. It's just their way of speaking.

The war rages right under our window. One shell breaks a pane on the porch. It's cold. Time to leave.

Alyosha returns. Seems to me that he has grown during the few days in the hospital. Actually, they have all grown this summer. And gained weight. Alyosha, by his account, gained all of four hundred grams. But somehow they're distributed over him inconspicuously. And—does it just seem so to me?—he now tends to walk rather than run. And he appears to be ruminating over something. His eyes are the same, clever and shiny, but there is something new in them.

"Shurik was gonna see me in the hospital," he confesses to me. "My teacher told me. But he's gone."

19

"He went south," I say in an apologetic tone.

"Everybody's gone south. My daddy too. Maybe he'll meet Shurik there? And Stepanka's gone too. I've got no friends anymore."

Yes, Stepan is already gone. I thought that the kindergarden departure would happen all at once, joyously, noisily. Not at all. It has been a week now that parents have been seeping into the camp and quietly, stealthily, taking their precious children away. They have taken Vova, Andryusha, pretty Inga. I met Stepan and his mother at the bus station. He was carrying some sort of bundle all by himself. Good-bye, Stepan, our little Russian fairytale soldier.

Kostya and Tanya come to the fence.

"My daddy'll go south too and meet Shurik," says Tanya.

"And when'll Shurik be back?" asks Kostya.

"Don't know, my friend."

We stand there silent, all four of us. It is lucky they don't remember the pictures.

"Day after tomorrow I'll leave, and he'll never see me again!" says Tanya.

"But why, Tanechka? You'll give us your address and he'll come to see you in the city."

"No, he won't!" says she.

She is tired of waiting and hoping. But what words now crop up inside her. "Day after tomorrow!"

With Alyosha too we speak for the last time.

"And remember," says he, "how we called you bad guys?"

And he now has the "and remember." Alyosha is grown. He understands the sweetness of remembering.

"And remember," says he, "how I fell from the tree, and Shurik gave me an apple?"

Must have been a good apple if he still remembers it.

"When will they come for you?" I ask him.

"I'm going with the teacher," he says. "It's hard for Granma. We're moving to a new place. Dad's got a separate apartment for himself. Granma says ours is a very good neighborhood. The air is so good there, as good as outside the city. Granma says the main thing for me and mom is the air."

"Granma—is that your mom's mother?"

"No, dad's. She says this year she an' me'll study German every

20

day. I think I forgot it all during the summer. Remember, I kept asking you how you say table in German?"

And, dreamily, pensively:

"Der Tisch!"

And now—there's nobody behind the fence. The bedroom windows are boarded up. It's quiet. Sometimes yellow leaves light up the birch tree. The summer's over.

Soon Shurik will come. We didn't arrange a farewell party for the kids. We didn't write down their addresses. We didn't print their photos. We didn't do any of the things we promised. Shurik never even gave them a ride on his bicycle.

And how much we could have done!

After all, we were like giants among them. Like Gullivers. Like Olympian gods.

We could have bought shoes for Alyosha. Till the very end of summer no one brought him any shoes, and on cold days he walked around in his worn-down white sandals.

And for Stepan we could have bought milk chocolates in a little bag—and never did.

We could have picked apples in the landlord's garden, let the landlady get mad. What bliss it is to pick a red apple and give it to a child. Or even just a green one. Can you ever forget the first apple a kindhearted Gulliver picked for you?

Giants must be good giants. We were ordinary giants, mighty, but indifferent.

They, however, did a lot for us, even if they didn't know it. Who was it that said that among children your soul heals up? We had a difficult year—and all summer we recuperated.

Some day they will all have their "and remember." Too bad that they won't remember us as good giants.

And why, during that long, long summer, did we never understand that we are almighty?

All we needed to do was arrange a party, write down a few addresses, give them a few bicycle rides, buy candy in a little bag.

And—say good-bye to the little woman, Tanya Serova.

1966   *Translated by Helen Reeve*

Witches

AMONG the patients in the huge postoperative ward are three female intelligentsia and Auntie Pasha.

Auntie Pasha—she's only in for tests—is lying between two of the intelligentsia: one has had her gall bladder removed; the other, her appendix. The third intelligentsia, an actress who has been awarded the rank of Honored Artist of the Republic, has been put a little way off from them, near a screen, across an empty row of cots. But she's been here for quite a while—she's about to be discharged—and nobody even knows exactly what kind of operation she had. Now she's sitting on her bed, wrapped in a brown hospital gown, having a lively conversation with the well-dressed visitor beside her. It's not a visiting day, but they've let her visitor in anyway; after all, she's an Honored Artist, and the visitor, from the looks of her, is an actress too.

"Look how she's sitting!" exclaims the younger intelligentsia admiringly. She has a small face with a sharp little nose, and a nearly-grown-out permanent. "We can't do that, our backs would get tired right away."

"What's so wonderful about that?" rejoins the other woman, the one with the gall bladder—or rather, without the gall bladder. She was born in Siverskaya, but at first glance she makes you think of Asia: yellow skin the color of weak coffee, lightless eyes, smooth raven hair without any gray. "It's all for show. And look what an audience she's got here. Thirty people."

"Artistes!" says Auntie Pasha. "A woman lived in our apartment once that looked like her. Also an artiste. A ballerina."

"You can always tell a ballerina," sighs the younger woman. "By her posture, by her walk. Why, once I was on vacation in Yevpatoriya and saw two ballerinas. What figures, what grace!"

"But when they retire, they get fat right away," says Asia. "You remember, there was that ballerina—Kapustina. Her husband works with mine, I see her often. Now she's a real hippo. But she used to be so. . . ."

25

"The visitor's leaving!" says Auntie Pasha, raising herself up. "Oh, it *is* her! I swear to God, it's her! Verochka!" she cries. "Verochka!"

The visitor, who is already walking to the door, stops, turns her head in its sable hat, looks hard, exclaims "Oh!"—and with a light step approaches Auntie Pasha.

"Polina Artemyevna!" she exclaims, coming close. "Well, I never would have thought." She gives her a big kiss on the cheek, and Auntie Pasha, pleased, grumbles, "What's this Polina Artemyevna stuff? Just plain Auntie Pasha."

"Well, how are you? What are you in here for? You're just the same, you haven't changed a bit!"

"In more than ten years? Come on! Now you—you really haven't changed at all. You must be eating well. I'm just here for tests. It's all right here, the doctors do their job. The food's bad, it's true—but then where can you get decent food these days? Naturally, I'd rather be eating something a little more interesting. But, anyway, the main thing is, they're not going to operate. They did their tests, and they didn't find anything. Soon I'll be discharged. Well, how are you? Are you still living with your Jew?"

"Auntie Pasha, for almost ten years now I've been—"

"Jews make good husbands, they say," says the young woman with the permanent to no one in particular.

"Our Verochka's not bad, either," says Auntie Pasha proudly. "You'd never know she was—How old are you, Verochka?"

"Going on fifty-two, Auntie Pasha, but who's counting?"

At this, everyone expresses genuine surprise. Verochka is wasp-waisted, with quick movements, and smooth skin that doesn't wrinkle even when she laughs—and Verochka laughs a lot. Her eyes are light blue, her gaze piercing. She calls out, "Olga Mikhailovna, come over here!"

Olga Mikhailovna, the Honored Artist, approaches slowly, waddling a little, and sits down on a chair next to Auntie Pasha's bed.

"You're so pretty, Olga Mikhailovna, pretty as a ribbon!" croons Auntie Pasha. "Peaches and cream. What do you eat, to get that way?"

"Heart trouble, that's where the peaches and cream come from, Auntie Pasha. Not good health."

"Don't be afraid, I won't cast a spell on you. I don't have the Evil Eye!"

"So you know each other," says Verochka. "That's my Polina Artemyevna, all right. Always lucky. In our apartment she was known as the Lucky One. She smashed two fingers at the factory. They amputated. Am I lucky! she says. A little further, and it would have been my whole hand! Now I'll get full disability and my pension, and I can still do my housework. That's our Auntie Pasha."

Verochka, telling this to Olga Mikhailovna while the others listen, dissolves in laughter.

"You always loved a good laugh," says Auntie Pasha.

"It's too late for me to change," laughs Verochka.

Both intelligentsia smile and look at her with pleasure.

"Do you have an apartment to yourselves?" asks Auntie Pasha.

"All to ourselves, Auntie Pasha. It was very lucky we moved when we did; now, we couldn't find one. In the center of the city, right in the center; and ceilings *that high!*"

"You were lucky." Cautiously Asia joins in the conversation. "We got one in Dachnoye. It's a wonderful apartment, a real gem, but the ceilings—they just press down on you."

"*Khrushchoby,* or new buildings?" the young woman wants to know.

Then everyone joins in. Each woman has something to say about the housing question. Asia has finally managed to get away from her son's family: "Do anything you want, but don't live with your children, that's what I say!" Olga Mikhailovna confesses that in her whole life she hasn't spent a single day in communal housing. But now—the irony of fate!—she is thinking about having someone assigned to her. When her husband died, she was left alone, and the apartment is a big one, and all his books and papers still there, they are valuable; well, it isn't really that—but on the other hand—or maybe it would be better to move into a smaller place?

"They ought to give you a place in the Nest of Gentlefolk," says the younger woman authoritatively. "A person like you—an Honored Artist and all. They really should."

"What Nest of Gentlefolk?"

"Why, you know, the new building in the Petrogradskaya area, where the director Tovstonogov lives, and people like that. That's what they call it, the Nest of Gentlefolk."

"Oh. But they aren't giving them away. It's a cooperative nest. And why should I buy an apartment? And where would I get the money?"

"If only you had grandsons," says Auntie Pasha. "Now me, Verochka"—she goes back to their original subject—"I'm still living in our old apartment. The tenants change, but I stay put. Where else would I go? Two families and I'm the third. A sunny room, fourteen square meters, with heat and hot water—and a building from Stalin's era, not like they build them now. And I know all the people in the shops; when they have sausages they always save me some."

"Do you remember, Olga Mikhailovna, I told you about that apartment?"

"The place where they denounced you?" the Honored Artist asks.

"What do you mean, denounced?" asks Auntie Pasha. "Who denounced you?"

"Why, you did!" laughs Verochka. "You were the one, Auntie Pasha, don't you remember? The one who told the neighbor ladies I was a witch? And there were more people living there then than there are now. A family in every room. They were so mad they could have killed me."

"Come on!" Auntie Pasha waves her away with her mutilated paw. "I only mentioned it to them. Who would have wanted to kill you, I can't imagine."

Verochka runs her eyes over the group; they're all watching. "Pretty soon they were all telling me to my face—*Vera, don't you come in the kitchen for half-an-hour, I'm baking.* They were afraid that if I went in, their dough wouldn't rise. Or—*All it takes is for you to go out to the kitchen, and my cup cracks, or my plate.* And Auntie Pasha gave them the whole idea, our Lucky One. Not that anything of hers broke—she was the Lucky One."

"It's a terrible thing, superstition," says Asia, frowning.

The younger woman is disappointed. "I thought you bewitched their men."

Verochka shakes with laughter. But Auntie Pasha declares firmly, "Nothing of the kind. What didn't happen, didn't happen.

As for my warning people about her—I had to, Vera, I told you so then and I tell you so now. Maybe you didn't even realize it yourself; but people had to know. That's the way it is, like it or not. In the country people used to believe that witches were taught to be witches. If a witch was dying, say, she had to pass her knowledge on, you know, pass it on to somebody else. But that's all old wives' tales. Witches don't get taught to be witches. They're born that way."

"Why are you lecturing us, Auntie Pasha," the younger woman says disapprovingly. "You're not at a meeting!"

"We should be ashamed of ourselves, listening to this stuff," Asia says.

"Why? I'm not calling anybody names, am I? I'm being very genteel. And I've seen this business since I was a child. In the country once, we had a witch, and you know what we used to do, girls? We knew what to do. As soon as a witch goes inside her hut, stick two needles into the molding above the door to make a cross."

"And then what?" the actress asks with interest.

"And then there's no way she can come out, that's what. She stands there turning around and around, she wants to go out, but she can't as long as nobody pulls out one of the needles. Our own mother used to get mad at us. But you can't tell a witch just by looking at one; they look perfectly ordinary. After all, it's not their fault they're witches. Remember, Vera, I taught you how, and you caught an *artiste* that way once."

"When?" Verochka looks at Auntie Pasha with huge, astonished eyes. "I can't seem to remember." And suddenly, for some reason, she blushes.

"Oh, come on. You were always saying that anybody who got mixed up with those two—her and her husband—died all of a sudden. What they didn't know was whether it was the *artiste* or her husband who was to blame. And how did you check it out? Just the way I said, you stuck needles into the curtain in her doorway."

"That's interesting," says Olga Mikhailovna. "Verochka, who did you do that to? You never told me about that."

She looks at Verochka curiously, and Verochka avoids her eyes, and suddenly—

"Oh!" The whole ward cries out, "Oh!" The lights have gone out. The huge room is plunged into evening twilight. They hear running and shouting in the corridor. "An electrician, an electrician!" "What's going on?" "It's never done this before—" "An electrician!"

"Only three o'clock, and so dark," sighs Asia.

The younger woman ventures, "All the same, there's something to it. I knew someone myself—" She sits up straight in bed and, making sure she has everyone's attention, she begins. "I know this woman who can tell when somebody is going to die. Not that she knows, exactly—she feels it. All of a sudden, she starts to feel uncomfortable with somebody. So uncomfortable that she can't control herself. The person comes to see her, and she says she has some kind of urgent business and runs off. He calls her up, and she speaks to him coldly even on the phone. And, mind you, it's not that she dislikes him—she just feels uncomfortable, that's all. The first time she couldn't understand it at all. Then she gets a phone call: the person went to a resort and drowned. Then it happened a second time—all of a sudden she starts to dislike somebody, and he dies. And then a third time—"

"Well, that one's really dangerous!" says Auntie Pasha, and secretly crosses herself under her bathrobe. "Bringing death on people!"

"But she didn't bring it on them—that's the point. She just felt it coming."

"Well, then, was she a gypsy, or what?"

"Why drag in gypsies? She was as Russian as you or me."

"No, that kind of nastiness you can't forgive! A cup, a plate, that's nothing. But bringing death on people, why, someone like that, I'd—"

"With your own hands?" asks Verochka innocently.

The lights flash on; the ward sighs with relief. "Ah!" Auntie Pasha says sweetly. "You, you—God bless you! What am I, a murderer or something?"

"They used to kill people on account of superstitions like that," says Asia. "In the country, not all that long ago. But for us— now, in Leningrad—to be serious about witches! I teach history; I know. They used to burn women on account of slander like that!"

"Yes," says Verochka, "It's a good thing, Auntie Pasha, that we aren't living a hundred years ago. They'd have burned me alive, probably, the people in that apartment, wouldn't they?"

"Oh, for pity's sake," says Auntie Pasha angrily.

Everyone laughs, and Verochka loudest of all. She stands up, gives Auntie Pasha a kiss on the cheek, and says, "I haven't laughed like this in a long time. Thank you Auntie Pasha."

And she walks away with her light step. Olga Mikhailovna sees her out. Asia falls back onto her pillows; the young woman looks after Verochka as she walks away; Auntie Pasha leans over and rummages in her nightstand. And all of a sudden she screams, "Oh, no, look! That devil—what has she done? God help us!"

"What? What happened?" The young woman is frightened. She leans over the nightstand and says, "What got spilled there? Milk?"

"A bottle of milk was sitting in there," says Auntie Pasha in a wavering voice. "The bottle cracked. Cracked all by itself, did it? I never thought she'd lift a hand against me!"

"Who?" asks Asia without raising her head.

"And I was thinking"—says Auntie Pasha—"I was thinking, I'll just have a little milk. *Now* what am I to do? She's already started getting back at me!"

"Who?" says Asia, not understanding.

"Why, that Verka—that's who! Because I gave her away in front of that *artiste*. In front of Olga Mikhailovna. She used to tell me about her, how people died because of her—and now her husband's dead. Oh, what an evil woman!"

"Come on," says Asia. "You knocked the bottle over yourself somehow—" But her voice lacks conviction. The young woman looks at her reproachfully.

Auntie Pasha grows thoughtful. "I'll have to write to them where she works," she decides. "Let them know about her. Then we'll see!"

1981   *Translated by Ann Harleman*

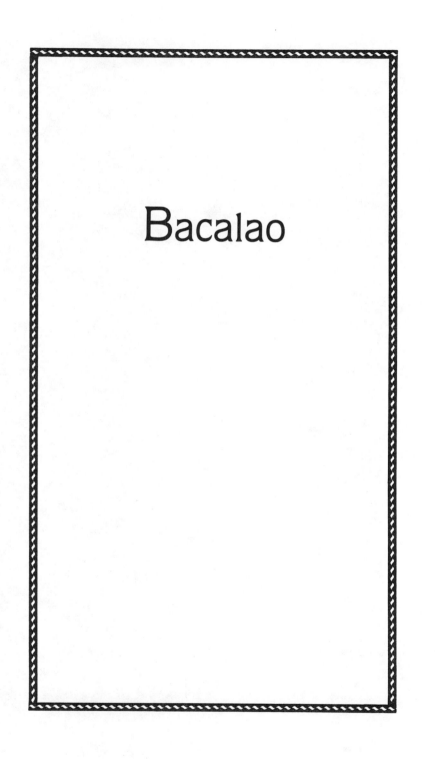

Bacalao

HE was a communications officer. I would run into him at division headquarters where I was working temporarily as a translator. *Bacalao* is not a first name, not a last name; it means "cod," and used figuratively, it means "skeleton." Broad-shouldered and with a pink round face, he did not look like a cod, nor like a skeleton. But that's the term the Spanish use to tease their B.A.s. Nineteen now, Carlos Garcia de la Fuente had received his baccalaureate degree two years back, in the fall of 1936, in Madrid itself.

This B.A. title intimidated me a bit; up to that point, I had encountered Bachelors only in Cervantes's works. Gradually I learned that a Bachelor was simply a person who had received an undergraduate education, and so, by the rules of their country, I too was a Bachelor. My timidity passed, Bacalao and I became friends, and he started teasing me. It was his way of becoming friends.

He teased me like a schoolboy, or an unbearable younger brother, even though we were the same age. He made fun of my accent. He laughed at me when I wasn't smiling. "Women are supposed to be cheerful, playful, not serious!" He was amused that I smoked, that I held my cigarette in my right hand. "Only *señoritos,* the young gentlemen, hold their cigarettes that way!"

I got angry with him, made biting remarks about the fact that he was short, that he was insufferable, that he had dubious vocal abilities. (He very much liked to sing.) He laughed off what I said, invoking in passing Santa Virgen del Pilar, a name good Catholics weren't supposed to take in vain.

"*Santa Virgen del Pilar!* All right, let's assume I don't know how to sing, and you do. Let's assume that. But when you sing, what is it? The important thing isn't how you sing, but what you sing, that's what everybody thinks nowadays. When you get back to Leningrad, your fellow students will ask you to sing something in Spanish. You'll pick up the guitar. . . ."

"I don't play the guitar."

"No matter, you'll take it in you hand, for show. And you'll start singing *Rossio*. All our cooks sang it here before the war. Do you realize—a newspaper even ran an ad: 'Looking for a cook who does not sing *Rossio*.' Honest, it's the truth! And then your *novio*—a clever fellow, I could see from his picture—will say: '*Santa Virgen!*' or whatever you people say over there, 'Is that a Spanish song?' He'll sense right away that it's all just *Españolada*, fake Spanish, for the tourists. One must sing *flamenco*. Like Manolin."

Manolin was his driver. They drove a small blue Renault with well-worn seats. Manolin had mended and sewn them up himself with an owner's zeal quite unusual for a driver from Madrid. He was tall, rather tall for a Spaniard, spoke rarely, had a calm manner and a haughty bearing, all of which fits our image of a thoroughbred beauty. He sang *flamenco,* the ancient Andalusian melodies embellished with Mauritanian runs, that thrust upward like a Gothic cathedral—his head back, his eyes closed. You could almost see these runs glide along his throat. Bacalao always listened, mouth open in rapture. As soon as Manolin stopped, though, Bacalao began joking around with him. He warned me that Manolin only appeared to be calm and cool, that he was actually quite a ladies' man, a real Madrid *chulo*. There may have been a bit of truth in this.

"Rita, you better be careful with him. He's *mucho pinta,* a tricky fellow."

As he said it, he put a finger to his eye, as if to say *Look out. Be on the alert.*

Manolin smiled calmly dignified, said nothing, went on busily doing something. He was always puttering around when he wasn't singing—poking around the motor, cleaning his pistol, mending clothes, his own or Bacalao's. They had both joined the war in Madrid.

"Did you know, Rita, that this silent Manolin fought against the Moors like a Cid Campeador? Oh, he is brave! Ah, but do you know who Cid Campeador was?"

They called Madrid *Foro,* a word taken out of Madrid's slang, out of *calo*. They taught me some slang expressions: *chupa* for jacket, *traija* for chain. . . . They were homesick for Madrid. Bacalao made melodies of the names of city streets and blocks: Alcala, Puerta del Sol. Manolin would exclaim: *"Viva, Madrid, mío pueblo!"*

Manolin's wife and daughter Teresita were back in Madrid. I was sure I would recognize them on the street, that's how often he showed their pictures. To tell the truth, he also had pictures of other women in his wallet, tenderly inscribed to him. I asked about them but he only smiled awkwardly. Bacalao, though, never mentioned his family. From Manolin I heard that his mother and his father, a professor of literature, were killed when their house was bombed.

Manolin was a Communist, and Bacalao a leftist Republican, like the President, Don Mañuel Asana. They both fought under Carabanchel, and when Manolin was wounded, Bacalao carried him out of the fighting on his own back. Later, they parted ways. The educated Bacalao became a lieutenant, Manolin a driver. They met again only here, in Catalonia, at the Ebro; they never parted again.

As always, the Ebro's water was heavy, dark yellow, muddy; there was no play on it, nor any silvery, scaly glitter. A bright noontime sky hovered over it, but the river did not reflect it; the river seemed indifferent to that calm blue above. Lumbering, weighed down with worry, the river rolled its muddy waves as if fulfilling a burdensome service, flowing away from us to the southeast, to Tortosa, a place taken by the Fascists last April. In the evening, when the sky turned pale, triple-engined Fascist *Junkers* appeared from Tortosa or Lerida over the river. . . . We watched them, our heads turned up—all of Franco's air force was on our front now. And someone was sure to say: "That's all right, let our brothers in the Levant have a breather today."

A week ago our division headquarters moved to this small town on the right bank of the Ebro. We'd seen the town earlier, before the offensive, observed it every day through binoculars and with the naked eye: white two-storied houses with rust-brown tiled roofs. To us only a name, the town looked like a mirage, postcard flat. Not a town, just a settled spot to be taken; and the river not a river, just a water boundary. On the left bank, in the green valleys between the hills, officers taught soldiers how to cross that water boundary: precisely, swiftly, silently! The soldiers lifted the nonexistent oars in unison, just like boys playing at crossing the river. At night, heavy trucks, lights dimmed, sped along the slate-blue asphalt roads, delivering boats to the Ebro. The Fascists had to be deflected from that central front at any cost.

We crossed the Ebro during the night. Right away people made up a song about it, with two refrains, one contemporary, boisterous, and one traditional, lyrical:

> Our Army's on the Ebro,
> Bombara, bombara, bam! Bombara!
> Crossing it at night, all right,
> Ah, Manola! Ah, Manola!

The song went on to mock the fright of the Fascist traitor and to praise the wonderful courage of the Republicans. The song spread until you could hear it everywhere: in unit formations, at stopping places, at headquarters after dinner.

However, our attack stalled, Franco had moved up his reserves. Endless, exhausting battles were fought over each hill.

And so the town we'd observed from across the river has become ours. Actually, it wasn't really a town, just a *pueblo,* a village, much like its sisters on the left bank—similar two-storied houses, a market square with a fountain, an empty stone church where people no longer prayed. . . . People lived on the second floors in these houses, and had very wide beds and round tables up there. The first floors were cattle sheds, with cattle in them. Through the cracks between the upstairs floorboards you could hear a mule sigh and shift from leg to leg.

Only one house in this village stood empty; where the *alcalde,* the village elder, used to live. From the white outside wall of this house a charcoal drawing of a sweetly benign, dashing-looking fellow gazed down at us, a kind of jack of clubs: languid eyes, parted hair, a moustache—so well known to us from caricatures: the Caudillo himself, their Generalissimus Franco!

Our soldiers stopped to examine this face.

"What a *cabron!* Cuckold! *Hijo de puta!* It's all his fault!"

"Now he's worried, the traitor!"

The portrait got whitewashed over. The abandoned house was commandeered by the staff, and the purple, yellow, and red Republican flag was raised above it. Early in the morning women in black came to find out about their husbands and sons, most of them in the Republican army.

"*Señor* commander, I mean, comrade commander, did you see my son Marianno, maybe? He was a *cabo*, a corporal. . . . My brother. . . . My husband. . . ."

Girls never came into the commander's office. During the daytime there were none to be seen, and soldiers peered up through the grilled shutters on the windows in vain. The girls showed up in the evening, in high heels, in well-ironed jackets, their shoulders straight, their eyes flashing, their hair in lacquered waves . . . for the *paseo*, the stroll around the main square. Here, by the fountain, was where everybody first met.

Paquita, though, I saw for the first time in broad daylight. Walking along the street, Manolin pointed out to me a skinny girl, quick like a lizard:

"This girl. . . . Just a child, wouldn't you say? She has the whole village in the palm of her hand, all the fellows are crazy about her!"

Sensing that we were talking about her, the girl turned her shoulder, and flashed her green, oval eyes.

"What a beauty!" exclaimed Manolin.

He couldn't keep quiet when a beautiful girl bestowed a glance on him. In his usual methodical way, he explained:

"This is an Andalusian custom, called 'tossing flowers.' One is supposed to toss flowers to lovely creatures."

He added thoughtfully:

"As a rule, though, it's better to keep one's distance."

The "lovely creature" turned out to be the niece of my landlady, *señora* Rosa. I saw her again that very evening. She curtsied, eyes down, and *señora* Rosa looked at me with pride: *See what a well brought up niece I have?*

In a short, washed-out dress and *alpargatos*, canvas slippers—with sharp elbows, sharp knees, a pointed little face. A prickly girl. But also a blinding green glance from under elongated eyelids, and a quick, mischievous smile. . . . She explained that she never went to the *paseo*, Mamita wouldn't let her. *As if anyone could keep you from it once you decide you want to*, I thought to myself.

She spoke good Spanish, something rarely encountered among Catalonian village youths. She had two sisters, both younger, who resembled her mother; but she looked just like her father. The father had been killed.

"He was a very good man. At the very beginning he joined to fight for the Republic. *Mamita* didn't want him to, but he went."

He was killed near Teruel. He had never been away from home before. She herself had never been anywhere except to the neighboring village where her other aunt lived; she would have to visit her soon.

She was a good student in school, her teacher praised her. She'd like to become a teacher herself, but *Mamita* said it was nonsense: one must marry.

"Do you have a *novio?*" I asked.

For a moment she hesitated, then looked at her aunt who gave her a nod.

"Sí, I do."

"From your village?"

"Yes, but he isn't here now."

I expected her to show me a picture of him, but she didn't. After she left, *señora* Rosa said to me:

"She's got a very strict mother, a good Catholic. Maybe you think that's bad. But it's good for bringing up children. Paquita'll wait for her *novio* till he returns. She's young, just sixteen, she can wait."

"Does she love him?" I asked.

"He's a very good fellow," answered *señora* Rosa, "a solid man. Helped the whole family when her father was gone."

That night I listened long to the mule's sighing. I felt sorry for Paquita.

She dropped in on me every day, not for long, just a few minutes at a time. I tried to keep her a little longer—it was impossible. She said nothing more about herself, she had questions. All her questions were about the Soviet Union. What do they wear over there? What do they eat? Does everyone have a car? How much do they pay for school? Was it true that children didn't have to obey their parents? Was it true that the snow never melted there?

She'd ask a few questions, then flutter away; she couldn't sit still in her chair. She had to hurry off: it's time, *Mamita*'ll start worrying. She never told me what she thought of what I said; she'd ask, listen, quickly glance at me sidelong, then ask the next question. The following day, a new series of questions would begin, usually with "Yesterday you told me. . . ." Once she asked:

"Will it someday be that way for us in Spain too?"

"You should join the Komsomol," I suggested.

She laughed, shook her reddish hair:

"*Qué ba! Mamita*'ll never let me!"

Then she ran off. I heard how downstairs soldiers greeted her with exclamations: "*Olé!*" "Good-look'n!" "Blondie!" You could tell when Paquita was walking down the street.

Several days later she went to see her aunt in the neighboring village. That was when I met her *Mamita,* a quiet, colorless, shapeless woman. She regretted having let her daughter go off.

"I can't understand why I agreed! In such terrible times! A girl alone on the road! God only knows what can happen."

"What are you saying, *señora,* we don't live in the woods here, Paquita is not Little Red Riding Hood! There're no gray wolves roaming the roads, the bombs have scared them off!"

"That's it, the bombs! What if suddenly . . ."

Then she and *señora* Rosa started talking to each other in Catalonian:

"Maria's *alpargatos* are torn, wouldn't it be nice if Paquita brought her a pair from her aunt."

"A young captain from Barcelona gave neighbor Alonsa stockings, and soap, and thread as a present."

"Ah, Alonsa is not shy! We'll see what her husband'll say when he comes back!"

"Some women've lost all decency, they think now that there's a war on . . ."

Paquita was back next day. She had spent the night at her aunt's. She was lucky—she'd gotten a ride both there and back.

"D'you know with whom? That driver Manolin that you were with when I first saw you! What a voice he's got!"

"Paquita, my child!" *señora* Rosa gasped. "You got into a car with strangers! A decent girl must never do that! *Mamita*'ll be very cross!"

"*Santa Virgen!* These are not strangers," said Paquita, "they're Rita's friends. We met last week when the Barcelona artists were here. Two danced the *apache* dance. D'you want me to show you how they danced?" And, with funny gestures, she imitated the dance with throbbing, music-hall passion.

"Paquita, you're quite a dancer!"

"*Qué ba!*"

She glowed that day, and had no questions. As she was leaving, she asked nonchalantly:

"They're married, no?"

So that's it, I thought.

"Manolin's married," I said solemnly.

Something flashed in her eyes, and she quickly lowered her eyelids.

I was having dinner with the commander's officers. Supper was the usual: lamb tough as shoe leather, *lentejas*—lentils with olive oil (that oil was my ruin!), and a light white wine. The officers discussed bullfights—outlawed during the war—and dropped the names of various *toreadors*. Bacalao asked:

"Rita, tell me—who was the first toreador? Hah, of course you don't know. Theseus, that's who it was! He defeated the most famous bull of that time—*el Minotauro*. Oh well, how could you ever understand the pleasure that people find in bullfights?"

Manolin seemed preoccupied.

"Manolin, you really seem to win over many hearts!" I said.

"Didn't I tell you?" Bacalao laughed. "He's a real Picci! Do you know the song 'Picci conquers all the hea-arts,/Not a single girl can slee-eep,/Can you find one who's not longing/For this faithful Romeo/To be her own bo-oy friend!' Who did he conquer this time?"

"He knows," I said.

After dinner Bacalao saw me home. It was dark, the moon was not up yet, only a few large stars quietly glowed in the sky. Bacalao told me about an American by the name of Wallace who was wounded today at hill 506. Looking up at the sky, he added:

"With such a sky above, we shouldn't be talking about the war. We ought to sing!"

"Please don't," I begged him.

"Then I'll recite you a poem. Don't worry, not mine, but Lorca's:

Her smooth skin was more
Tender than pearls and lilies,
Lighter than the moon's glitter
Spilling over window panes.

"What a poet!" he said. "Hundreds of years of global spasms of suffering just to produce such a poet. And now—gone! Killed in Grenada! I saw him. He used to visit my father. I thought at that time: 'I've just seen an Immortal!' Now—the Fascists simply kill him. Nobody'll ever again write about love that way!"

Suddenly he smiled:

"I might! After the war, I'll start writing poems about love. About a girl with green eyes."

"Why green?"

"Ah—such eyes will adorn any verses. And what eyes does your *novio* have?"

I'd have been glad to know what eyes my *novio* had. I had no *novio* at all. How could I admit to that? Everybody had seen this picture I was carrying, everybody knew that he was a student and that we would marry as soon as I get back to Leningrad. But the student whose picture I carried with me to Spain probably didn't even know my name.

"Would you like him to be here right now?"

I sighed. "Of course!"

On our staircase I bumped into Paquita, in a hurry to leave. "You didn't come and didn't come, I waited and waited. Now I have to run, it's late. See you tomorrow!"

The next day she came back, and started in again: "Is Don Mañuel Asana a good man? Do they have mules in Russia? How do people get married in Russia?"

"Tell me about your *novio*," she once asked. "Tell me how it all started for you, how did you realize that you loved him?"

"You have a *novio* too, you know all that as well as I do."

Her face grew dim. She shook her head.

"You don't love him?"

She bent her head so low that her hair covered her face.

"I love another. You know who."

"Paquita! But you've seen him only twice!"

She raised her head and laughed.

"We see each other every evening, after I leave here. Listen, tell me yourself: how could I not fall in love with him?"

"What about your *novio?* What about your *Mamita?* What'll happen?"

She tossed her head impetuously.

"*Novio, Mamita.* . . . What are you saying? Do your young women marry without love? No! And I won't either!"

I knew I had to have a talk with Manolin.

By morning we were moving out of the village and I didn't get a chance to say good-bye to Paquita. A few days later, Manolin handed me a note from her, just a few words: best wishes and warm regards. I read the note while Manolin sat next to me, fixing his pen.

"I wanted to have a talk with you," I said. "You know that she has a *novio,* a decent fellow . . ."

"Do you know who he is?" asked Manolin.

"No, why?"

"He is the son of the *alcalde,* the one who fled. He is not in the fighting against us because he is lame. Anyway—he is on the other side."

"She told you this?"

"That's the point, she didn't, she said nothing. I told him everything myself."

"Him—whom?"

"What do you mean—whom? Bacalao! He said he didn't want to see her any more. She kept coming, crying. . . . He said he no longer trusted her. You know, first love is easily hurt! He meant to marry her. Lucky, it was I who told him. What if he'd found out from somebody else?"

"But she loves him!" I exclaimed.

"That's all right!" he said. "She'll console herself with one of these *enchufados.* There's plenty of them in the village."

Those who shirked the war were called "enchufados," "emboscados."

Our headquarters was moved into the hollow between the hills. We slept in huts made of branches, *chabolas.* Sappers built an adobe house for a mess and meeting hall and dug a shelter. Water was a problem. To wash, I had to walk over the hill into a thicket of reeds where we'd chanced upon a small stream that was, by some miracle, still trickling away. A red-hot August had dried out all the grass, covered the olive leaves with hot dust, and cooked the bunches of grapes spread over the slopes to a frenzied purple. There was no cold water left in nature; even my little stream was as warm and sticky as the water in my flask. The biting flies hurt worse than the mosquitoes; and the wounds they left on our arms and legs wouldn't heal.

The sun set in the opening between the hills. There, one evening we watched before our very eyes two planes fight it out: a Republican *Mosca* fending off a Fascist fighter. Small, weightless, almost transparent in the paling evening sky, the planes tried to climb above each other, noiselessly, like moths—far away. Oh, but how we shouted! Officers, soldiers, cooks, the division doctor—an Austrian who happened to be with us. . . . Something elemental in us yelled and shouted. We invoked magic, we prayed, we wished ardently; our pilot must have felt a surge of energy, because the Fascist fighter suddenly burst into flames, sent out an enormously long tail of smoke into the sky, and then went down, down, down. . . . A black toy figure separated itself from it, struggled in the air, then a white umbrella opened above him. The Fascist pilot had jumped out with a parachute.

Our division commander Alvarez asked me and Bacalao to come with him to visit the neighboring international brigade. He'd been told the pilot had come down in their area. The commander of the "interists," a huge blond German, was in the adobe hut, speaking on two phones at once:

"*Io contg'attacco!*" he shouted in his throaty Berlin tenor.

Our lively, black-eyed Alvarez, from Asturia, watched him, his eyes squinting in amusement.

"*Biurocrato, eh?*" he asked.

Alvarez had worked for about a year as a coal miner in the Donbass.

"*Biurocrato!*" echoed the German, putting down one receiver. "What can you do if people yell at you on two phones in three languages? For the fourth time today they're climbing hill 511. It's time to have supper, and they're still at it. Translate this for him, Rita, he doesn't understand my Spanish."

"That's all right," said Bacalao. "Did you read the paper today? Negrin said, 'The people fighting on the other bank of the Ebro aren't just heroes, they are gods!' "

"And a machine gun?" our host yelled into the receiver. "Two machines guns? *Ach, feiner Kerl!* I'm saying, you're great! And rifles? How many? I'm asking you—how many rifles? Right. Good-bye! Good-bye and thank you!"

He put the receiver down and turned his flushed face toward us.

"They've got a good commander over there. He took the hill again! Captured two machine guns. . . . Now we can have supper. You stay here. We have a cook, a Frenchman."

"Where's that pilot?" asked Alvarez. "Still alive?"

"They took him to Army Headquarters. A brazen fellow, *frecher Junge.* Fascist."

"Spanish?" asked Bacalao.

"German, my countryman."

"They'll gobble up everything," said Bacalao.

We were sitting there on a low stone wall that must have been a border to somebody's vineyard some time back. The wall was as hot as an oven when the stones heated up during the day.

It had been a hard day. The Fascists began bearing down on the area held by our division, their air force bombing the bridges again and again. The pontoniers stayed with the ferries. Not constrained by my presence, the French pontonier captain swore in pretty strong Spanish at Franco, at the bad woman who'd brought him into the world, at the long summer days, at Chamberlain, at Hitler and Daladier. We found out from the newspapers that Chamberlain had gone to see Hitler in Berchtesgaden to sign an agreement with him. It meant the Sudeten would be handed over to the Germans and then, probably, all of Czechoslovakia too.

"They'll gobble up everything," said Bacalao. "They'll sail over Paris, you'll see. France, the epicurean garden of Europe! Maybe people'll understand then that Daladier and the rest of those. . . . Ah, what's the point in talking. They understand it now too, but they like to play ostrich—like Australian chickens."

From beyond the hills came a rumble of artillery.

"We're a people of *Don Quixotes,*" said Bacalao. "Now we are a reconnaissance in force for all of Europe. Others are laughing at us; they're watching to see how long we'll last. For three years they've been watching. *Santa Virgen!* Today, in the interbrigade I saw some Czechs. Hah!"

"Have you heard—how's Wallace?" I asked.

"He's back in the battalion. Wounded in the shoulder. You know, a wound is good for seeing your family. You can show it to them: look, the bullet passed this close to my heart. But Wallace's folks are in Texas. A bit too far away!"

Again the rumble, this time closer.

"They're aiming at something," said Bacalao. "Did it give you a scare?"

"No, no, didn't have time."

"On the whole, women don't get frightened easily. I remember once, the war had started and women were still at the front. . . . We were storming a hill. The machine guns were banging away, you knew well enough not to raise your head, but they would go crawling ahead as if they didn't hear anything . . ."

He sighed. "But that's not courage. Just inability to recognize danger."

Suddenly, turning his pink face to me, smiling, he flashed his blue-white teeth:

"Have you ever seen Goya's pictures? But there're none in Russia, I believe. Still, what I was going to say . . ."

Some huge ball whizzed low over our heads and hit the hill with a bang. All went dark. The stone wall under me was gone—I was on the ground, I felt a sharp pain in my neck, I gradually realized that I was alive, I felt someone's hand squeeze mine, then release it. A voice was shouting "Killed, killed!"

My darkness lifted. I slowly sat up. Bacalao was lying next to me, face up, pale, eyes shut, on his jacket a large dark spot was spreading. Officers came running from the dug-out. Manolin came too, yelling "Killed, killed!" A medic tugged and struggled to undo the straps of his bag on the run. Opening his eyes, Bacalao said:

"I'm alive, *Santa Virgen!* Stop yelling!"

And shut his eyes again.

Manolin fell silent. The medic cut Bacalao's jacket open. Looking around, he noticed the commander next to him.

"It's not his stomach. He got it in the hip and shoulder. My commander, this requires an operation. We must get him to the hospital on the other bank."

"I'll take him," said Manolin. "Just help me carry him to the car."

Our cars were parked by the road behind the hills.

Bacalao was put on a stretcher. I picked up his cap with the two lieutenant's stripes, which was lying on the ground, and put it on his head. He looked at me and said:

"Paquita . . ."

"I'll bring her to you," said Manolin.

The next morning we drove to staff headquarters. The dust on the road had settled overnight. It wasn't hot yet. We were driving along with the windows down. Suddenly the driver turned to us:

"My commander, look! The girl from the village, she used to go with Bacalao!"

"She must be crazy!" exclaimed the commander. "What is she doing here?"

Paquita was walking quickly toward us, a small bag swinging in her hand. She must have left the village before dawn.

The driver stopped the car. We got out, Paquita rushed to me.

"Crazy girl!" yelled the commander. "What are you doing here? D'you want to get yourself killed, hey?"

"*Qué ba!*" she said. "Who'll kill me? My commander, I need to see my *novio, teniente* Bacalao. Or, is that not permitted in wartime?"

Clearly, she had prepared this statement. She didn't yet know that Bacalao was wounded.

The driver in the car opened his door to hear her better. Almost mechanically, she flashed her green eyes at him. He startled, as if pushed, and mumbled: "What a beauty!" The commander got angrier:

"Get in the car immediately!" he ordered. "That's all I have to do, driving girls down the road. We will have to take you to your mother for a good spanking, right?"

"My commander," Paquita said emphatically, "I really must see my *novio*. He quarreled with me, and I can't live without him.

You were young once, too (the commander was twenty-eight), I'm sure you understand."

"As if he was your first *novio*," remarked the commander.

Apparently he knew the whole story. Everybody knew everything from the very beginning, except me.

"My commander . . . ," began Paquita.

She suddenly burst out crying like a kid, covering her face with both hands. Big, pea-sized tears ran out between her fingers.

"He talks to me, just like you . . ." she continued crying. "But I . . . I. . . . Tell him, Rita . . . tell him. . . ."

"You must go home right away, Paquita," said I, putting my arms around her. "Listen . . . but don't get upset . . . Manolin'll come fetch you. . . . He'll tell you what happened. . . . Only, don't get upset. . . ."

She raised her head and looked straight at me. Her face turned ashen.

"Oh no, no . . . he's alive . . . only wounded. . . . Not seriously, not seriously, do you hear? Why do you stand there as if you don't understand? Get in the car, we'll take you home! Manolin's probably already waiting for you there. . . . Get in!"

"No need to!" said Paquita. "You must hurry along. . . . I'll walk home!"

"Get in right away!" barked the commander.

Paquita climbed in. She was shaking, but still managed to ask questions carefully, in detail, methodically: Where was he wounded? What did he say? Did he really say—Paquita? Did he? And Manolin promised to bring me to him? Promised, for sure?

Our driver kept watching her in his mirror; he sighed in sympathy. The commander sat straight, did not turn around. But when we let her out two kilometers from her village, he said:

"Crazy girl! So—the war can go to hell, just so she gets her *novio*, hah? I should let him have it, your Bacalao! It's all right, he'll be back. With a bride like that, he'll live!"

Then he smiled wryly, and added:

"And me, I'm an old man in her eyes, hey?"

Commander Alvarez didn't get to live to his old age—he was killed within a month, at the start of a massive Fascist offensive in Catalonia.

Bacalao, though, got well. He and I met again in the beginning of February, in a small town right by the French border. The last days of the resistance. Barcelona was already under the Fascists. Over the radio, Falangists shouted: "Franco! Franco! Franco!"

"You're a captain now, Bacalao!"

"Yes," he said, "like Consalo of Cordoba!"

He tried to joke as before. But his face was tired and tough; his round cheeks and chin had hardened. He appeared to have grown up.

"I haven't grown up," he said. "I've grown old. A man gets old when he has more friends in the cemetery than in the cafe. I'm an old man now."

"Paquita!" I exclaimed.

"No, not Paquita," he said, "but Manolin. Killed in Barcelona. . . . Bombing. . . . Came to pick me up from the hospital. . . . I later went to the morgue. . . ."

His mouth twitched. He frowned.

"He didn't need to come," he said. "My fault. He came to get me."

"Don't talk nonsense!" I objected. "What's that got to do with you?"

"You haven't experienced it yourself yet," he said. "The living are always guilty before the dead."

"Of being alive?"

"Rubbish. Of not protecting the other one from death. How would you know that? You have a *novio* in Leningrad. Your friends are waiting for you at home."

"Why do you talk that way?" I asked him.

"Don't mind me," he said softly. "I know how you love Spain. And our dead are dear to you. You are—our sister. But you have everything still ahead of you."

"You do too."

"I do. Only . . . when you say a simple word, say, 'street' or 'house'—what do you have before your eyes?"

I saw blue-green slabs of sidewalks, speckled by colors from acacia, a sunflower-seed vendor sitting in a recess of the corner house, curly grass between cobblestones. A childhood street, an Odessa street.

"I too used to see my childhood street. There was a cafe on our corner. Now I see rubble. Our house was hit by a bomb. For two years I keep seeing just this. Do you understand? When I say 'friend,' I see Manolin. When I say 'foe,' I see Franco with his moustache. He, though, is alive."

Again his mouth twitched.

"Know what, Rita? I'm a Communist now. *Tovarich!*"

He pronounced the word in Russian.

"Do you want me to tell you why I became a Communist? Because Communists will fight to the end, against Franco, against Mussolini, against Hitler. Right?"

"Right."

"And don't feel slighted that everything is still ahead of you. I'm not talking only about joy. You understand?"

I understood. He was indeed much older now than I.

"Listen," said I. "Why don't you tell me anything about Paquita? Where is she? What's happened to her?"

"Won't take long to tell you that," he said. "Where she is—I don't know. What's happened—I don't know. I only know she left Barcelona."

"Was she actually in Barcelona?"

"Manolin brought her there when I was in the hospital. She lived with a Communist girl friend he had. She visited me. When Manolin was killed, they left Barcelona for the border. Apparently, the French had opened the border. Maybe they're already in France. Paquita in France? What'll happen to her there?"

"She loves you," I said.

"She says she does. For how long? You know her, she's a child. And my war will be a very long one. Even if we leave this place, I won't stay in France. I'll come back, get through to Madrid. Madrid is holding out! *Viva, Madrid, mío pueblo!*"

A light morning haze hovered over the mountains; below, in the valley, the romantic, incredibly delicate-looking almond blossoms had opened; a woman was hanging out laundry amidst the almond trees. Bacalao gazed at her for a while.

"It's hard to leave your native land," he said. "This woman wouldn't be able to. Listen, if you see Paquita. . . . Anything is possible; you and I met again. Tell her that I love her, that I'll fight for her, and that she mustn't, she doesn't dare . . . nobody else. . . ."

It was hard for me to keep looking him in the face, but I did.

"Maybe you better not. Can you use words to make someone love you or remember you? Well, give me your hand, let's say good-bye . . . *tovarich!*"

I walked a few paces away, turned around. Bacalao stood without moving and watched me. Meeting my gaze, he raised his fist above his head and smiled.

Spain, Spain!

Twenty years later I saw Spain again—in Moscow, in a movie. Watching the screen, I recognized the narrow streets, the trees, the wide highways. But the people moving around on the screen I did not know, and couldn't know. They were the other ones, from across the river, the ones who had painted Franco's portraits on the white walls of the houses and now hang them in their apartments. The ones who threw bombs on Barcelona. The ones who killed Manolin, and Alvarez, and so many, many others.

I watched intently, closely. . . . I didn't bother with the actors, I forgot that this was a film. This old woman who had medals left her instead of her dead sons—she gave her children to Franco, all, down to the last. Maybe some of them died by the Ebro, by that very bend of the Ebro? And this one, the last of them who was still alive, an involuntary murderer, was with them, also yelling: "Franco! Franco!"

When his body crushed by an automobile was left lying on the road, a woman who sat next to me said in the darkness:

"Retribution!"

She said it in Spanish.

The light went on, I glanced at my neighbor—and recognized her. It was Paquita.

I recognized her only because at that moment I was ready for such an encounter. On the street, by daytime, I would have walked right by her. Twenty years do not pass for anyone without leaving a mark. She was not heavier, or gray—she was dimmer.

"*Madre mia!*" she exclaimed. "What a meeting!"

We walked out hand in hand. Paquita was examining me.

"You're still the same! Of course, time passes. . . . So, you still recognize me?"

"Paquita, of course. . . . And you were in Moscow all this time?"

"Since 'thirty-nine."

She told me how she worked as a teacher in a children's home. First, she'd worked in a place for Spanish children—that had felt like being home. Then she'd taken up studying, finished a technical college.

"What about Bacalao, what does he do?"

I had no doubt that they were together.

"Bacalao?" she asked me. "Ah, you haven't heard anything. Bacalao is in jail, in Franco's jail."

I stopped. My legs turned to stone. She slowly nodded her head, up, down.

"Since then, since 'thirty-nine."

"Didn't he leave with the troops?"

"He did, then went back again, illegally. . . . He wanted to get to Madrid, to fight to the end. How I cried! How I begged him . . ."

"You met?"

"What else? He found me in Argeles, in camp. Ah, that camp! Behind barbed wire, everybody together: men, women, children. . . . The barracks full of holes, we all got soaked when it rained; it was crowded; sick people moaning. . . . Yes, France greeted us in style! And—there he was. I had begun wondering if he'd gotten killed. I said to him: 'My love, my darling, stay with me! We'll struggle together!' How I loved him!"

She wiped her eyes.

"I was silly then, didn't understand a thing. I thought the war was over, whether good or bad, it was over, and it was time to think of oneself. But he said 'No, you cannot.' And left. He arranged for me to be sent to the Soviet Union, but himself, he left. He didn't want me to stay in France."

"And how did you find out?"

"That he's in jail? Got a letter through the Red Cross. I've been getting letters since then, every now and then. The last one reached me this year. He wrote that he's grown old. How can he get old? I think he must be the same."

She looked straight ahead as if trying to make out something out there, far away. When she stopped talking and her dimmed face no longer quickened with emotions, it turned sorrowful.

"I've seen jails only in the movies. But when I wake up at night sometimes, I hear guards walking on the stone floor, and tortured people shouting. . . . I hear his voice 'Paquita!' For him, I'm the same as before! Time has passed for you and me; we lived through 'forty-one; then there was 'forty-five, and then the other years. Fascism is over for everyone except them. . . . Over there, it's still 'thirty-nine."

She again wiped her eyes.

"My *Mamita* is still alive. And Aunt Rosa too. They write me, asking me to come back. How can I? How do you return to 'thirty-nine? Also—he'll be looking for me here. They can't understand that. They feel sorry for me because I'm not married. Our neighbor Alonsa married my former *novio*."

Suddenly she stopped, clutched my hand.

"Twenty years, Rita, just think! Twenty years! A whole lifetime! He won't recognize me when he comes. I'm an old woman, Rita. But he'll come, I know he will! I believe it!"

Tears streamed from her eyes. No longer did she try to hold them back. They washed away the wrinkles, the weariness, the years from her face. I saw again Paquita, the green-eyed girl from the Catalonian village.

"I believe it! I do, I do!"

1961   *Translated by Helen Reeve*

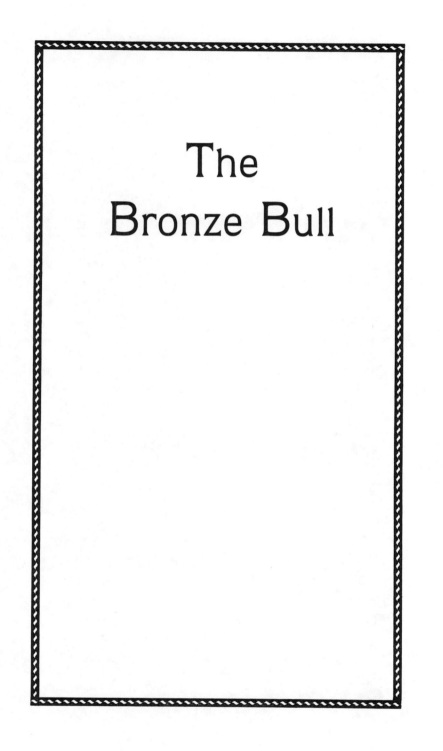

The
Bronze Bull

AFTER the rains, came the summer—that sudden Leningrad summer when each sunny day seems to be the last. The sun hurries to accomplish all it can in its allotted time, and leaves the sky only at the very last moment. And when the sun does go down, the old stone facades of the city take over: they breathe, they pant and strain, like asthmatics, hurrying to give off warmth they can easily spare. From dawn to dusk half-naked bodies sprawl on the somewhat dirty sand near Peter and Paul Fortress: those who can't wait for their vacation are soaking up their share of sunshine. There are few attractive bathing suits here. The water is greasy and cold, like leftover soup. People don't stretch out here for long—just till the lunch hour is over, or until their shift starts. Also, you won't find any solid, fat people here—this is a beach for the young.

This time of year only the occasional foreigner glances into the antique shop: women whose faces are covered with melted makeup, who look like abstract paintings, and their companions, well groomed, with polite grins. They distractedly glance over the candelabras, the chandeliers, the marble busts, the dead birds painted on wooden panels. They stop in front of the old china. Mary Grigorevna, turning over the delicate cup so that the hallmark on the bottom is visible, lowers her eyelids, raises her straight eyebrows and says, in French or English: "Real Saxony!" And purses up her lips as if pronouncing the word "you."

Mary Grigorevna always fulfills the plan. And the store always fulfills the plan because of Mary Grigorevna. Actually, Mary Grigorevna worked here even before the store really existed. It was just an ordinary pawn shop where they sold furniture, pictures, and crockery. Mary Grigorevna worked in the crockery department. From that department grew the present antique store.

The director says: "With Mary Grigorevna you don't need any kind of appraiser. If I were running things, I wouldn't even keep one on. She knows everything—absolutely everything! There's no point in keeping on an extra person."

But he had one anyway. Whether it was worth it or not, the extra person was mandated by personnel regulations. And he didn't reassign Mary Grigorevna to this duty. First, because she did not have the necessary education and, secondly, who would take her place at the counter?

Lyuba was in her first year of working for the store, and hoped it would be her last: in the fall she was definitely going to enter the Precision Mechanics/Optics Institute. The night school. Then her whole life would immediately change, and she herself would change too. She would become happy, light, agile, adroit; she would do all the assignments in such a way that the instructors would immediately realize how lucky they were to get her as a student. She would let her hair grow and put it up in a twist. She would get new, beautiful things like boots with tiny, tiny spike heels. . . .

As to just how all these changes were to come about—Lyuba had never given it a thought. She was simply sure that all of this would come to pass—it must come to pass, because it was so boring to live in the old way. Lyuba had gotten tired of the dusty objects, of Mary Grigorevna's voice, and of the fluorescent lights. In the midst of all this she felt completely out of place. What's more, when he passed by, the director would shake his head as if it were Lyuba's fault that no one was buying the eighteenth-century chandeliers. . . . Meanwhile, Mary Grigorevna would say in her drawling voice: "Lyuba, be a good girl, get the customers interested, then they'll buy anything."

In Lyuba's opinion, all these people with their greedy, calculating eyes who crowded around in the store, standing for a long time in front of her counter, were not customers at all. They were gawkers, uninterested, indifferent idlers. They appeared in the store regularly, looked over the items carefully, searched for faults inquisitively, noticed each new candlestick, but did not notice Lyuba at all, as if she were a statue in a park, devoid of any artistic value.

Sometimes someone—of course, not one of the gawkers—would buy a candelabra with little roses and shepherdesses or a terracotta bust of Tchaikovsky. Lyuba would wrap up the purchased item and think: They can keep all this old stuff! But Mary

Grigorevna from her place would nod to the customer, purse up her lips, and say about the candelabra: "A marvelous thing! Such a pseudo-naive pastoral! Eighteenth century!" And about the Tchaikovsky: "I love unglazed porcelain. The noblest material!" *What she comes up with to say about all this junk!* Lyuba would think.

Her sympathy was reserved for another class of visitors: those who were trying to get rid of their junk—the consignors. They would enter the shop with a deliberately uninterested air, would look for their things on the shelves, and having caught sight of them, would go out sighing. Lyuba wanted to console them: never mind, it's just not the season now, but as soon as fall comes. . . . But she didn't say anything, she was too shy. She was shy with everyone, with the director, with Mary Grigorevna, with all the antique junk, but most of all with herself. She had long arms, long legs, a long thin torso—she wasn't a girl, she was a reed! All of this bothered her, made her awkward. She hunched over, stuck her head between her shoulders.

"Are you really only nineteen? I thought you were much older," Anna Petrovna, the cashier, said to her. "When I was nineteen, I was a real live wire. But you're like some kind of Sleeping Beauty."

Lyuba didn't answer. She usually didn't have an answer for anything, as if she were unconcerned by what was happening around her. Mary Grigorevna noticed that sometimes her eyes would light up, or a suggestion of a murky smile would slide across her clouded face and then immediately vanish as if washed away by a ripple of a spring stream.

Spring that year was gray, and summer began with rain. Leningraders with trepidation awaited Sampson day. Sampson day decides everything in Leningrad. If the sun shines on that day, the summer will be dry. If there's rain—it will pour for seven weeks straight. Sometimes the omen lets you down, but sometimes it does come true. Lyuba, who could never get enough sun, was also waiting for Sampson day. It fell on a sunny Sunday. She went to the Peter and Paul Fortress and lay there the whole day like a lizard on the still cool sand. A girl was sunbathing next to her. She was doing it scientifically, by the clock. Every ten minutes she would turn—from side to side and from back to front. This girl struck up a conversation with Lyuba; Lyuba had to raise her head. And when she raised her head, she saw him. . . .

A tall fellow in a blue shirt and sunglasses making straight for them, smiling a blinding smile. It seemed as if the smile itself were sailing out by itself to greet them. Involuntarily, Lyuba smiled back, but he didn't notice her. He approached her neighbor, took off the glasses, stretched out his hand and said cordially:

"Hello, Tanechka! Tomorrow some people have to face descriptive geometry, and here you are cooling off. I mean warming up."

Shaking his outstretched hand the girl answered: "I'm not Tanya, I'm Tonya. And I don't have descriptive geometry, but resistivity of materials."

"That's unimportant," he said, not at all embarrassed. "By the way, I'm Kostya. Anyway, you took your resistivity of materials exam the same day I did."

"You can take an exam without passing it," the girl observed. "And I think I'll fail it the second time, too. So I ask myself why, on a beautiful day like today I. . . ."

Lyuba had absolutely no desire to listen to this senseless conversation. She got up and went to the water, glancing at Kostya as she went—at his blue eyes, his blue shirt. . . . He has an exam tomorrow, and here he sits, talking nonsense with that Tanya-Tonya, with her unappealing, mincing voice, disturbing people who want to enjoy the sun and quiet.

When she came up onto the beach again, he was gone.

But the next day he showed up in the shop.

The day was ending. Mary Grigorevna was changing from the slippers she wore indoors into her fashionable street shoes. Lyuba was already anticipating the happiness of that brief time each evening when she mingled with the crowds of animated, hurrying people, all of whom had someone, somewhere, waiting impatiently for them. No one was waiting for Lyuba, and she had nowhere to hurry to, but in the crowds she seemed to be no worse off than the others. The battered red sun would be setting behind the House of Books, and on the pavement the morning's puddles would be drying up. And the salesgirls from the big stores, the ones she lunched with at the automat, would be hurrying along in the same human stream as Lyuba. In the evenings their faces were entirely different, smartened up. They showed none of the morning's anxiety, none of the afternoon's fatigue. They sailed through the crowds, showing themselves off; the city was theirs. With their many-colored slickers and their light scarves—this was their time, their hour.

It seemed to Lyuba that this was the only time of the day that was really hers—see her moving along the splendid street among the beautiful perfumed and coiffed women, waiting for something amazing to happen, for someone, at that moment, to look at her face and find it not sleepy but mysterious. Anything was possible in the evening, at sunset!

In the small room where Lyuba worked there were no windows, just fluorescents that shone with their cold wintry light. And only occasionally the bulbs of the chandeliers would be lit and shine like yellow dandelions. What could you expect to happen in a room like that?

So when the fellow in the blue shirt stepped up to Lyuba's counter, removing his sunglasses with the familiar gesture, Lyuba thought for a brief moment she had summoned him up with her close-of-day anticipation of amazing occurrences.

I don't know you, she would say. And he: *But I recognized you anyway.* She: *But I've never seen you before.* He: *You just didn't notice. Yesterday, at the beach. . . .*

The fellow approached, touched the mane of a bronze bull that had stood in splendor on Lyuba's counter for several months. "Still not sold, miss?" he asked.

Lyuba was silent a moment, then asked: "It is yours, then?"

Of course it was his. How else could one explain his appearance in the store? The bull had belonged to his grandmother, but she had died, and he was the heir. At this point Lyuba had to call Mary Grigorevna because she did not know what forms he had to fill out as an heir. Mary Grigorevna knew it all, explained it all, and said in conclusion, sadly shaking her head:

"There aren't many enthusiasts nowadays for these beautiful things. Somehow they don't look right in a modern apartment."

"Just as soon as we got a new apartment, Grandmother said we should sell it. But I think it's too bad. I'm used to him!"

"Of course it's too bad," said Mary Grigorevna. "Things like this are history. . . . Now I remember that someone was telling me about the bulls they used to have at the slaughterhouse. . . ."

"Mary Grigorevna," the cashier called out. "What time do you have? Isn't it closing time?"

The fellow left. Anna Petrovna said: "A loafer."

Mary Grigorevna objected. "Why a loafer? Just a modern young man."

The director came up and addressed Lyuba.

"Comrade Ivanova, you have to understand your job. The sales-person isn't here to be part of the furniture, but to converse with the customers. You're a young girl, you have to be more friendly."

He looked at Lyuba disapprovingly. Meanwhile, she was look-ing at him and thinking how bad the fluorescent lights were; a person's face seemed dead somehow, bluish, and it wasn't the skin you saw so much as the structure of the skin: pores, vessels, capillaries. . . . The director said:

"You don't look very healthy! You should get out in the fresh air more, take up some sport—swimming, rowing."

"How can I get fresh air, Dmitry Prokofievich," Lyuba replied. "It just keeps raining and raining."

"Junker Schmidt! My word of honor, Summer will come back!" said Mary Grigorevna sadly.

The director was about to walk back to his office but stopped, frowned and said:

"Not Junker, but Lieutenant Schmidt!"

"I was quoting Kozma Prutkov," Mary Grigorevna answered meekly, "lines from his poem."

"Ah!" said the director. "Yes, yes, of course."

Lyuba put on her plastic raincoat (at least it didn't squeak when she walked, like a slicker) and suddenly looked closely at the bronze bull. He stood, with his bronze head lowered angrily and his long, dagger-sharp horns pointed outward, straining the fold of his weighty thick neck; in the electric light his bronze body shone. A ferocious beast! Who had enraged him so?

Of course he had a history. All of these things, each of which was older—not only older than Lyuba, but even older than Mary Grigorevna—had their history. There was the marble girl, wear-ing the kind of bonnet they wore a hundred years ago. And the cast-iron snuff box with the figure of a sleeping warrior on the lid—not a snuff box, but more like some kind of tombstone. Things lived longer than people. What was there to be happy about in that?

She was thinking about this later, in the metro car. And she also thought about the fact that Kostya hadn't recognized her. That's all right. When he comes with the papers she would say: *You didn't recognize me, but I recognized you.* He'd say something in reply. Then she: *No, it's not surprising that I recognized you, I just happen to have a good memory for faces. . . .* And then he'd say: *I remember you too, it's just that I didn't recognize you right off.* She: *And how is Tanya—or was it Tonya?* He: *Oh, I haven't seen her since!*

Meanwhile, Sampson day didn't let Leningrad down: on the very next day summer started. At lunchtime Lyuba went to the Peter and Paul beach and lay in the sun for twenty minutes, completely happy. If only the summer weather would continue for a week or so. A fellow in dark glasses passed close by. Lyuba raised herself up on one elbow. No, it wasn't him.

Lyuba began to go to the beach every day at lunchtime. Mary Grigorevna observed: "Lyuba, you look really nice with a tan. But this is no way to live—you're not eating any lunch at all. Or do you have dinner in the evening?"

"Yes, in the evening," answered Lyuba.

"Are you expecting someone?"

"No one. Why do you think that?"

"Well, it's just that I see you looking at the door all the time. Heavens, even if you were expecting someone, why would you blush like that about it? What's his name?"

"There's absolutely no one," Lyuba insisted. "Mary Grigorevna, what were you saying about the bulls at the slaughterhouse? Is there some kind of story about them?" "So you think," Mary Grigorevna wondered skeptically, "it's the same one?"

Mary Grigorevna sidled with some difficulty out from behind her counter and went up to the bull, with her head doubtfully on one side.

"It's by an unknown artist, eighteenth century approximately, not Russian work. Yes, maybe it's the same one! Of course, I'm no expert on bronzes. But just look, such a ferocious beast! He's just about to impale you with those horns. You know, I never saw the famous Farnese bull, but in Paris, at the Louvre. . . ."

"Have you been to Paris?" asked Lyuba.

"A long time ago, Lyubochka. Thirty years. My husband was working at a Trade Delegation there. It's all ancient history for you, but for me it's like yesterday. I remember everything so well, so well. . . ."

Like the last time, Kostya came at the end of the day. He had a different shirt on, a checked one, and had an airline bag over his shoulder. It seemed to Lyuba that he had gotten paler and more hunched over. But then she remembered about the fluorescent lights. Kostya took his papers to the director's office, and Lyuba said:

"Mary Grigorevna, let's turn off the lights and put the chandeliers on. It's almost time to go, anyway."

Mary Grigorevna nodded. Lyuba switched the lights. Yes . . . yes. Today, today he would notice her. And sure enough, as soon as he came out of the director's office he came up to her.

"Miss, are you the one who's herding my bull?"

Lyuba answered with such animation that Mary Grigorevna raised her eyebrows in amazement.

"It's nothing, he's no trouble at all. Doesn't require any feeding, he doesn't butt anyone, doesn't even bellow."

She started to laugh. He joined the laugh and said:

"I've got a request for you. Please see that he goes to a good home. Okay?"

He leaned on the counter, bending his long spine, and looked right into Lyuba's eyes. Feeling as if she were getting lighter and lighter every second as if she'd fly away any minute, Lyuba answered:

"Okay!"

"They should cherish him, look after him, polish him up. . . ."

"Of course!"

They were silent for a moment. Then he said:

"I was picking mushrooms today, not far from here, and I decided to drop by."

"What do you mean, picking mushrooms? In a store?"

"Of course not in a store. I was just gathering them."

Lyuba looked at him with hurt in her eyes; was he laughing at her? In response, Kostya opened the strings of his bag and said:

"Just look if you don't believe me!"

She looked in the sack, on the bottom were mushrooms, small, mealywhite, just picked, still on their blotchy little stems.

"Those are champignons!" he said. "I can see that you don't

know all the secrets of the big city. Champignons grow right in town. And not in Siversk or in Komarovo."

"Where then?"

"Ah! So you think I should tell you where I find them? The mushroom picker's guild forbids that. It's a real secret!"

For the last time he smiled and then left. Lyuba stood unable to speak, transfixed. Mary Grigorevna said:

"I see what's going on!" And she pursed up her lips.

"Aren't you ashamed of yourself, Mary Grigorevna. How can you?" cried Lyuba in indignation. "I would never talk about you that way!"

"Lyuba!" said Mary Grigorevna forgetting, in her surprise, to purse up her lips. "What's wrong with you? Are you crazy?"

Lyuba turned away. And on the way home she stayed angry for some time at people who suddenly take god knows what into their head and just chatter and chatter. . . .

But the next day, as soon as she came in, Lyuba said:

"Mary Grigorevna, please forgive me for yesterday. I was upset."

"Well what was the matter? You surprised me. I didn't expect such a temper from you."

At this Lyuba's eyes flashed and Mary Grigorevna thought the better of insisting on an explanation. But when Lyuba had set off for the beach Mary Grigorevna said to Anna Petrovna, the cashier:

"Obviously, she told her mother everything, and her mother advised her to apologize."

"Are you talking about Lyuba? But she's an orphan. Her mother died—not quite a year ago. Her neighbors got her the job here. Doesn't have a father either."

"What are you saying," said Mary Grigorevna with surprise. "Oh, poor little girl. That's why she goes around as if she's out of her depth. But then how can she think of the institute? To live on a stipend. . . ."

"She wants to go to the evening classes. Whether she'll get in or not. . . . But she's a kind of self-reliant girl. Just so quiet. . . ."

August approached, and the hot days didn't end. And the bronze bull stood on the counter as before, waiting his fate.

The life-size bronze bulls had stood in Leningrad since the

1820s. At first they put them on Gutuyev Island, opposite the stockyard building. Then, forty years later, they moved them to the new slaughterhouse on Zabalkanski *Prospekt,* and it wasn't long ago, after the war, that they were moved again—carted to the new Meat Plant building. But long ago, when they were first set up, people came from all over Petersburg to Gutuyev Island to see the new work by the sculptor Vasilii Ivanovich Demut-Malinovsky. On that day they were driving cattle into the stockyard. And suddenly, an enraged bull broke out of the herd. He was frightened by the crowd or by the neighing of the horses; perhaps the sunlight glinted off the bronze and caught his eye—with a roar the bull threw himself at the crowd. A cry went up, the crowd surged apart, pushing and falling over each other. Suddenly, a man threw himself right into the bull's path—he was dressed like a peasant—raised his fist, and hit the bull between the eyes. The bull fell like a stone.

No one knew who the man was, or where he had come from. It was said that the sculptor Vasilii Ivanovich Demut-Malinovsky, who of course had been present at the stockyard and seen everything, brought the hero home with him, gave him something to eat and drink, and bestowed upon him a bronze figurine of a bull, which he had brought with him from Italy. At first he had thought to give him a copy of his own bulls, but then changed his mind, thinking that they were too peaceful, and gave him the long-horned ferocious one from Italy.

From that day to this no one knows what became of the hero and his bronze reward.

"And you think, that this is the one?" asked Lyuba, amazed.

"Anything is possible," said Mary Grigorevna. "Leningrad is a city of wonders. And our store isn't just a store, it's a shop full of wonders—haven't you noticed that yet, Lyuba? Here in your department is that oval mirror and you sometimes look into it with totally understandable pleasure. . . . Yes, yes, you've gotten very pretty lately. But just imagine whose faces that mirror has reflected in these two hundred and fifty years. These things are . . . are. . . . They were made by hand, Lyuba, a real master would sign them, like artists sign paintings. . . ."

"Yes, of course . . ." said Lyuba distractedly. "But who told you that story, about the bull?"

"Alas," sighed Mary Grigorevna, "he's no longer with us. He was a marvelous person, a poet, an expert on the past, an appraiser. He came to our store like you would come to a library: each object told its story to him. And I wonder, when we're gone—I'm not talking about scholars, there will always be those— but just ordinary people like me, who remember things because they're interested—who'll be left? I understand that young people don't like to be told this or that is their duty. But all the same. . . . Take that young man. He probably wasn't even interested to find out where his grandmother had gotten such a statue, was he?"

Lyuba shrugged her shoulders. It was one thing to talk to Mary Grigorevna about old bronze, quite another to talk to her about Kostya. Probably it was good to be interested in things, but should one really show the same curiosity about people? But maybe Mary Grigorevna didn't see the difference. For her things seemed to be very much alive. But did Mary Grigorevna know that there were places in Leningrad where you could gather wild mushrooms?

All the same, after this conversation with Mary Grigorevna, Lyuba began to walk the streets of Leningrad with a different attitude. A city of wonders! How many times had things changed in the past two hundred and fifty years? The water in the river, the trees, the glass in the windows, the parquet floors in the houses, and the street lamps. . . . But yet something remained. What was it? Form? Or the essence of things, their soul?

Sometimes she and Mary Grigorevna left work together. Then they did not go down into the metro: Mary Grigorevna didn't want to go underground.

"Plenty of time for that!" she would say. "When there's so many wonderful things to see above ground, why should I go under before I'm ready?"

Lyuba agreed, and accompanied Mary Grigorevna as far as Old Nevsky. They went past the Pioneer Palace, here, a few years before, Lyuba had attended a young physicist's club, then a singing group, then a biology club. . . . Mary Grigorevna was saying:

"Imagine it's some one hundred and thirty years ago. A winter evening, snow . . . and the carriages are driving up. And there is one carriage in particular. . . ."

Lyuba could see clearly an agile man with sidewhiskers jump

out of the carriage and offer his arm to a tall woman with ringlets falling around her oval cheeks. . . .

Mary Grigorevna had been all alone for a long time. She had no one except the people with whom she shared an apartment. Once they had had a young daughter to whom Mary Grigorevna became very attached. She had even taught the girl French. And ten years ago, when she was offered a one-room apartment of her own, Mary Grigorevna refused. How could she part with her friends? And who would they put in her place?

But her neighbors' daughter grew up, married, and moved to a co-op: her father died, her mother aged, began to complain eternally of her son-in-law and his mother, of her daughter. . . . And Mary Grigorevna began to feel at home only in the store. There she was needed, even indispensable.

Lately she had become attached to Lyuba, to this spiritless, silent girl who said next to nothing, but listened attentively. Until the moment when she would sink into some daydream of her own, which had no relation to anybody else. This girl had no past and no present—nothing but the future.

And since a new tie was a new anxiety, Mary Grigorevna was always anxious. What did she do in the evenings, this lonely girl? What did she eat, whom did she go out to meet? And that habit she had of going to the beach at lunch. Who knows what might happen? Every day on the radio incidents were reported: Citizen N, being in a state of intoxication, decided to take a swim. . . .

On that day Lyuba did not appear after the lunch break. Mary Grigorevna was beside herself. She tried to convince herself that nothing had happened—it was just that the silly girl had started to daydream by the water, or that her watch had stopped. . . . But the director could show up any minute!

At that moment, three people entered the store—a woman and two men. The woman was beautiful, like a bird of paradise. Mary Grigorevna glanced at her, couldn't believe her eyes, looked again. . . . She had seen that sweet, mild face somewhere—in a dream, or in a film. . . . The woman's voice was low and soft, her movements were free, and she held her head a little forward and down, probably as a girl she had been self-conscious about her height. Mary Grigorevna with her unerring eye immediately established her age—she was thirty, for certain. She saw that the woman bore her beauty serenely, habitually, and as unthinkingly as an almond tree bears blossoms in the spring. She saw also which of the two men was the woman's real companion, by the way she listened to him, submissively hanging her small head.

This companion of hers was of medium height with a face that was uniformly pale, elongated, and thin. He held himself extraordinarily straight—was he a dancer, a mime? Marcel Marceau without his makeup? It was as if he were moving to some kind of precise musical rhythm—and one, and two, and three. . . . Even though he was of middle height, he somehow managed to look down on the people around him, with a little hauteur. But this hauteur was softened by the sad expression of his small mouth, and his velvet black eyes. It was clear that the third member of the party was the translator.

The three looked over the cups and tea services on the shelves without approaching the counter, and exchanged observations. Mary Grigorevna determined that they were speaking Spanish; she caught several familiar words: "Por qué?" "mucho" "esta bien." South Americans? Unlikely. They didn't look it. And that Lyuba was going to miss seeing them! Mary Grigorevna addressed the translator:

"What would you be interested in?"

"I don't know myself," said the translator. "We were walking along the street. 'A shop?' 'A shop.' 'Old china?' Old china.' For some reason all women like old china."

Lyuba flew in and, not looking at anyone, took her place behind the counter. Her face retained the traces of an expression that had animated it somewhere outside of the walls of the store—an expression of impatient expectancy and aspiring readiness. Lyuba said, as soon as she caught her breath—she must have been running:

"This is crazy! I was sure I had enough time, I thought I had the time all figured out."

Mary Grigorevna nodded. She was very relieved. Now she could look after these customers. With the help of the translator she got it clear that the bird of paradise really understood something about fine china. Her companion turned away with a bored expression. He was not interested in china. Suddenly he gave some sort of exclamation, slightly raised his shoulders and with the cautious step of a tightrope walker approached Lyuba's counter.

Mary Grigorevna saw that he was looking over the bronze bull—stroking its withers, pulling at its horns. Then he turned his head slightly, and at that silent gesture the bird of paradise went to him, excusing herself from Mary Grigorevna with an embarrassed, trusting smile. The translator followed. But there, at Lyuba's counter, the translator was not needed: Lyuba was herself talking with the man in his own language, stumbling ever so slightly, occasionally searching for the right word. Mary Grigorevna craned her neck to overhear: Yes, of course, Lyuba could speak Spanish. What a secretive girl! When had she had time to learn that language? And just look, her whole face has changed, and her laugh, and even her voice was different—lower, more gypsy-like. No one could call her a sleeping beauty now. A small crowd had gathered around her counter—everyone who was in the store.

The translator turned to Mary Grigorevna with a distracted face.

"He's very interested in that bull," he said. "He says it's no ordinary one, but real, a beauty, a hero. There aren't any more like it today, he says, they've gotten smaller. Of course, he knows a bit about such things."

"What things?"

"Well, bulls. Didn't you understand who he is?" Mary Grigorevna shrugged her shoulders.

"How should I know? But it did seem as if her face were familiar."

"Of course! You've seen her in the movies. Did you see . . . ?"

He named a picture that Mary Grigorevna did not remember. And it wasn't really the visitors who interested her now, no matter how much they knew about antiques. She was interested in Lyuba: What was she at that moment relating with such expression to the man? Maybe, the legend about the bull? But why would he be interested in that?

"He's a toreador, you understand? A famous *torero*," said the translator in a whisper.

His simplehearted face shone with eternal boyish delight at daring professions—musketeers, toreadors, or cosmonauts.

"The best sword of Spain, can you imagine it? Hemingway himself admired him. Your salesgirl there, she recognized him right away. She's an interesting girl, that one."

"What's she telling him about?" asked Mary Grigorevna.

"Probably asking him about the bull fights," laughed the translator. Lyuba began to wrap the bronze animal up in paper, tried to turn him over, and looked around for help. The translator caught the glance and flung himself to the rescue; the toreador began to applaud quietly.

The bull was already paid for, wrapped up and tied with heavy string, but the toreador was still conversing with Lyuba. Then he took her hand and carefully kissed it, not taking his sorrowful, velvet eyes from her face. And his wife also pressed Lyuba's hand, said something, smiling quietly. And they left—the toreador with his heavy package, the translator with the bird of paradise. At the door the toreador turned and said to Lyuba, seriously and sorrowfully, *"Suerte! Mucho suerte!"*

"What did he say to you?" inquired the director, who had appeared in the store at the last moment.

"He wished me happiness," Lyuba answered in a ringing, excited voice.

"And he invited me to Spain. I said I would come when they no longer had Fascism there."

The director frowned:

"But why would you want to go to Spain?"

"Well, anyway . . ." said Lyuba pensively.

When the store had emptied, Lyuba went up to Mary Grigorevna.

"I was so surprised," she said. "I had read about him and seen her in films, and suddenly here they were. I kept thinking that it wasn't real."

"Did you notice her face?" asked Mary Grigorevna. "You look at her and it's as if you're hearing music. It goes through you, makes you want to cry."

"She's good looking," agreed Anna Petrovna, the cashier. "But him—maybe he's a celebrity, but he didn't appeal to me especially. Looks like an umbrella."

"No," said Lyuba, "he had a good face. I don't know what kind of man he is but. . . ."

"I read somewhere," said Mary Grigorevna, "that after thirty everyone is responsible for his own face. It shows what he's done with his whole life. It shows the soul."

"He has a sad soul," said Lyuba. "He told me: 'I guessed right away that you were Spanish.' "

Mary Grigorevna smiled. Lyuba raised her eyebrows.

"Why do you laugh? I really am Spanish, half anyway. They brought my mother to the Soviet Union in 1936—she was from Madrid. She was twelve, and so she remembered everything very well."

"So that's why . . ." said Mary Grigorevna.

"How else could I have learned to speak Spanish? They didn't teach it in school. Mamma said that Papa just couldn't learn Spanish. She'd say, 'If you won't speak with me, I'll forget it altogether.' Of course she was just saying that. Could you ever really forget your native language?"

Mary Grigorevna thought to herself: here's the third generation already come up since that time. But it was such a short time ago: Paris and the broad-shouldered fellows in their wide-brimmed hats and gray Moscow-made suits on the Paris street—Russian pilots who were flying missions into Spain. They showed up in the trade bureau, noisy, happy, hopelessly foreign in that city, cautiously observant, curious, eager. She remembered one especially, a huge lad from the Volga region, with a rumbling bass voice. He even had an appropriate name: *Velichko,* the great one. When the same boys came back to Paris—was it a few months, or a year?—she asked about him.

"Velichko isn't coming back," they told her. "He was killed." There were many who did not return.

Lyuba was saying:

"My mother's friends come to see me. They also don't let me forget the language. They keep recalling how they were taken away to the Soviet Union, away from the bombs and the famine. I told the toreador about them—I think he felt for them a lot. He said, 'Maybe your mother and I used to play together?' And Papa's older brother was killed in Spain—he was a tank driver."

That's how things all come together, thought Mary Grigorevna. *I thought you didn't have a past. It turns out that you do. You have your father's past and your mother's and your uncle's. And all that past belongs to you. You don't understand that yet.*

"And it all happened because of the bull!" said Lyuba. "I'll tell Kostya about it today."

"Oh? His name is Kostya?" asked Mary Grigorevna.

"Of course. You know who he is. And by the way, I told him that legend of yours about the bull. He'd never heard anything about it. But Mary Grigorevna, that's not because he's not interested. He's very interested!"

That's why you've changed so much! thought Mary Grigorevna. "Well, then! I hope everything goes well for you. There's no such thing as a life without troubles, but may your troubles be light!"

"He told me today—we meet at the beach—that he thinks it's the very same bull."

"It's very possible," said Mary Grigorevna. "And just look, Lyuba, how many new friends you have because of the bull! There's Kostya and the toreador. . . ."

"And you!" said Lyuba.

"Now then, Lyu-ubochka!" said Mary Grigorevna with pursed-up lips, drawing out the syllables. She was terribly flattered.

1966   *Translated by Martha Kitchen*

Scorpion Berries

for Natasha Troshchenko

From the neighboring garden, over the fence, heavy branches hung to the ground. In the summer, small amber berries shone in the dark greenery—it was a white cherry. But it was forbidden to pick the cherries, although Babushka had no such tree in her own garden. And even if the ripe fruit fell to the ground, it was forbidden to eat any.

Once, in that first summer after Mama's death, when Galya came to Leningrad, Papa brought her a bag from the store.

"Annushka, take a look at what I've brought you!"

Galya ran up for a look, wrinkled up her nose, and said: "But I don't eat those! Those are Scorpion berries!"

Papa laughed in surprise and cried: "What? What? Say it again!"

"Scorpion berries," Galya said firmly, "they grow in Scorpion's garden. Babushka doesn't let me take any."

And she walked away, her firm little cleft chin in the air.

Papa stopped laughing and didn't ask any more about it: who did not know that Scorpion was Babushka's neighbor, Sidorenchikha, who had hanged Galya's calico kitten on that very tree!

The branches of Babushka's apple tree hung over the fence into Scorpion's garden, and no one over there ate the apples either. Well, Scorpion's Shurik used to pick them, but he would try to eat them so his mother couldn't see.

And the day that Shurik drowned in the river and they carried him home dead, and Scorpion herself came out into the garden—huge, disheveled, terrifying—and, slouching against the wall, began to howl, then Babushka, Galya's Babushka, climbed without even using a stool, up into that very apple tree and shouted down at her:

"So who's had the right of it, Scorpion. Why doesn't that God you're always praying to help you now? No! God sees the right! You wanted my Katya to lie dead like that, you wanted my Galya to lie dead like that—but God heard *me!* For you there's no forgiveness! Not in this world, not in the next!"

"Babushka," Galya called to her in a strangled voice, faint with horror and shame. "Babushka, come down! He's dead, Babushka!"

"Get to the house, child, this isn't for you to hear! So, Scorpion, you've got nothing to say? You just think back, just think back. . . ."

"May you stick fast to that tree and never get down! May your shameless eyes dry up in your head! May that little gypsy wench of yours. . . ."

"Keep your heathen tongue off the child!" shrieked Babushka in a voice Galya'd never heard her use. "Keep it off!"

"Babushka, come down, come down!"

It was that summer when Galya, grown taller and more slender, began to lie awake at night, thinking. Sometimes she would cry quietly into her pillow. Babushka would wake up, rouse Dedushka.

"Wake up old man! . . . I thought I heard . . . Galya! Are you awake?"

When Galya gave no answer, Babushka would get up with a grunt and approach her bed, treading heavily over the floorboards in her bare feet. Her roughened hands would fumble over Galya's neck, damp beneath the braids.

"The child's suffocating! You can't get a breath of air, it's so close in here! Lord have mercy!"

She would go out the door and, trying not to make a sound, open up the heavy wooden shutters. At once it became lighter in the room: the mirror, with the collection of photographs fanned out behind it, glinted softly in the moonlight. The corner where the icons used to hang appeared strangely empty. On the way back to bed, Babushka, yawning, would open the window, and in one breath the room would be flooded with the sounds and smells of a July night: a chorus of frogs, the fragrance of jasmine and stock, cicadas chirping, the sleepy cry of a frightened bird. . . .

"That damned Scorpion with her evil eye! She's put a spell on the child!" Babushka would complain.

The dry July ended, the rains and the thunderstorms came and moved on; Galya began to feel better and be more cheerful. But if she happened to meet Scorpion in the lane she would try to run by unnoticed. Once she could not resist looking back: the old witch was standing with her enormous feet, in men's boots, planted far apart. She glared after Galya with eyes that glowed like coals. Galya was eleven at the time.

But now she was fifteen, her childhood nightmares forgotten. She no longer called Sidorenchikha "Scorpion," and she was no longer disturbed when Babushka would tell stories about the wicked neighbor:

"She's selling half the house, the damned drunk: she needs the money for vodka! You wouldn't know anything about that, you haven't been here for ages. Well, Scorpion's started to drink—she started right after Shurik died. First she drank up what money there was, then she started to sell things off, then just this spring she took it into her head to sell half the house. And listen to this: the buyers would come during the day, and at night she would dig up fruit trees from their side and plant them in her own or-chard! That's just like her, the damned Scorpion!"

"Oh Babushka!" Galya said. "Is all this any of your business? So she sold the house, so she dug up some trees. There are people like that in the world. We just have to reeducate them!"

"Reeducate Scorpion? Her? Do you know that she murdered her own mother? Murdered her for the land, the orchard, and for that very house. And you talk about reeducating her!"

"Murdered?"

"Well her mother couldn't read or write, so Katka, Scorpion, as soon as her father dies, has all the land deeded over to *her*. She got all of Gavrilovsky Lane that way. And when her mother found out about it, she died—died that very night. A heart attack! And then came the Revolution. . . ."

"See, Babushka, and you said she murdered her mother!"

"You think she had to do it with a knife or an ax? You don't think she could cut without a knife, or poison without poison? But how could you understand? You're nothing like your mother, my Katya, my wise one, my darling. . . ."

Babushka went off into the house, leaving Galya alone with her own thoughts.

What did all this matter, after all. Yesterday Galya had received an airmail letter from Leningrad that began with the words, "Dear Anya . . ."

In the Ukraine, Galya, Anya, and Anna are the same name. She was Anna on her birth certificate, and everyone in Leningrad called her Anna or Annushka. "They called me Anna at my birth, the sweetest name to speak, to hear. . . ."

"Babushka, call me Anna."

"All right, Galya dear. Where are you going in that old dress? And with your hair. . . . You look like a wild heathen!"

"I'm just going to get the bread, Babushka."

"To get bread? You'll pass right by Scorpion's house! Go change into your good shoes and put on your pink dress. No, you won't be too hot in it. Let her see you, let her envy me—the shameless old drunk!"

Once outside the gate, Galya kicked off her good shoes and sighed blissfully as she worked her small feet into the warm dust. Ah-h! Papa said she should always go barefoot in the summer. If only he would come soon. When Papa and Aunt Nina were around everything seemed easy and calm, so uncomplicated!

Aunt Nina was Papa's wife, Galya's stepmother. She and Mama had been in the same class at school. Galya didn't remember Mama very well. Occasionally, she would suddenly recollect her mother's low, tender voice, or her necklace of jet beads, or her large sallow hands resting on a blue blanket: she was always ill. . . . Her face, however, Galya could not recall.

But if Mama's face was forgotten, Galya could never forget how Aunt Nina brought the news that Mama was dead. It was then that Babushka took the icons out to the garden and chopped them up with an ax. Grandfather stood by and cried, the tears running down onto his long mustache. For a long long time there was a dark spot in the icon corner—until they repapered the room.

It was strange all the same, that Babushka didn't mind Aunt Nina's marrying Papa. She was angry with God, but not with Aunt Nina. When she and Papa came to take Galya back with them, Babushka gave her up without a fuss, only making them promise to send her back for summer vacation. For the last few summers Galya had been sent to the Crimea instead: Papa got the idea it would be better for her health, for her lungs. It was funny how he was always worrying over her.

And not waiting for her to write first, Zhenya Popov had sent the first letter: "Dear Anna . . ."

Before the letter came it had seemed to her that . . . well, that she wanted to be friends with Zhenya. But now that feeling was gone. He had written, true, but there was no romance in the letter. When love really came, would she be written to, spoken to, in that calm, ordinary way? Or would she hear those wonderful words—the ones she herself spent some time thinking up. *My love! My heart faints within me when I hear the soft sound of your footsteps!*

"I'll have a loaf of the white, please."

The young salesgirl in the bakeshop was new. There used to be an old lady behind the counter who would always say to Galya "I look at you, and it's Katya to the life—the hair, the eyes, the way you walk!"

Whenever Babushka heard that she would just shake her head—imagine comparing Galya with her beloved Katya. She explained it once this way:

"Ekh, Galochka! If a pine tree dies, you'll never see another pine grow up on that spot!"

"What kind will grow there, Babushka?"

"A fir tree will. It's green, like the pine, and it isn't afraid of the winter either, but all the same it's not a pine. So your mother was my pine tree, and you're my little fir tree that came after her."

No, Galya couldn't take her mother's place with Babushka: no one could—not her sons, not her grandsons.

Galya loved her grandmother, although it wasn't easy being with her. And she loved the little whitewashed house with geraniums and fuchsias in the windows and warm dust beneath her bare feet. . . .

A warning beep from behind her. Galya jumped to the side of the road. Quietly, like a boat, a long automobile drove by in a cloud of dust and stopped in front of Scor . . . in front of the neighbor's gate. So Sidorenchikha's older son, Pavel, had come from Moscow. Pavel, who had the little boy named Borka. Borka was probably already old enough for school by now. He'd been such a little thing when she saw him last.

Galya was not acquainted with him. Feudal strife. If she were to tell Zhenya Popov that in our own time, in our own country, in Gavrilovsky Lane, there existed such Montagues and Capulets, he would never believe it.

No! Galya would not like to live her whole life in Gavrilovsky Lane. Everything there remained suspended in the past—and what, really, was so wonderful back then? This horrible feud—which used to frighten Galya, but which now seemed even a little funny—it too came from the past, probably started over something silly, a goose, perhaps. . . .

At Babushka's gate Galya wiped off her feet with the hem of the pink dress and put on her shoes.

"Babushka, the cherry tree at the neighbors' is in bloom. Just think, a cherry tree suddenly flowering in August!"

"I wonder what that's a sign for?" said Babushka pensively, pursing her lips.

"It's a bad sign, isn't it?"

Galya's humble voice had a note in it that offended her grandmother.

"Go ahead and laugh at somebody else's misfortune!"

"I'm not laughing, Babushka. But, do you remember, when that chicken of yours began to crow like a rooster—you killed it right away."

"Right. That's a bad sign. Why should she crow?"

"But afterwards you were sorry. She was your best layer."

"Right," Babushka repeated, not listening. "Oh this muggy weather! There's a storm coming, my bones feel it. My fingers are stiff as wood!"

The sky was clear. In the yard a tall poplar stood as if dreaming, gilded, in the intense heat. . . . Galya went into the orchard. She was about to answer Zhenya Popov's letter. And into the envelope . . . into the envelope she could put a white cherry blossom. After all, that was something interesting—a cherry blossom in August!

She approached the fence. There were very few blossoms on the tree, you could even count them. But Galya hesitated. For some reason it was difficult for her to pick one of the pink and white little stars. She hesitated and stood by the fence and listened. In the neighboring house, the terrible old woman was shouting in anger.

"So you want to cheat me? Just like winning the lottery? No! You think: Sidorenchikha's gotten old, she won't see, won't understand? Think I'll sell you my house for a drink of vodka, for a scrap of herring? You'll never live to see it! I'm going straight to the executive committee!"

"Mama," it was the quiet, Moscow-accented voice of her son. "Just stop it now, really! You yourself signed the papers. Right here they say. . . ."

"So you're against me too! A son against his own mother! Good people, bear witness! The son is on the side of his mother's enemies! He doesn't care about his mother's property, doesn't need what she has to pass on to him!"

Galya went back into the house without picking the cherry blossom.

The evening was dim and stuffy, the birds were calling out easily, and Babushka was restless: she banged pots, pulled out dresser drawers for some reason, lost her temper with Grandfather. He was silent, tugging at his grey Cossack moustaches. Galya could only be amazed at how this old Taras Bulba knuckled under to his wife. *When he was young he probably was like Andrey,* she thought.

The storm broke in the night. It came from far off, and at first seemed to have abated along the way: the thunder rolled so lazily, as if it were not really in earnest, and the warm rain drops were scattered. But then the poplar in the yard began to murmur as if in alarm, there was a blue flash of lightning at the window, something split with a crash—and the storm began to thunder and rage, banging the shutters—Galya lay awake and listened as Babushka got up, drank some water, scolded Grandfather for something in a whisper, looked for a candle. The storm had affected the electricity somehow, and it didn't work.

"Why can't you sleep?" Grandfather inquired. "Just walking up and down like that. . . . What's the matter?"

"Something's happened at Scorpion's," said Babushka, and her voice was suddenly very clear. "When I went to close the shutters I saw the ambulance."

"Well, I should go see," said Grandfather. "What if something's wrong with Pavel or with the kid?" The wooden bed creaked as Grandfather sat up.

"Where are you going snooping in the middle of the night? Think they can't manage without you over there? Look at him—

now he's a doctor! You go back to sleep. Scorpion's had a heart attack: she almost got cheated over the land sale. She's lived like a greedy animal, now she'll die like one."

The bed creaked again. There was a sigh. And again Babushka spoke softly:

"Petro, are you sleeping, Petro?"

"No," came Grandfather's hoarse voice in answer.

"It'll be a hard thing for her to die. Her with so much on her conscience! How will she like standing before that God she's always praying to?"

"People used to say," and from Grandfather's voice you could tell he wasn't sleepy any more, "people used to say that when a witch died you had to take the roof off a house, or tear up the floorboards. So her soul would have a way to get out. A witch's soul is sinful, heavy. . . ."

Silence. Galya could hardly breathe in that room. A human being was dying—even if she was greedy, even if she was bad—and her grandparents were happy about it. And what if they really did need help next door?

"Galya, where are you going?"

"Babushka, I'm going over there. . . . I can't just. . . . After all she is a human being! Maybe they need someone."

"So you think she's a human being, do you?" Babushka sat bolt upright, and by the dim candlelight Galya saw her face—cold, motionless, almost like a stranger's. "Then go on over!" the old woman said in a strange, cold voice. "But don't forget to ask how much the Germans paid her for Slavka, for his pure soul! Ask her how much she was paid for my Katya's tears!"

"Nastya!" Grandfather warned.

"Well? She's of an age where she ought to know the truth! What if I die, who'll tell her then? Hasn't anybody told you about Slavka? Not Nina, not your Papa? Well, they asked me not to tell you either, not to torment you with it. But I won't keep still anymore, my tender-hearted one, if you're getting ready to go over and comfort Scorpion!"

The huge dark figure of Babushka crossed the room and stood with its back to the window, arms folded. Again there was thunder, a long angry rumble that died out reluctantly.

"They went to school together, Katya and Nikolai, your

papa. . . . But Slavka only came in the higher grades. They sent him from another school. He was a wild one, and had talked back to the teachers there, so they sent him away. He was short, curly-haired, big-eyed—looked like a gypsy. They said his mother was a gypsy or a Rumanian: got married to a different man every year. I don't think Slavka even knew who his father was. He was always mocking people; he made fun of everyone. That's why the teachers didn't like him. But your mama, as soon as he got here. . . . I scolded her for it, tried to convince her, forbid her to let him in the door. . . . What good did it do? She just wasn't the same!"

Babushka sighed heavily, and the candle flame wavered, trembled. "How many nights I lost sleep over that hooligan, how I cried! I knew that Katya's happiness could not be with him. He wasn't a reliable boy, for him everything was a mockery, every-thing was jokes. . . . And with a mother like that. . . . I'd say to Katya, 'What are you thinking about? You'll have a miserable life with him! Better to give him up,' I'd tell her, but what good did that do? Once—they were already in college then—him in that Communications Institute or whatever, Katya was studying to be a teacher—once I even locked her up in her room so she wouldn't go running to him. What do you think she did? She jumped out the window!

"But suddenly something happened between them, between Katya and Slavka. To this day I don't know what it was. I just know it wasn't because of anything I said. Before, he'd come and wait for Katya underneath her window every night. I wouldn't let him in the house, so he'd stand underneath her window, whistle some tune, and Katya would jump out to him. But after they had this fight, he didn't come any more, and she just sat in the house and cried and cried on into the night. She wouldn't talk about it."

"She was proud," said Grandfather. "That's the way you all are—the worse for me!"

"Yes, that's so," Babushka agreed readily. "And Galya's like *you*, too ready to forgive. Well she sat and sat, and Nikolai kept coming to see her, trying to cheer her up. And then it seemed like she had cheered up. She and Nikolai got married on the first of June. Not in May! . . . in May take a wife, toil all your life. Your Grandfather and I were happy then."

"It was you that was happy."

"And you? You saying you weren't happy? You said it yourself. He was a good lad, a steady boy who'd loved Katya since they were children."

"He loved her. But did she love him? You were her mother, why didn't you tell her?"

"What could I tell her? What?"

Their conversation went on, filled with pain from the past, and both of them for a moment forgot about Galya, who listened almost without breathing, her legs, dangling from the bed, growing colder and colder. The storm began to move off, the thunder was quieter and less frequent. The candle guttered on the table, and Babushka's long shadow, wavering, climbed up the curtain to the ceiling.

"All the neighbors came to the wedding, and Scorpion was there with her husband and little Shurik. Her husband worked at Grandfather's factory—he was a metal worker too, but his real work was at home. Everybody brought their scissors to him for fixing. That's what he was a master at."

"He didn't fix them, he sharpened them," Grandfather corrected her.

"Well, then he sharpened them. It was Scorpion who made him keep doing it, otherwise why would he? They had money, clothing, all kinds of things in the house! And their stock—a cow, piglets, chickens. . . . They lived like noblemen. Slavka, when I was still letting him come to the house, used to go over to the fence and shout 'Hey, Sidorenchikha! The Komsomol committee says they're coming over tomorrow to liberate your property.' Oh, how she hated him.

"If it weren't for the war, maybe nothing would have happened. But suddenly—this was on a Monday, the second day of the war—Katya comes into the room with Slavka right behind her. I couldn't believe my eyes."

"What was to believe or not believe?" Grandfather muttered. "Even I saw it, how she kissed him in front of us and in front of her husband."

"She was sending him off to war, so she kissed him," said Babushka sternly. "He and Nikolai went to the front on the same day, together. Even your Grandfather went as a volunteer—just think. A hero of the 1918 war, how could they do without him?

I cried and cried, but how can you tell him anything? Stubborn old devil, God forgive me. And then the evacuation, with the Germans coming closer all the time. . . . Slavka's mother was dying then, in the end she died in Katya's arms, so we didn't leave. By the time we buried her there was no leaving at all, not on foot or any other way.

"Scorpion's husband was in the hospital too, then: it turned out he had cancer, and he died while the Germans were here. And Pavka and that other son she had, Vasil, they were sent to the front. So she was left alone with Shurik, and she started to drop in on me. Seems like she was lonesome all by herself. And she kept needling me: 'Where are your Bolsheviks,' she'd ask. 'They've helped you out a lot, haven't they? Where are they now? Might as well go look for the wind.' I'd ask her how she could talk that way—'You've got sons of your own in the Red Army.' 'What sons?' she'd say. 'They're no good, they don't fear God.' She was already a great churchgoer, went around in a black dress, like a nun. 'I have one son left, Shurik, and I'll make a real man out of him. He'll get all my property.'

"Katya and I lived quietly. I don't even like to remember the first winter, but in the spring we put in potatoes in the yard, and things got a little better. I'd do the housework, Katya would teach at the school, when it was open. The light had simply gone out of her, she went around all in black—Lord knows where her looks went. I was even a little bit glad, because she wasn't going to catch a German's eye like that, but my heart ached. She'd come home from school, eat whatever I'd made, and go sit in the corner. She sat and sat, and wouldn't talk. That winter, though, she cheered up a little. When they chased the Germans out of Moscow.

"But the Germans had more victories that summer, and Scorpion kept running over here to rub it in. Katya didn't say a word. We had a radio then: I'd turn it on, she'd turn it off. Once she turned it off and said, 'God, there must be partisans somewhere! How could I find them? What can I do?'

"Another winter went by. And then I was asleep one night—this was in the middle of March—and I heard a noise. Somebody was whistling under our window, very softly. I think, who is it, who's trying to break in?

"I was frozen, couldn't even say a word. Then I heard Katya jump for the door. . . . She doesn't even ask who it is, she opens up. I shouted, 'Katya, what are you doing?'

"In comes a small man, dressed nicely, in an overcoat and a hat. You couldn't see his face. Why was it I couldn't recognize him even in the dark, recognize the grief he was going to cause? The rascal was still laughing. 'Well Aunt Nastya, will you take me in today or is it again *au-revoir, bonjour, Cecile?*' That was a saying of his even in school. 'The war's over for you?' I asked him. 'I was captured and just escaped,' he said.

"Katya stands by him holding his hand, as if she didn't believe it was him. Doesn't say anything. But I took a good look. Did he think he was going to fool me? Think I'd never seen any prisoners? He had gotten a little thin, it's true, but he still had some meat on his bones. They don't look that way when they've been in prison.

"He stayed with us. I put him in the storeroom, where the pickle barrel is now. And I watched him close. He would hide during the day, go out only at night. Then he'd disappear for a few days, then show up again at night. I already had a bad feeling about him. I knew he wasn't keeping out of sight for nothing. But Katya, when he wasn't there, she didn't sleep. She'd just talk to me about him, how brave he was, how fearless. She told me he was a partisan. He'd been sent to our town as a go-between—jumped in with a parachute! He'd always been wild and he still was.

"He'd even send Katya out to do things for him. Before, she used to just sit at home, but now she was never there. And she was smiling again, all lit up. She'd read me the reports from Moscow— they'd started getting them. But I saw that it wasn't just reports between them. I'm alive too, I saw and understood. 'Katechka,' I'd say, 'What are you thinking of? What are you doing with your life?'

"How she looked at me, riled and angry. 'Mama,' she said, 'for me, life without Slavka isn't worth anything anyway. And don't remind me about Nikolai. I'm not really doing him wrong.' "

"Not doing him wrong!" said Grandfather heatedly. "A wife to act that way and not be doing wrong to her husband!"

"You're saying she was? He married Katya, and didn't he know that she dreamed about Slavka at night?"

"Well, why did she marry Nikolai? Who made her?"

"Who, who. . . . It was her cursed pride, that's who. . . . That fool of a Slavka took offense at something, or she did—and that's the way it turned out. She probably thought she'd forget him. And she would have, if it hadn't been for the war. Listen, Galochka! When Slavka started to live with us, we were more afraid of Scorpion than of anything. She'd stop by, and I'd try to go out somewhere, so she wouldn't be sitting around the house. Maybe that made her angry, or maybe she just started to watch, but one Sunday I met her in the street, her and Shurik coming from church. And she says, 'Seems like I've been hearing that whistling on the street at night—it's calling up the Devil, they say, Lord have mercy. So you've got suitors coming around now?' My heart just fell. Must've been Slavka coming home at night and whistling for Katya so as not to wake me. 'Don't know,' I say. 'Who'd be coming to us? Maybe, it was just a drunk passing by.' 'But it seemed like I knew that tune.' And it was as if she was raking my soul with her eyes. 'Seemed like I used to hear it a lot. It's not that hoodlum come back, is it?' 'Who'd that be?'—As if I didn't understand.

"Yes. I told Slavka: 'If you come back at night, don't whistle any more, no matter what. Knock, and I'll open up for you myself.' He looked at me closely. 'All right, *Tyotya* Nastya, I understand. Capitalist encirclement.'

"Then Scorpion comes to see us one evening, and goes straight into the kitchen. It was all right, Slavka was in the storeroom, hiding. Well, she starts up with her usual talk: 'Your Bolsheviks have given you a lot, haven't they? Helped your Piotr, when he was in the Red Calvary.' 'And did it help your man to hide behind the stove like a mouse?' We were talking the way we always did. I said: 'Don't you wag your tongue too much, your sons will come back from the Red Army and ask how you've been spending the time waiting for them.' She said, 'Why do you keep bringing up my sons that way? Would they be like they are if it weren't for the Soviets? My children would be merchants. We'd be rich people. Do you know how much my land would be worth if it weren't for their damned Revolution?'

"I just looked at her and didn't say anything. What good was it to talk to a block of wood like her? And then I hear the door creak: Katya'd come home. I didn't have time to draw a breath, and she was already in the kitchen and taking her jacket off.

"As soon as Scorpion looked at her, my heart fell. Well, I thought, it's all up with us. Now she'll know everything. Because Katechka was already expecting, and you could see her stomach."

"Why are you telling the child things like that?" Grandfather was angry. "Expecting, expecting, for shame!"

"Don't listen to him, Galya. You're of age now, and it's time you knew the truth. As soon as Scorpion looked at Katechka, her face became so spiteful. 'Well, goddaughter,' she asked, 'you aren't pining for your young husband, are you?' And Katya—what ever got into her—answered her sharply: 'My husband is with me, so why should I pine?' 'Where are you hiding him? Why don't you show him to the family?' 'That time will come!' 'What are you waiting for, for your Reds to come back?' 'They just might!' 'So, your husband is a hero with them?' 'Maybe he is!'

"They threw the words back and forth so fast-one-two-three! Like a machine gun. Katya was standing in front of her—they were the same height—and looking at her in such a way! Her face burning, her eyes shining! I can see her right this minute.

"I stepped in then: 'Now go, Scorpion,' I said. 'You've seen everything, you've sniffed everything out, now go! There's nothing more for you to do here!'

"And she went out like a dog that's been whipped. But she stopped at the door and said: 'Well and good, kinfolks, I thank you for your tender welcome. I won't forget it, and neither will you.'

"As soon as she'd left, Slavka came out of the storeroom, dressed, with his coat over his arm. It was already fall, and the rain was pouring down. He said, 'I can't stay here any longer, or I'll ruin you and not get to finish my work. Thank you Mama.' (It was the first time he'd called me Mama.) 'And now' (he nodded to Katya), 'let's kneel and ask her forgiveness, if we've done wrong. . . . Let her give us her blessing. . . .'

"And where did he get that word? He never used to know it, that's for sure! So they knelt down in front of me, and I started to go for the icon. Then I thought: how can I bless them with the icon when they don't believe? No, I'll just bless them with a parent's blessing. I said: 'My children! I give you my blessing, forever and ever amen. Live in love! Don't forget God, and be kind to others!' I said it the way people usually say it.

"So, Galochka, that's what I said to your mama and her husband. They were not wedded, but promised."

Babushka gave a long, wavering sigh.

"Slavka left us. And we never saw him again, dead or alive. The police came to us that night, searched and searched but didn't find anything, and then they took your mama Katya away. And she sat in prison until October, when our boys came back and set her free. They had interrogated her, tortured her, beat her so that her kidneys were ruined. . . . She lived for another seven years, all the time in hospitals and sanatoriums, but was she really there? I never saw her face shine again.

"Later, the partisans told us about Slavka. He went from here to another house, some railroad worker's. But it seems they were watching that one. The police came to take them, and they started shooting. There were so many police and Gestapo there you couldn't even count them! When Slavka was left alone, he threw a grenade and then blew himself up. He was a wild one."

"He was a hero," said Grandfather harshly. "A hero of the Soviet people!"

"I say he was wild!"

There was a short silence.

"Babushka," asked Galya in a trembling voice. "Wasn't the baby born, then?"

And again silence fell.

"Why wouldn't it be born?" said Babushka. "It was born—a baby girl. We call her Galya."

The room was filled with a ringing and a mist, and it seemed to Galya that someone had thrown an enormous pillow over her that wouldn't let her breathe or think. Through this pillow she heard:

"So what are you telling me to do, my little granddaughter? Go to Scorpion? Look after her? Comfort her? If she were dying in front of my eyes I wouldn't give her a drink of water; if she had to go begging, I wouldn't give her a piece of bread! When her Shurik drowned, I knew! That came to her because of my Katya, because of Slavka, because of you, Galochka, my tenderhearted granddaughter."

"But why," Galya could scarcely speak. "Why wasn't she tried afterwards? Why didn't you go and tell?"

"Why! Why! Because she's my sister! My own sister! Two years older than me."

"*Tyotya* Nastya! Please come and pay respects to my mother."

"Thank you for the invitation," Babushka answered in a measured tone, and tied her snow-white kerchief more tightly beneath her chin. "But I'm not coming. There's nothing for me to do there."

Uncle Pavel—fat, yellow-faced, tired—did not try to persuade her any further: he turned and left. Babushka remained by the window. She sat silently and watched. Since that night she had been silent, as if she had said everything she had to say. She silently set the table, silently came and went. Just as silently, she handed Galya an envelope with old letters—all that Mama had left.

Galya had been reading the letters for three days. They were written in Papa's familiar handwriting—straight, up-and-down letters. It turned out that he'd had the same handwriting since childhood.

"Katenka! Slavka and I are going to get the tickets. At 7:30 we'll be at your house. The code whistle is 'Tell me, girls. . . .' "

"Katya! My sign is NNN—no matter what." This was written on a scrap of paper. How had that been saved?

"You can laugh at me for not having any pride. For me there is no one but you. I know that you can't fight love, otherwise you would love me. But you haven't stopped thinking of me as your friend? Why then. . . ."

This was a three-cornered note written at the very beginning of the war. My God, how had it managed to survive?!

"I should have known that you wouldn't stop loving him. Forgive me, Katya, if you can. Let me remain your friend—forever, till death, till the end. . . ."

The last letter was in a yellow envelope with a return address—their Leningrad address.

"Katenka, my dear! Let me come get you and Galochka. There are doctors here, professors, friends. We'll put you on your feet again, I swear. . . ."

Grandfather came in cautiously. He had been at the neighbors' since daybreak, helping to knock the coffin together. He had a guilty air and his moustaches were drooping.

"Nastya!" he said softly. "Maybe you should look in for a minute. She was your sister after all. Well? Nastya?"

"You go see her," said Babushka not turning her head. "Go ahead, my tenderhearted man."

"What about you, Nastya?"

Babushka remained silent and gazed at the street. Grandfather gave a quiet cough, looked at her straight, stony back, made a gesture with his hand and went out, trying not to make his shoes squeak.

Was there no letter from the other one? Not the smallest note or letter? Did he not write, or not like to write? Or, maybe, had Mama destroyed it all so as not to have to remember, not to have to recall? Only one photograph remained, a little "five minute" one with a torn corner. There was a dark, cheerful face, the long lips laughing. . . . And that strong cleft chin—that's where Galya got it. . . .

Into the room without knocking ran a little boy about six years old. He had on short pants and an embroidered Ukrainian shirt. He ran up to Babushka with no hesitation, not looking to one side or the other.

"Babushka Nastya," he pronounced in a surprisingly light, somewhat chirping voice. "Come to our house! We all really want you to!"

Of course it was Borka, Uncle Pavel's son. Quite a little fellow he was! Babushka was looking at him, and he was already tugging at her arm, pulling her up.

Babushka stood up.

"Let's go, Galya," she said, and again pulled her kerchief tight under her chin. "You must come too. Cover your head."

It was such a golden, crystalline, dewey splendor out of doors on that morning, with the poplars, the apple trees, and the calendula in the flowerbed breathing freshness. How happily the sun shone, as if it were May and not August, and the long summer days were still ahead. . . .

There was activity in the lane. All of the familiar old women were standing by the neighbor's gate. They remembered Sidorenchikha as the owner of all the land on which their houses stood, on which their children had grown up. . . . With her were departing their last recollections of a hard, poor, hungry time . . . a time that had nonetheless been their youth. They had come to bid farewell to that time and to their memories.

When Galya and Babushka entered the murky, close room, people stepped aside. Galya saw the high table, the candles, the armfuls of flowers still moist with dew and a yellow, stony face with darkened eyelids. She did not immediately understand that it was Sidorenchikha. Uncle Pavel approached Babushka and tried to escort her to the coffin, but she gently shook him off and went forward with a firm step, not leaning on anyone, not taking her eyes from the dead face. The priest—a youngish man in a black cassock, with long hair and a trimmed beard—stepped aside, visibly cowed. Babushka sat down on a chair by the corpse's head and folded her heavy, stiff hands on her knee. It became perfectly quiet.

"Katrina my sister," Babushka began in a level voice.

Galya felt a slight, swift chill run down her spine.

"I forgive you for killing our mother with your cruel greed. . . ."

From a far corner the frightened priest made the sign of the cross at both of them.

"I forgive you," Babushka continued, "for betraying my daughter Katya to the Germans.

"I forgive you for destroying my promised son-in-law, Slavka, and for leaving his little daughter fatherless.

"I forgive you for trying to put the evil eye on my granddaughter Galochka.

"I forgive you for hanging her kitten, for taking away an orphan's last joy."

Babushka's words fell slowly, one after the other, as people gazed at her and listened. Even the priest stood with his arms at his sides, not making any more signs of the cross. Next to him a rosy-faced woman in a black kerchief stood with her mouth open in amazement.

"And I forgive you for having me work for you, from youth up, like a field hand, all for your greedy, gluttonous belly.

"And I forgive you for trying to separate a man from his wife."

Grandfather made a gesture of annoyance and turned aside.

"I have no guilt before you!" She concluded proudly. "I say this in front of witnesses: I did not envy your property, I did you no harm, I waited for your conscience to strike you. I have nothing to repent of before you."

Babushka rose.

"And now, Father, you may sing the requiem. I won't go to the cemetery, but I'll open the gates."

The priest bowed, crossed himself, and said something to the rosy-faced woman. She lowered her eyes and, without changing expression, began to sing in a colorless voice:

"Rest with the saints. . . ."

A small hand crept into Galya's moist palm.

"Let's go," whispered Borka. "Papa said that we don't have to stay to hear this."

After the smoky gloom and the thick incense, after Babushka's heavy forgiving, which was like a cursing, and the strange, thin singing, Galya was again gripped by the calming quiet of the morning in the orchard. And once again—not for the first time in those days—it seemed to be all a dream she had had. But in the orchard, dead and dark, stood the small, low, neglected house with its shutters closed. Behind the shutters was death, which had taken up residence there long ago.

Soon they would carry her out, that horrible woman who had lived by hatred alone. Could one really live on hatred? They would carry her out, and life would go on without her. Her memory would fade. Other people would come, they would paint the house and start to live.

Borka sighed and said:

"We're not staying here. Papa said we don't need this house."

"He's right," said Galya. "You don't. It's not a good house."

"Papa was happy in Moscow," Borka sighed again. "But we came here, and now he doesn't laugh any more. Is your papa happy?"

"Very happy! My Papa is wonderful!"

He was wonderful, but why, why had he and Aunt Nina hidden the truth from her? Did they think that she wouldn't understand? But after all, she was already fifteen years old. And what should she do now? Admit that she knew everything? Knew, and loved

Papa even more because of it all? He'd been so good, but why was he afraid of the truth?

Borka tugged at her hand.

"Let's go," he said in a mysterious voice. "I know a place. . . . Let's go!"

He ran ahead, looking back at Galya with his finger to his lips, and stopped suddenly by the fence, at the spot where the cherry tree leaned over with its splendid branches, looking like long white flowing sleeves.

"Here," he said triumphantly. "Now lift me up, and I'll pick the flowers. Before, my Babushka wouldn't let me. She said they were yours if they were on your side. But now I can, can't I?"

"Now you can. Take them all if you like. We're not greedy."

She lifted Borka up, and he hastily picked the little white stars.

"Don't be afraid," said Galya. "It's even good for the tree. It shouldn't be flowering now, it's like the tree is sick. Jump down, I'm going to pick them too."

This one is for Papa. This one is for Aunt Nina. This one is for . . . Zhenya Popov?

"Why is the tree sick?" asked Borka, standing on tiptoe. "Should it have some medicine?"

"Good people will come to live here," Galya said in a singsong voice like Babushka's, "and they will give it medicine, and care for it. And it will flower, like all trees, in spring. . . . Trees also have to be looked after, and cared for, and loved. . . . And then there will be berries."

"I like berries," said Borka.

Doleful singing was heard in the orchard. At the door appeared the priest, waving some sort of long lamp out of which came clouds of blue smoke. Behind him was the rosy-faced woman. Then, by herself, not leaning on anyone, came Babushka. Behind her, Grandfather, Uncle Pavel, and two other men carried out the long plain coffin. The old women from Gavrilovsky Lane walked after the coffin sedately, without talking, their eyes lowered.

Babushka went to the gates and opened them wide.

"God speed you!" she said in a ringing tone.

When the last old woman, eyes on the ground, had gone out

into the street, Babushka turned, met Galya's glance and said sternly:

"Let's go home. There's nothing else for us to do in this place."

"Take me with you!" Borka pleaded.

1959   *Translated by Martha Kitchen*

Elizabeth Arden

IN 'forty-eight we got rich.

By some miracle, my husband, an editor at a Leningrad publishing house, was given a half-time appointment at the Pedagogical Institute. The working of this miracle is even now mysterious to me; I remember only a cultivated voice on the telephone. "My name is Kastorsky. Yes, that's right—Kastorsky. Tell him I've arranged a half-time appointment for him."

That's how dreams come true. I had dreamed of an income of three thousand rubles (about three hundred, now) as the pinnacle of good fortune. At the publishing house my husband made twelve hundred. A half-time appointment at the Institute—fifteen hundred, because my husband had a Ph.D—took care of everything. He'd have to lecture on things that didn't interest him at all, but— a half-time appointment! The remaining three hundred, I earned—by typing, writing reviews, translating. With this three hundred rubles we paid our Simonovna, our Nanny Tasya, our nurse–cook–housekeeper—in short, a member of the family, just as my own nanny had been. Only Simonovna didn't live with us—she lived with her daughter Shurka, a furnace stoker in a "dormitary" on Krestovsky. But sometimes she stayed with us, spending the night on a metal folding cot in which the mesh hung like a hammock. When we came home from an evening out and immediately, without turning on the light, threw ourselves down on the opened sofa bed, sinking into the cozy depressions between the unruly springs, I would listen for a few minutes with inexpressible pleasure to her snoring, to the sound of the children's quiet breathing. That snoring filled us with peace: we could sleep, sleep. If one of the children began to cry, she would get up; if one of them called out, she would answer; in the morning she would pick them up quietly and take them out to the kitchen. . . . Wonderful, unforgettable nights.

When we got rich, we began to have Simonovna stay overnight once a week; now we could afford it. Besides that, I ordered a coat for myself from the furrier's: the outside was old, but the fur trim was new—red opossum. And for my daughter a new outfit— a little hat, scarf, and mittens; we'd asked a friend to bring it from Tallin. And we celebrated our fifth wedding anniversary, we even served pheasant, since pheasants were no more expensive that autumn than chickens. And I went to a cosmetician.

I started going to cosmeticians when I was nineteen because of my freckles, which I'd thought of ever since childhood as the mark of Cain. My struggle with freckles was long, exhausting, and hopeless: sometimes they'd go away, but then they'd invariably pop out again. The beauticians would say what dry skin I had, and suggest nourishing creams, egg masks, deep-pore cleansing. . . . For the last five years, which had been devoted to the primitive struggle to stay alive, I'd given all that up; but now that we'd finally gotten rich—True, we still owed three thousand to a friend who had a full-time appointment and no children. But he was in no hurry, and kept saying that now, after reform, it wasn't three thousand but three hundred. We said, Not for one second, and asked if he'd wait until spring. In short, I went to a cosmetician.

I didn't go just anywhere—I went to the Hotel Yevropeiskaya.

Nowadays a lot of fashionably dressed workers from the State Security Agency hang around the Yevropeiskaya, because only foreigners can stay there. But in those days, as I recall, businessmen from Moscow stayed there, and members of the Writers' Union—not even the top people. And I went, and nobody stopped me, and I found the beauty salon on the second floor.

The cosmetician looked like an advertisement. She had firm, smooth, white skin that shone with pink along her rounded cheekbones, below which there were dimples, above which there were wide-open, light-blue eyes that expressed a quiet love of life. Whenever we happened to occupy the same physical plane—when she bent over my chair to examine my skin, which it was her job to "treat"—an unaccustomed feeling of seamless peace descended on me; the eternal clutching loosened, my blood vessels dilated, I felt warm as winter crops beneath the snow.

I started going there three times a week. And every time, when I settled back in the chair that tilted like a dentist's chair and the pink-and-white cosmetician bent over me, smelling of lotions fresh as cream, a peaceful warmth enveloped me like a blanket.

"You know how o-l-l-d I am?" she asked. The tip of her tongue, in the dark pink depths of her mouth, trembled: *l-l-l*.

No, I didn't know how old she was; neither did her other client, a woman who looked like one of Pharaoh's lean cows.

"Sixty!" she said gaily. "No one believes it!"

I didn't believe it either. And I don't believe it now. Sixty! At that age, even Catherine the Great looked like an old country squire's wife. No, she was probably forty-something, but she added to her age for the sake of advertising. The West!

She was "western." She looked German, but she wasn't. (Germans—not prisoners of war, ordinary Germans—had in fact begun to appear in the streets of Leningrad; but they were men. Engineers, people said, from the Zeiss factories. But in all that time I'd seen only one woman—a prisoner of war, six feet tall. When a rumor swept through Leningrad like the wind, of the capture of a forest witch who ate partisans, and all of Leningrad went running to the Zoo to get a look at her, she appeared in my mind's eye in the form of that German woman: six feet tall, and in a German uniform.)

Probably she was from one of the Baltic republics—from Tallin, or Riga. Maybe she'd gone back there after the war, from somewhere in the States? Otherwise why would she have Elizabeth Arden products? As far as I knew, no, absolutely no, foreign cosmetics were sold officially in the Soviet Union (except in the new territories that had appeared after 'thirty-nine). There were some around during the NEP years (I remember a word, *lorigan-koti*—I think some writers who were considered fellow-travelers even used the word in print); but that was in my mother's day— a very, very brief day, as I realized even at the time. One of my earliest childhood memories is of a blue faience bowl with designs on it that held macaroni, which I called "rations" (I thought for a long time that that was what macaroni was called); later, when I was school age, Nanny and I used to stand in line for macaroni— real rations, then. But the whole of my mother's era, with its L'Origan-Coty and its pastry shops, was sandwiched in between these two closely spaced memories.

I can't remember at all what that western cosmetician was called. No matter how I try, I can't. Because, to myself, I always called her "Elizabeth Arden"—then, and for many years afterward. Those two words, Elizabeth Arden—musical, melodious words—were printed, no! *engraved,* on tiny cups and bottles and boxes. And on pink, textured, glossy, incredibly foreign powder boxes that closed with a big button, closed unequivocally with a smooth triumphant snap that never failed to call up from some childish depths a happy feeling of the triumph of man over mechanism.

Elizabeth Arden would stroke cream soft and thick over my lean face, a nourishing mask. The headrest of the chair inclined backward, and I would gaze with pleasure at the clean, even, carefully white-painted ceiling—a rarity in postwar Leningrad. You could close your eyes and hear, to the music of water gurgling in the basin, the nourishing mask sinking into your skin; you could look out of the corner of your eye and examine the "lean cow" who sat mute and uncomplaining in the next chair, yellow from the mask, fixed eyes open wide.

Now and then male voices were heard in the room. The electrician would inquire whether the motor was working; a workman would ask if everything was all right with the iron; the plumber would want to know something. Elizabeth Arden would laugh: it was all right, everything was fine. The men tramped around, wouldn't go away. The manager would come in (grey suit, 52 Long), checking, asking questions, giving pep talks. The cosmetician asked why they'd fired the linen woman for that floor; the manager rejoined in a velvet voice, "Now, why worry your head about that? You should be asking when we'll have a party and invite some interesting men!"

In one of Priestley's books or any classic detective story set in the West, she would have been a spy: a foreigner, a beauty, a cosmetician. . . . A spy whom the powers-that-be had already suspected for some time and were playing like a large, hooked fish. But that's in novels. In reality she wasn't a spy at all, just dumb. She'd come here from the Baltic States, no doubt thinking that this place was like any place where there were women. Yes. But even so, things won't work out for her, she's too conspicuous. They'll call her a spy anyway, she can't escape it, even I can see she's doomed; and probably the "lean cow" can too—that's why she keeps staring so. It's like going to the theater to see a familiar play, but the actors are new. That's what makes it interesting.

She dried and smoothed and pulled at my skin as if it weren't skin but taffy. I *became* taffy. But all she had to do was take a step or two away from me, and she'd fall right back into a detective drama. The play goes on, has been going on for quite a while, and you're still in the wings; but then comes your entrance. And then—my own. There's no escape. The time will come for all of us, like death. We're not supposed to talk about it, and we shouldn't—why talk about what you can't escape?

And if suddenly there were a chance to escape? Well, who are we? Not Party members, and my husband's job nothing wonderful, and the children small, and mostly—mostly we go along with the majority. During the war we went along with everything. We call Stalin a great man—of course, what's the point of talking about it? Who doesn't, now—after the war? But what about the business of "rootless cosmopolites"? . . . And the disclosure of pseudonyms? . . . And once I refused to work for the NKVD—but look when that was, way before the war. And once I called Lenin a second-rate journalist, and the man I was talking to got scared. . . . And another time I said to somebody, "The conquered dictate terms to the conqueror"—but that was just something I'd read in Feuchtwanger. *Yes, you'd read it somewhere; but remember the reason why you said it.* And once a fellow student, walking home with me, suddenly inquired in a very businesslike tone, "What do you think about Zhukov's fall?" as if he were completing an assignment. That time I didn't go for it, that time I told him flatly, I don't think anything, what I think about is where to get winter boots for my son. *Yes, but before that, way before that, you and he were inseparable, you could talk about anything.*

Come on, that's all just worrying—empty fears, night fears, because we're so well-off, so secure, so lucky, living so well. Our home, our sixteen-square-meter room, had everything we needed: three beds, a sofa bed, a desk, and best of all, a six-hundred-ruble oak wardrobe in mint condition, with pull-out compartments. And German curtains that I bought at Gostiny—eight hours standing in line, but what curtains! And books—we can even buy books now, there's a bookcase in our communal kitchen with plenty of room. And there's always milk for the children, and sometimes even tangerines—"halvesies" the children call them, because we give them each half. And my fur coat. And Elizabeth Arden!

Elizabeth Arden. I desperately wanted one of her powder boxes—glossy, with a button clasp. The powder wasn't white or pink or rachel, but something completely different, the color of the *fil-de-Perse* stockings that Mama had during the NEP years. The color of plenty: Mama had so many of those stockings that they lay in a heap—she would throw them in the pile if they got a run. They were so delicate. I would stretch a stocking over my hand and look at it closely. At the beginning of the thirties I started wearing them on the sly; under a long skirt the runs weren't visible, especially if you mended them properly. They lasted me until I was seventeen, those stockings.

To get a pink box, you had to go through a "full course of treatment." Ten sessions at thirty rubles each, payable in advance. Only then would I receive a box—the reward, the prize, for having served my time.

I served it conscientiously. I threw back my head in the dentist's chair, inhaled the creamy fragrance of Elizabeth Arden's fingers and her décolletage, and listened to her gurgled advice.

"Nef-er f-r-r-own," she'd say, smiling, rolling the *r*'s softly. "Your face should alvays be ser-r-rene."

"What if you have cats in your heart?" the lean one asked, raising long-suffering eyes.

"Vat does it mean—cats? Soch an eggzpression!"

"What does it mean—storm?" asked my two-year-old son. He knew how to find the subject of a sentence right away, taking the bull by the horns. *Covers the heavens with mist* didn't satisfy him. "But a storm won't come to us? Never, ever?"

No storm came, but at two in the morning he woke up wailing anyway, insisting there was a dog under his bed, or a cow, or some other memory of life at the *dacha* which, in a city apartment, resurfaced in nightmares.

"I gave you as nursemaids the wind, the sun, the eagle," I sang, walking the dark room with him in my arms. He scrunched down into a more comfortable position and grew heavy. Then he opened wide-awake eyes and said, in his practical way, "Where is the wind, really?"

My daughter answered him from her bed in a fresh morning voice, "It lives in the chimney, Nanny Tasya said so. And it howls there."

Toward three o'clock they'd quiet down—sometimes it would take till as late as eight. At ten Simonovna came and I was set free like the wind in the chimney, filled with tender and delighted love for my fine, precocious, unusually interesting children. But you had to work to live: I would sit retyping the enormous thousand-page manuscript of an out-of-favor member of the Academy who had translated almost all of ancient Chinese poetry in the meter of Lermontov's "The Novice." The work was easy, even fun; the only sad thing was that I'd been paid in advance.

If there was time left, I worked on a novel about my classmates Dodik and Dusya. The idea for the novel, the plot and the story, I already had. Love between two schoolmates, then his betrayal, then the rekindling of love just before the war; and then the war. It had to have the eternal themes of love and fidelity and death. And ephemeral things, too—war, betrayal, treason, Fascism. Anti-semitism.

Our friend—the one to whom we owed three hundred rubles— had an Aunt Manya who didn't believe in kleptomania. "Why isn't there a sickness where you come and *leave* things?" she'd ask. "Why is there only a sickness where you come and take things?" In the same way, many of my contemporaries didn't believe in anti-semitism. The way most naive atheists don't believe in God: "Well, have you ever seen him?" They haven't seen it—it doesn't exist. Of course, sometime, somewhere, before we were born, i.e., practically never. But now? Ridiculous!

Deep down I suspected that everything you read about in books really exists. And so, from childhood on, I kept waiting for love and war, Paris boulevards (where little Liza sells spring violets) and the partitioning of Poland, the terrible pains of childbirth and palace revolutions. Only as far as the Tsar was concerned did I understand once and for all that there was no Tsar and never would be—much to my distress, since I had been raised on turn-of-the-century books, Russian patriotic children's literature ("And do you know, little ones, that our country is also a tsardom-stardom?")

In general, I waited for everything. And when I saw it face-to-face, with amazement and a catch in my breath, I recognized it.

That was the way I recognized anti-semitism. Not immediately, because it crept up on us—it arose—gradually. Afterwards it seemed to us that the first faint signals sounded in 'thirty-nine, when the Pact was signed (it was then that we came face-to-face with the partitioning of Poland)—but old-time Odessans—oh, those old-time Odessans—by the beginning of the thirties had already composed a Biblical joke: "What's the difference between Moses and Stalin?" "Moses led the Jews out of Egypt; Stalin led them out of the Central Committee."

The young people of Odessa knew this joke, of course; but what did we care? We were at last embarking on youth: romances and rumors, kisses (a single peck), dances (slow foxtrot and tango: "*Zigeuner, du hast mein Herz gestohlen!*"; "*Wszystko mnie jedno!*"). In Odessa, youth lasts a long time. It begins at about twelve and goes on and on; by fifteen everyone has accumulated memories, disappointments, petals fallen from life's first flower. . . . We didn't talk about impersonal matters. In any case, not before 1937. All of Odessa tacitly agreed: Look what those bandits Marx and Engels have done. But no one thought about it—because no one said it out loud.

Various other Odessas rustled, breathed, sometimes hid themselves alongside us. In Cathedral Square, before the Cathedral was blown up, a tiny, slovenly, big-eyed old woman used to sell books; once I heard her talking with a customer in French. I began speaking to her in French, too: the unknown, hidden Odessa of the past was very alluring, and she belonged to it. Her surname was Rennenkampf. She showed me some snapshots of herself with Ida Rubinstein and D'Annunzio in Venice. Gondolas and huge hats. "She wasn't beautiful," she said of Ida, "but she was very slender. Thin, thin, thin!" Later, from her story, I recognized Ida in a portrait by Serov. "I am a firm believer," said the old woman. "And I know the Lord will repay me for what I've been deprived of here." She was a Catholic, from a Jewish family.

Those few years of youth: spring, when the sap is running. . . . That's the imbalance in human civilization—those few years of spring, unbroken spring—how can we endure them without going crazy? It's all very well for animals—spring ends, and then right away comes reproduction. . . . But we never gave it a thought; we were busy with other things. The only thing that mattered was who looked at you, and how, and "he said—she said," and, oh, hands, lips, eyes—You remember. . . . When

Dodik stood at the blackboard favoring his game leg (a few years before, he'd dived from a boat and there'd been an underwater rock), Dusya didn't look at him. She just lowered her eyes and listened; she was all ears. He was courting a pretty high-school girl at the time, a blonde none of us knew very well. Later he lived with her for a few years; then the Germans came, and that was the end of that. Dusya remained faithful. He perished. Dusya said to me, "Don't write about this as a Jew."

I would have liked to write about it like Vera Panova, lightly, ironically, dealing calmly with sexual feelings. But the words wouldn't behave; "locks of hair" and "single glances that expressed so much" kept creeping in. And thoughts about the Jewish business, which one really shouldn't, one mustn't, it's in bad taste. Not because of censorship, but because there were more important, universal human considerations.

Meanwhile, that year all we talked about was being Jewish.

We had talked about it before, we'd always talked about it—joking, without fear, at least consciously. Naturally, there were signals that clicked for each of us, warning clicks like the ones you hear on your telephone when it's tapped and someone is listening in, reminder clicks. Mine clicked several times in nineteen forty—it clicked loudest when I talked with a Jewish family (Mama, Papa, daughter Ruth) who were moving from Central Europe to Sweden. I had met them in Moscow, at the Hotel Savoy, and we'd talked. They were going to Sweden because Ruth was so talented, she needed. . . . I asked, "Ruth? Are you Jewish?" "Yes," said the woman, a tall, well-built, very European woman; and she blushed. That was a click I could interpret: they blush, that's what they've been reduced to there. And in the back of my mind was Feuchtwanger, *The Oppenheim Family* and *Exile,* and that it could only happen there, and so we ought to be thankful—people can be arrested here, but so what, here we don't have *that,* we never have to blush. . . . I remember my avid curiosity about that woman and others like her, obviously wealthy, who were passing through the Hotel Savoy on the way to Sweden, to America (if Sweden was too close for them), because they, their very existence embodied the history of literature, the history of religion, the history of the Middle Ages—in short, History. . . .

We certainly never had to blush. I remember how, in our first year at the University, we jokingly called ourselves *Natsbol*—an ethnic majority. Not *Natsmeny,* but the opposite: *Natsbol.* In our department at the University, we actually *were* the majority. And everywhere I went, in all the close-knit little groups in which I found myself, right up until 'thirty-eight, until Spain, that was how it was. Even in Spain, we translators were our own kind of *Natsbol;* but we worked for others, the real majority, real Russians, whom we regarded with puzzlement. Though we knew they were more important than we were, we were astonished at how different they were, how uneducated, how ignorant (back then, people didn't say "dim"). I think now that we girls must have been caught unawares by the unexpected sexual attraction we held for these people, these grown men; but still the greatest surprise was how unlike us they were. The Spaniards even seemed more like us, despite their foreign ways, customs, and, of course, language—a truly foreign language, not the language, in which the words seemed familiar but the meaning was foreign, spoken by our *consejeros.*

No, we never had to blush; we only wanted desperately to be Russian, and sometimes we mistook the wish for the reality, especially when we were abroad. There we were Russian! We were Russian women in Spain (even though we girls had the choicest of Biblical names), and our boys were Russians in Germany when they went there as victors. Our boys, yesterday's students and graduate students, Germanists. Our boys, Germanists and humanists, who believed that one shouldn't beat prisoners, shouldn't take revenge on the defenseless inhabitants of a conquered country; our boys who paid for their internationalism, their far-above-nationalist clemency, sometimes quite dearly. Read Lev Kopelev's book.

Afterwards, returning victorious to Leningrad, our boys were ready to take up their peacetime lives at the point where they'd been interrupted—their graduate studies, for instance. They couldn't.

One I remember better than others. He began the war as an enlisted man, finished it a major; began the war as a member of Komsomol, finished it a full-fledged Party member; began as a youth, finished a grown man, a serious one who had seen everything. His student nickname had been the Enthusiast. There are more anecdotes and stories about him than I can tell; we were all a little in love with him—all of us liked him so much, and his simplicity was somehow captivating. In Germany, among a conquered people, he'd been like that, too: kind to everyone, as he'd always been. And suddenly he was not allowed to return to graduate school.

He wasn't angry, I remember—he was baffled. And the rest of us felt a sort of malicious pleasure ("Nice guys finish last"), a sort of triumph ("I told you so"), but mainly, mainly, we felt: Here it is. *Here it is.* Here it is, we're face to face with it. Now try to say it doesn't exist. Anti-semitism. State-sanctioned anti-semitism.

When we recognized it, we called it by its name; and that was dangerous.

Children in kindergarten, in primary school, complain: He calls me names! Criminals growl, frothing at the mouth: He called me *scum.* Caliban doesn't like to recognize himself, even in a nickname. Nickname, appellation, name. Besides their nicknames, ancient peoples had secret names known only to their parents and the priests. To name is to know. And to know? You remember who first decided that knowledge was dangerous.

But the joy of knowledge? The joy of recognition? Here it is—familiar to us from Feuchtwanger, from Ehrenburg, from newspaper articles; here it is, clear to everyone, sanctioned by the State. Here you have it: the conquered dictate terms to the conquerors. And we shuddered with joy, talked about nothing else, told jokes, made fun of our friend the Enthusiast and others. Made fun of two brothers, university professors, one of whom was registered as a Jew, the other as a Russian; the rector called in the older one and thundered (the rector was a passionate man), "Put your family in order!" Made fun of the professor who said, "How can I be a Jew? I was raised on Pushkin," and was advised, "Write that on your questionnaire: *Jew, raised on Pushkin.*" Made fun of Rabinovich (his mother was an Ivanov), who got a job in the Public Library as a Russian and was told by his exasperated boss, "With a surname like that, I'd rather have a Jew." And many, many others; it was impossible to remember them all. We found a kind of joy in fear. Ordinary, inescapable, lifelong fear—the narrow-minded, lower-class fear described by Afinogenov—took a new form.

But it was not this that my novel of young love and war was about. Not this exhilarating fear.

I wanted to write about the dawn of love, which, as my generation and the ones before it knew well, was the only good love; among my young contemporaries only the literary scholars can remember it (Nadson did make it into the Small Series, after all). The ghetto, the Holocaust—that would come later, later.

But I couldn't even manage the dawn of love. I didn't have enough skill or time. I had to type Chinese poetry and go every other day to Elizabeth Arden; at night I had to sing about the sun, wind, and eagle; and in the evenings. . . .

Every evening, or nearly every evening, our friend, the one who'd lent us the three hundred rubles, came over. He and his wife both had full-time academic appointments, and they were expecting a baby any day. He came by streetcar. For those days, he lived a good distance away; it was before the subway, when Avtovo and Okhta and Vasilevsky were the remote outskirts of Leningrad. Nevertheless, he'd come every evening, or almost, and we would talk, the three of us. He was born and grew up in Odessa and he remained an Odessan all his life, like Zhabotinsky: unashamed, unchanging, unwavering, believing that the Odessa City Theater was the second in the world (to this day Odessans argue over which is the first), and Odessa's women! . . . His wife was from Odessa, of course. He was a Party member. And a Marxist.

And he had an austere mind. He was a philologist in the Leningrad sense of the word—a scholar, not given to frivolity. But Odessa sharpened that scholarly mind. And Odessa irony destroyed him. Not a sense of humor—one could live with that. But irony. "Not a Russian emotion." In the early fifties, a Moscow schoolteacher said to a boy whose German surname sounded suspect to her, "Why are you smiling so ironically, Vizen? Irony is not a Russian emotion."

Irony gave birth to his best work. In 1948, when even jokes had ceased, he composed a song to the tune of "Cut-glass Tumblers."

> I'm just standing there,
> Hands in my pockets,
> When suddenly along comes

A gentleman I don't know.
He says to me softly,
"Where can I go
Tonight to spend
The evening raising hell?
Find a few broads,
Find a little wine?
No matter what it costs—
It's all the same to me!"
And I answer him:
"Yesterday morning
The last thieves' den on Ligovka
Closed down!"*
And he said, "In Marseilles
There are such bars,
Such liqueurs there,
Such cognacs!
Girls dance naked at your table,
There are ladies there in sable,
Lackeys bringing wine,
And tuxedos worn by swine!"
He offered me francs
And a glassful of pearls
If I would give him
The plan of a Soviet factory.
We grabbed that gate crasher,
Relieved him of his suitcase
Relieved him of his francs
And his glassful of pearls
Then we turned him over
To the NKVD.
Since then, I haven't come across him
Anywhere in prison.
The authorities commended me,
The Public Prosecutor shook my hand,
And immediately they put me
In Maximum Security.

---

*Stop! A few years later, a verse—rather, a couplet—of Galich's topped this one. So good that when my article on it was published in a Russian newspaper, the editor inserted that couplet in the original song. Here it is: "The Soviet underworld holds its own soviet/The Soviet underworld told the enemy, 'Nyet.' " A wonderful couplet; but it's Galich's.

From that time on, kids,*
I've had just one desire:
If only I could see
that Western Marseilles!
What girls there,
What bars,
What liqueurs,
What cognacs!
Girls dance naked at your table,
There are ladies there in sable,
Lackeys bringing wine,
And tuxedos worn by swine!

The song was absolutely perfect. It made its way into folklore, into *samizdat,* into our thesaurus (I'm thinking of the expression "plan of a Soviet factory"). As a student our friend had written poetry: ". . . but white nights and scarlet lips! Violet eyes and *changeant* suits!" Those violets, right out of a flower basket in a song, became for us the standard of bad taste, Odessa bad taste. But does it do any good to talk about taste—good taste, bad taste? The main thing is to be true to yourself. And western Marseilles, where girls danced naked, is sung by Odessa, twin sister to Marseilles, impoverished but not disheartened, who still knows how to laugh at herself, at her own golden, baroque, French, ancient-free-port past—and at her rich Mediterranean relative.

"Nothing is sacred!"

Not true; she did hold something sacred. Or rather, her children did. Herself: Odessa. I'd be with the family at holidays, and someone would propose a toast: "To Odessa!" And everyone would stand up—*stand up*—and drink, without any Odessa jokes, almost without speaking. Just like Gogol: To Sech!

It's true I never heard these toasts until after the war—from the ones who came back. But the years went by, and to the very last, my generation drank to her.

To Odessa.

---

*This verse too Galich later improved on a little. The song survived for a long time anonymously and developed according to the laws of folklore: whoever wanted to, improved on it.

Nothing sacred? For every single one of us, there was something. But we could laugh at the whole idea of anything being sacred and still hold onto it, because the most sacred thing of all was laughter—the small joke that gave back the Odessan measure of things to a world stupefied and maddened by seriousness. What didn't Odessa laugh at! She laughed at the poverty of wartime communism: that deathless song, "Lots of Noise Over at Shneerzon's." Laughed at the "temporary difficulties" of the Five Year Plan: "Papa, Mama, daughter, son/Run around the city in search of kerosene" (to the tune of "The Red Cavalry"). Laughed at the ulcer, repeatedly laid bare in the *un*censored Russian press, that was eating at Soviet society. Two people meet. "Hello, Abramovich!" "Listen, Rabinovich, these days every other person is an informer. I'm not; so you must be. Goodbye." Laughed at their own brand of patriotism: "So that's what Sasha Pushkin is famous for—oy veh!—because it was here that he recalled the wonderful moment!" Laughed at love: "The queen of your heart there's called Marukha/You play knives for her./And when you leave you say, 'Slut,/Tomorrow I'll take you to the movies' " (to the tune of "My Heart's in Tatters"). Laughed at Stalin and his "passportization": "Joey Stalin, Profiteer/Gets a passport;/And me, a poor handyman,/They throw out!"

This gay little folksong about passportization (to the tune of a *Freilakhs,* what else?) Odessa belted out on every street corner, in every trade school and Factory Workshop School, at a time when the whole country—well, not the whole country, but its "leading representatives"—were already beginning to compose beautiful songs to Stalin the Wise, the Native Son, the Beloved (who, by the way, composed the first one?). . . . But Odessa, twin sister of western Marseilles—she sang him not a hymn but a folksong; a folksong! Just give her the signal and, tasteless Southern dame that she is, she'll bust a gut. What crude sacrilege— calling Stalin, that great tragic figure, "Joey Stalin, Profiteer." Just up and calling him names! Odessa is forever calling names. Because of that, she. . . . At any rate, they had to declare her one of the "hero cities." Unwillingly, but they did it. That too was set to the tune of a folksong. "Ah, Odessa, beauty at edge of the sea! Ah, Odessa, the woes you've seen! Ah, Odessa, the only hometown for me! Odessa, long live Odessa!" Also to the tune of a

Freilakhs, though the "ah" was somehow sad and Nekrasovi-an. . . .

And then even Odessa fell silent. Official radio deafened her; Rumanian melodies stunned her; the tragedies of the ghetto took away her powers of speech. On the trains that went past Razdel-naya station, singers sang plaintive, despairing songs: "In Odessa all you hear is, What's in it for me?" Passengers would smile politely; the singers didn't pass the hat. To tell the truth—it wasn't worth paying for.

Then suddenly, in the deaf, stupefied, dumbstruck year of 'forty-eight, the marvelous, colossal Odessa song "Glassful of Pearls" spread to every corner of the country. It captured every-thing—not just the thirties but the tumultuous forties as well: spies, thieves, our illustrious Chekists, the dream of going abroad, which was our myth of an afterlife. It turned out that it was, it *was* possible to laugh at all that. And the greatest irony was that this "Glassful of Pearls" had surfaced in a Leningrad crushed and beaten-down, ever-rebellious, ever-humiliated, gloomy and miser-able, which had long ago forgotten its own Robin Hood, Lenka Panteleyev. And then suddenly: "The last thieves' den on Li-govka." And each succeeding couplet in the song was a surprise, a gift, a burst of laughter, a truth.

Oh, I'll use our friend's real name, I don't care. He was called Achilles. They made up a saying about him in the second year: "His body's not the best/But he's Achilles in all the rest." Of course it was the mythological name, so strange sounding to Russian ears, that inspired this epigram. He was slight in build and short, with beautiful fair hair and the eyebrows of a fair Mephistopheles. At the University not many people liked him: irony is poison. The Odessans at L.G.U. could be counted on one hand; Odessans mostly headed for Moscow, where they would be understood. At Leningrad University, Odessa jokes gave rise to misunderstand-ings, denunciations, and personal files. Achilles too had a personal file—because of a young lady—but it coincided with 'thirty-seven, when the Komsomol suddenly began throwing out its own mem-bers. At the end of that operation, as Achilles himself observed, there were more Komsomol members kicked out than left in, that is, the minority had expelled from its ranks the majority. For this observation alone, he'd have really gotten it in those days; but they didn't catch him. So it finally ended up that Achilles outlasted most of his fellow members. The war caught up with him when he was a graduate student in Leningrad during the blockade. At the end of the war, he was a docent and worked in the Public Library. Why the Public Library and not at the University where he'd done his graduate work? The usual reason. The rector of the University was Voznesensky, whose brother was the head of the USSR's Gosplan. Achilles nicknamed him *persona brata*. Everyone thought that was very funny—everyone except Voznesensky. And Achilles had to go to the Public. There he managed to do some serious work—a bibliography of translations of Heine.

And then—"Glassful of Pearls." We sang a lot in those days, maybe so we wouldn't have to talk. "Everybody" was approaching thirty, "everybody" had found some niche in life, "everybody" still got together for wedding anniversaries and birthdays (back then, International Women's Day and revolutionary holidays didn't call for family celebrations)—sat at the table, ate a lot, drank a lot, and sang. It was at one such table that we first heard Achilles' masterpiece. His voice was high and off-key. We didn't look at each other: we felt awkward because he sang out of tune, because he was singing his own song. At that time we only sang other people's songs. Vertinsky's "Foreign Cities," his "Over the Pink Sea," Blok's "I Called to You, But You Didn't Turn Around," a gay little tune and a terrific refrain: "Never forget, my darling,/ Our feelings, thoughts, and dreams! We part for now, but dear, be sure/Our paths will meet again." All tried and true. And suddenly there was this underground song, and on top of that, to the tune of "Cut-glass Tumblers"; and on top of that, in an off-key falsetto.

"If I would give him/The plan of a Soviet factory!" We were afraid. Tactlessness had taken a dangerous form. Then suddenly, a happy ending: they grabbed him, grabbed that gate crasher, hurrah, no need to be afraid, they relieved him of his suitcase and his francs. And there followed unexpected things, captivating things: "Since then I haven't come across him/Anywhere in prison." "And immediately they put me/In Maximum Security." "Ah, if only I could see/That western Marseilles!" We wept for joy.

All this happened at the beginning of 'forty-eight—the first year without ration cards, the year we got established in life and got ready to turn thirty, a year of good prospects, when our families decided we could afford a second child.

Achilles had a unique, almost ballet dancer's walk—moving lightly, toes turned out, as if he were about to execute a step. Every night, with his dancer's walk, he'd come into our kitchen (which the investigator would later call our salon) rubbing his small hands from the cold—it's no joke, half an hour in an unheated streetcar—and he'd say, laughing, "Look, there you sit, and I've been out saving the world from yet another Nikolai Ostrovsky!"

It would turn out that he'd talked an almost illiterate handicapped veteran out of writing his memoirs.

We'd sit and drink tea, and he'd ask, "Well, how's your Lizaveta?" (That was how he Russianized my beautiful cosmetician.) "Have they picked her up yet? Don't talk to her too much. If she asks you about Kravchenko, for instance, that traitor who 'chose freedom'—so called—"

"On the subject of that traitor I agree with Kostya Simonov."

"Sure, sure, you agree with Kostya Simonov. By the way, my cousin the lawyer came to visit us. She said one in five Soviet citizens has been convicted of something. Or will be. When the three of us were at the station, seeing you off, remember—Kostya Simonov and—what's his name—Sofronov, that's it. It will happen. One of us won't escape. Kostya Simonov, most likely."

And he burst out laughing. Not because it seemed so incongruous; just because.

Funny? Funny. Kostya Simonov was at his peak; Stalin had decorated him. He could do no wrong. When the Writers' Union threatened Veselovsky's parrots (it was a prelude to the "cosmopolites" campaign), the parrots defended themselves. Zhirmunsky announced that he'd written an article but nobody would publish it. From the Presidium, Kostya said softly, without emphasis, "Send it to *Novy Mir*."

And the hall began to stir—maybe because it still wasn't forbidden then to argue, and there was still somewhere to send such articles; or maybe from hearing the voice of a man who'd been showered with nationwide acclaim. He was the one they argued about; the one who filled their thoughts. Fadeyev, though also at the peak of his fame, didn't capture their imagination in the same way. He stood on the podium under the blinding lights, and his narrow raspberry face beneath white hair turned redder and redder from the heat of the lights and from his growing irritation. "Leningrad has always been a stronghold of Formalism," he shouted angrily, tying that moment to what happened in the twenties, when they all were young—both Rappovists and Formalists—and didn't fear him enough. He was taking revenge for some ancient injuries that we could only guess at; but still he only rolled out the first barrels, sent the first stones down the mountain, not foreseeing—as his defenders now insisted in their poorly written prose—what an anticosmopolite avalanche they would set off in their wake.

But who could have foreseen it? Who could see in the potholes of everyday life the rhythms, alternations, tensions—the kind of pulsations that could let him predict the direction of events? Who could hear, in the journalistic skirmishes between the thugs and the long-suffering intellectuals, the creaking of the old wheel of history? After all, things seemed to be getting better. Members of the families of Traitors to the Fatherland were returning and settling in Luga—that is, the wives who in 'thirty-seven had been sentenced to five and eight years (those who got ten didn't come back). The rumor came, the rumor spread, that Zabolotsky would return. Of his critics it was said that now of course they were writing about Nedogonov, but just let Zabolotsky come back and they'd rush to him and genuflect. The rumors of Zabolotsky's return grew as thick and stirred up as much emotion as if he were returning from the Isle of Elba. Vertinsky gave concerts; there were no tickets to be had, but we got them somehow, and finally we heard from his own lips:

> A casual rumor brought
> Kind
> and gentle
> words . . .

Things were getting better. There were the reparations from the war: you could buy imported women's underwear, not just on the black market, but right in the stores. There were confiscated films with Sarah Leander and Willi Birgel (in clubs, on the sly); there were radio broadcasts of football victories over the "Arsenal"; there were rumors that in the spring prices would come down.

Yes; yes; things were getting better.

Except that Simonovna—our children's Nanny—had made up her mind to go back to the country; but when she went she got frightened. "How am I supposed to live, they're starving there, there's nothing, absolutely nothing! I cried and cried, boarded up the house—and now I'm back again, if you'll have me." As if we wouldn't! That was back in 'forty-seven. But that was the country; as far as I could remember, people in the country were always starving. Swollen, frightening people sat in the bakery doorways; when she sent me out for bread, Nanny would say, "Hold on tight to your ration cards, there's a hungry man sitting there, he might grab them out of your hand." I was eleven then; it was nineteen thirty. The winds of Satan were blowing across the face of the earth: the wonders of socialism were ravaging the Soviet country-side; the wonders of capitalism were ravaging the American farm-lands. Somehow abundance itself was turning into famine. You couldn't believe it—and we didn't; we knew very well that the newspapers always lie.

Things were getting better. Sometimes I'd bring home tangerines, or apples, so the children wouldn't go without fruit. By the half kilo. Simonovna took an apple in her hand and sighed, "There are places where such an amazing thing can grow. An apple! And out in the country—" "What are you going on about, Simonovna? Apples grow around Pskov!" "But we're near Novgorod." "They grow around Novgorod, too." "I don't know how or why, but in the country, where we were, I never once saw apples growing."

And I remembered: in my childhood there were oranges from Jaffa, where my second cousin Mulya had gone to live. He sent me a letter from there that said, "But you can even get sick of oranges." That you just couldn't believe, either.

"Now they're planting eucalyptus there," Achilles told us. "Six million eucalyptus, for the number of Jews that were killed."

Achilles had a radio (we didn't), and he used to tell us what was going on in the world, according to the radio. About Kassyenkina, the Russian teacher who wanted to stay in America and then changed her mind, and afterwards mysteriously fell from a window of the Soviet embassy (that was how the papers put it: *fell*). Achilles heard her speak on American radio. About Kravchenko, who chose freedom and wrote a book about it and sued a French newspaper for libel. . . .

"Say what you like," I said, reveling in my own conformity, "he's still a traitor!" The men didn't argue. Only my husband asked, "But why don't you believe he chose freedom?"

It was the same words, but a different intonation. But what is freedom? If you start down that road, you'll have to decide everything for yourself—everything, right down to the meaning of the simplest words. But if you behave calmly, peacefully, the meanings of words will have already been decided long ago, and their direction predetermined. My God, aren't we all really measured by the Five Year Plan, and didn't we rise or fall with it? But the Five Year Plan and all that it measured—wasn't all that a product of reason? And the meanings of words had to be defined by reason; but by what else besides? By the ribcage?

But the ribcage resonated, like an oscillograph, and to entirely different meanings. To a strange meaning of the word "freedom," not the rational but the irrational one. A meaning that—if you took it seriously, rationally, as we had been taught—had long ago become ridiculous. Nothing more than "acknowledged necessity." Boring, but so what? It's logical. Weren't *we* acknowledging necessity?

The ribcage rattled. At words. Kravchenko said: Camps. A woman who had returned from the camps, once a member of the *nomenklatura*, a high-ranking bureaucrat (it was from her, in fact, that I heard then for the first time the fundamental word *nomenklatura*), said, of Stalin: "A madman." On the street a well-dressed man said in a sad, quiet voice to his well-dressed companion, continuing their conversation: "Yes. Article Fifty-Eight." And everywhere, everywhere, they said: *Jews*. With various intonations. But the word was in fashion.

My husband let me get on the bus ahead of him. An exhausted blockade-worker hissed, "Abrahamchik and his Sarah!" On the "Red Arrow" from Moscow to Leningrad, a sailor said to the conductor, "The Jews—what are they to us, leave them alone. If they'd just clear out a little faster—aren't I right?" Almost wordlessly the conductor agreed, with hardly more than a nod, and

went on sweeping. The playwright Pogodin and certain other critics panned someone called Surov; then Pogodin fell from view,
like Kassyenkina, and everybody forgot about him and began to
pan the critics in every issue of *Culture and Life*. Their names
began to stick in one's memory: Gurvich and Yuzovsky. Then the
number of such names began to grow. And a word appeared—
had already popped up earlier in connection with Veselovsky's
parrots. The word "cosmopolite."

But that word we remembered. Wasn't it a Nazi word?

The ribcage rattled. At words. And the vibration, the heavy
shaking, caused things long ago laid away to float to the surface,
things almost forgotten, almost buried in the memories of the
Odessans. For instance, the words of a very wise, middle-aged
Odessan: "Alas, the idea of nationalism is stronger than internationalism."

Achilles never said that. He just told us the news.

"Listen, did you know that the writer Yakovlev has turned out
to be?"

"Really?"

"Absolutely. He's turned out to be Holtzman."

From 'thirty-seven on, the phrase "turned out to be" needed no
complement: it was understood. In 'thirty-seven and 'thirty-eight
it was understood as: an enemy of the people. In 'forty-eight it
was understood as: a Jew.

Once again the winds of Satan blew around the earth. Jews in
America were exposed as Communists; Jews in the Soviet Union,
as anti-Communists. And once again we didn't suspect that those
winds were one and the same; and we wouldn't have believed it
even if we'd been told. But at that time we were reading Ehrenburg's *Julio Jurenito* and telling each other over and over about
the spade in the thousand-year-old hand and the little word *nyet*,
the Jews' favorite word.

Our friend Karel, who naturally considered himself a Russian
and a Marxist, voiced his thoughts. "The Jewish mind is funda-
mentally not synthetic but analytical. As you know, there's a time
for gathering stones, and a time for throwing them. The time for
throwing stones is over now."

For some it was over; for others it was just beginning. They
began throwing stones at "cosmopolite" literary critics in every

magazine, every newspaper; *Life and Culture* would sing solo, and a chorus would take it up as precisely as if under the conductor's invisible baton. We were lost in awe. Yesterday a critic—let's say, Basargin—sang the praises of Olga Berggolts; today he trampled all over her because of what she'd said about the blockade: "I froze in your unimaginable ice." And the next day we'd read in the papers that he was no Basargin, just the cosmopolite Blumenfeld who, back when Enemy of the People So-and-So was in power, had groveled before the Formalists, shaken hands, glorified Hemingway, made mincemeat of Makarenko. . . .

Simonovna told us that her pilot son's widow had gotten married and come to Leningrad. She too had boarded up her house. "There are a lot of houses like that—what else can they do? Little children have to be fed—what's there to feed them with? It's all right, she managed to sell her cow; and he's a good man, not a drinker." Simonovna too came every day with stories. About a boy on the streetcar: he sits there, frozen through, and no scarf on him, no mittens, nothing; and his mother is with him, blue face, voice like a man's. "She played around and got pregnant, and now she gets fifty rubles for him! I took off my own mittens and put them on him, put my arms around him, and she. . . . A bad mother!" Afterward our son would tell the same story in the first person: "I took off my own mittens. . . . Bad mother!" And he'd shake his head sadly.

One figure kept turning up in Simonovna's stories: some old fellow who had attached himself to them in the "dormitary." Frozen, miserable, full of lice; they'd heated water for him, washed him, steamed him, and fed him. Now every evening he paid them a visit, slept in a corner on the floor. Such a devout old fellow. He prayed all the time, it was all "God will reward you." His children had driven him out of the house, he was from the country, near where we were from. And then came Simonovna, all astonished and full of amazement, and told us that they'd arrested the old fellow, arrested him right there in the "dormitary"; it turned out he'd been the headman of his village under the Germans. "The manager says to me, 'He's a real criminal, Little Mother.' And I say, 'How would I know is he a criminal or what? I see an old fellow, so I'—'Look,' he says. 'Little Mother, see—an old fellow, and he's killed so many people, so many partisans.

And you, Little Mother, your sons were in the Soviet army; and you'd help someone like that. And I say—' "

"To all of these intrigues," said Achilles, "we have only one response: 'Haze rye.'

"Haze rye"—it's not a misprint. Someone or other had said that at one of the meetings in the thirties, accidentally garbling it; from that time on, it went into our thesaurus, like "Oh, Sophocles!" "Oh, Sophocles!" That one is a quotation. One of our fellow students was called "Louis Quatorze" because her bright curly hair reminded us of his wig. In her bosom were hidden inexhaustible stores of enthusiasm. In a student reading room once, she screwed up her eyes and said with relish, "What a dazzling mind that Stalin has. . . ." It was in 'thirty-eight. That pronouncement of hers didn't make it into our thesaurus, but people began to pick up their ears when she spoke. We were rewarded. On another occasion she again raised her head from her book and exclaimed, "Oh, Sophocles! What a great, truly great, playwright!"

Also preserved in our thesaurus for many years: "With parched lips he fell upon the clear source." The author: Glickman. In 'thirty-seven he used to walk the main corridor of the Philological Faculty, cringing nervously. "Well, Isaac," they'd ask him, "How's everything?" He'd answer loudly, "Light, bright, and cheerful!" Someone wrote the words on wallpaper, like a slogan, and signed it, "Glickman." The slogan hung in Auditorium Sixteen, the most popular one. Lev Lvovich Rakov, that dapper and handsome man, who'd been a friend of Mikhail Kuzmin in the twenties, then went to jail, then in the thirties taught us ancient history, then went to jail, then in the forties, after the war, was director of the Public Library, then—Well, in February of 'thirty-seven, Lev Lvovich Rakov stepped elegantly up to the platform, saw the slogan in front of him, did a double take, read it again, and asked, over the students' laughter, "Comrades, who is this Glickman?"

They explained. He snorted and shrugged his shoulders. "Glickman!"

"Who else?" we'd say now.

Glickman was a legend. Many years later I heard a complete stranger say about a girl's behind, "A source of inexhaustible delights for her future spouse." That was Glickman, too.

The main promulgator of Glickmanian aphorisms now teaches

Russian literature in the United States—probably he even took them there. Thus does culture spread.

New Year's of 'forty-nine was noisy and strange—a crowd of people only indirectly connected. Of course, a *milieu* like that was a *stukach*'s dream. Among other things, the word *stukach* hadn't yet come into use; *nasedka*, I think—yes, that's what we said. I remember even as a child hearing *provocateur*. Mama would say it to someone in front of me, lowering her voice: They say K. is a *provocateur!* And *informer*, too, I remember hearing even as a child. And there's the Hebrew word *moser* (from the verb *limsor* "to pass along"); and then there's the newest one (perhaps resurrected from the era of Word and Deed), *tikhar*. Terms for this concept don't live long; they very soon collapse. But when one breaks down, several others immediately take its place; one of them wins out—but not for long. Only the term *stukach* somehow came of age and now has even reached its full growth. Maybe because of the softening of the police regime during the last decades? Everyday language reflects the changes in everyday life.

So, then—New Year's. A table was extended the length of a whole room in an apartment where we'd never been before and would never be again; some of those at the table we knew from our student days, but they brought others with them whom we saw, with no great pleasure, for the first time. A pretty woman, slightly faded from eight years in Siberia as a family member of a Traitor to the Fatherland, brought along a suspicious-looking officer in civilian clothes, tiny, with a Jewish surname and effeminate manners. There was no conversation, just the noise of people at table. Then came charades (one of the words was "cosmopolite"). Then we sang: "She Brought a Chance Rumor," "Filibusters," "Over the Pink Sea," "Doña Marquita" (in honor of Spain), and "Glassful of Pearls", which we sang in chorus. There was no special song for the occasion. Later Achilles told us he'd tried to compose one and failed.

I went there after Elizabeth Arden. She made me a mask, washed it off, put on a light makeup and said with light reproach, "Don't theenk. Don't theenk about anything. Otherwise your money is vasted. Luck at me."

I looked, and suddenly I thought I saw in the depths of those china-blue eyes, fears flash their tails like fish. One terror in particular thrashed about. She lowered her eyelids, moved away from me, and began to laugh unconvincingly. Then she came close again and asked softly, "Vy do you luck at me like that?"

Startled, I shrugged. "No, it just seems that way, I only. . . ."

She said, "Do I luck bat?"

"Why, *you* always look as if you're about to go on a date! Of course not!"

She looked at me without pleasure and even tried to knit her eyebrows. She couldn't; so then she stuck out her chin just a little. "Today you vill luck good all night. I can give you—I can give you everything. Today. See!"

I gasped. I had gotten the longed-for pink box with the button! And several more bottles and jars. I had two more sessions to go, but I'd gotten everything. What a New Year's gift! I thanked Elizabeth Arden heartily, and she nodded; the fish stopped flicking their tails.

Elizabeth Arden had begun to be afraid. Well, that only meant that now she'd become a Soviet woman. Can it be that she's afraid of me? Well, why not? I'm pretty serious, I don't chatter, just listen; and it's not at all clear why I've now suddenly become preoccupied with my face, which is obviously beyond help.

It began to seem funny to me: these stupid women just up and landing in socialism, like chickens in soup. None of *us*, women of experience, would ever—

Oh? None?

None.

Of course I had to think for a minute: why had a certain Dusya begun visiting me? At the University she was ahead of me, we hadn't said two words to each other. And all of a sudden she came to my husband at the publishing house and said, "I read Ruth's reviews in *The Star;* you know, I work for Sovinformbureau; it would be good for us to get together."

So we get together and we write an article together. I'm flattered: not just some reviews, but real work. . . . Yes, but why me? Come on, why worry about it? I'm always careful. . . . But then why don't I just send her packing on some pretext or other? It's true I've always liked to look at her: gentle dark face with beauty marks, and velvet eyes. . . .

Well, this way I'll go crazy before long. Was this the reason our Moscow acquaintance was advised by his friend not to have much to do with us? What did that mean?

It tormented me. Just before the New Year I telephoned a friend in Moscow.

I won't say more about her, though the light and warmth of our life then and for many years afterward came from her. In the last analysis, who writes novels about the faithful working of the sun? At most, when it rises and sets it casts its rays obliquely across the picture being created. In poems it exists; sometimes, it even comes to the *dacha*. And it came to us, from time to time, arriving from Moscow, not very often. So I called her on the telephone and I said, "I'm worried. Do you remember how your journalist friend told you he'd been advised not to get too friendly with us?"

"Yes?" she said.

"But doesn't that mean his advisor had a very poor opinion of us?" Over the telephone it was impossible to ask explicitly whether he thought we were "workers."

She thought for a minute (though a minute on the telephone cost quite a bit), then laughed heartily. "No, of course not, it means something different, completely different. I talked to him. By the way, he asked me to send his love, he liked you very much."

It felt so good to be liked that I didn't ask any more about it. And besides, the telephone conversation was nearly over, and everything was different, completely different. Another New Year's gift.

Yes, it meant just the opposite: that we were under observation, and therefore it was dangerous to associate with us. But I didn't find this out until twelve days later, and even then I didn't connect it with the journalist's warning. It came, so to speak, from another department. When you're young, departments are strictly separated, and at each one stands a border guard.

We knew that They were *asking* about us. It didn't worry us particularly. You think, Who aren't They asking about? They have to know every detail of people's lives. Whoever can tell Them about somebody, that's who They ask. For the files.

Word had already reached us that summer, at the *dacha:* They're *asking*. They ask people you'd never expect—for instance, the one whom as students we'd called the Enthusiast. He said he didn't know much about us, which corresponded to the facts, since we hadn't seen each other for nearly two years or so. He let us know about all this through mutual friends; so as not to look like a liar in the eyes of the "organs," he'd stopped seeing us altogether.

They asked a woman I'd never been friends with. Also in the summer. I don't even remember anymore what she answered; but in the preceding ten years we hadn't said ten words to each other. In any event, even she managed to let us know about it.

We were angry, but mostly for propriety's sake; and, if you can believe it, we were even flattered—it meant we were starting to get established. After all, if the "organs" aren't interested in you, you have no social status at all.

We waited for Them to summon us so They could interrogate us about somebody. Just that—for the files. The "organs" have to know what air we breathe. An institution—it works like an institution, doesn't it? They'll ask us about somebody, we'll tell Them we hardly know him, then we'll let him know They've been *asking.* . . .

No one summoned us; but that didn't hurt our feelings. We didn't have time, anyway. Each day brought a great many problems; if you measured by problems, then we were living a very full life. On top of that, it turned out I was pregnant.

No doubt about it: we had no room for a third baby. I would have to have an abortion.

But abortions had been outlawed ever since 'thirty-six, after a national debate, widespread discussions, almost a referendum. I remember a line of verse about it (Dolmatovsky's I think: he, too, specialized in intimate subjects):

"Think—what if it's to be Mozart?"

No one tried to talk me out of it—everyone understood that it was impossible. I had begged my husband's parents, whom we lived with, for my son. But a third baby, in a sixteen-square-meter room?

Maybe that's why Elizabeth Arden's creams and potions didn't make me beautiful enough. But it was a pleasure just to look at them. Soon after the New Year I went to her again; I told myself that I had an obligation to, a matter of honor. She was surprised to see me, but she began doing everything she was supposed to; we talked, looking in the mirror. She said thoughtfully, "I vas teenking of fisiting my sister in ze spring; but Zey said I could not. Before ze war I did it all the time. Once a year I fisited my sister."

"You have a sister in America?"

She started to laugh, but broke off. "Vy America? I don't haf anybody in America; I'fe never efen been zere, America. But everybody asks, me, everybody says—"

"I'm sorry. I didn't mean—"

"I haf a sister in Shvitzerland," she said. "Lausanne. She has a drugstore—a fery nice pharmacy."

That day had begun with the milkman ringing our doorbell. In those days milk was still delivered, at least in the Petrograd section. Our "milkman" was Masha, a Finnish woman with part of her nose gone, the same one who used to come before the war. Sometimes others would ring our door, looking for customers. That day a new milkman rang the bell. It was ten o'clock.

And when the bell sounded—I was sitting in the kitchen—into my mind flashed sharply, pierced, rapped out the words: "NKVD? Too soon!"

It was as if someone had sent me the words in a telegram. Because they terrified me, those words, and I didn't even understand them at first; and the words NKVD had become obsolete by that time. Now there were ministries, and the Ministry everyone feared was called the MGB, the Ministry of State Security. But I wasn't afraid of that yet, I was afraid of what everyone else was afraid of; and so I was surprised at the words knocking in my brain. Only then did I realize that those words weren't my own thoughts; they had been sent from somewhere.

And of course it turned out to be the milkman; and I thought it was very funny, and I was already thinking how I would tell the story that evening.

And then the phone rang. I answered; and from the receiver came a woman's slow voice, murmuring, "Don't say my name."

I was silent.

"Can you come to the commission store on the Nevsky at eleven?"

"Yes."

"I'll wait for you there."

It was ten minutes after ten. I went back to the kitchen, gathered up my papers, went back into the room. I still had half an hour.

I didn't feel like rushing and I didn't feel like getting there too early either. The day was a typical Leningrad day, damp but not freezing.. I didn't feel like doing anything.

But why was I so terrified?

So she'll say again, They're *asking*. She isn't the first and she won't be the last. She's just setting it all up like a conspiracy because her husband is a Party member and has his university career to think of.

I'd known her from my student days. We didn't get together often: our lives followed different paths. But we did get together. I liked her: her face, her voice, the way she talked—intelligent, humorous. Never once did we talk about anything political, only held forth about which Jews weren't accepted here or weren't accepted there; and I'd make broad historical generalizations.

Why was I so terrified?

Maybe it was the fact that her call had coincided with my "psychogram"? And no wonder: she was anxious, didn't know whether to call, had doubts—and all this reached me in a single unconscious wave. By accident, I had tuned to the right frequency.

How frightened she was. And how bravely she overcame it.

A sleepless, sweating, mortal fear. The fear of anyone of my generation in 'forty-nine—it was fear squared, cubed. It was the murky, childish fear of the revolutionary years multiplied by the remembered fear of 'thirty-seven and raised to the nth power. By the end of the forties we had something to lose. And not just for a while, but forever. By the end of the forties there had emerged a collective experience distilled from the individual: No one returns from *there*. Granted, sometimes on the edge of the hundred-kilometer zone ghosts would appear—Eurydices—but not for long. Very soon they would sink back again into the depths of Hades, the kingdom of shadows; probably because (if there is any human explanation) they looked back, those Eurydices, and remembered. And when this became known, the Cerberuses seized them and took them away, took them away again. "We'll all end up *there*": it sounded at that time more concrete and more frightening than it does now. And you didn't want to believe it. How can it be that we'll all end up *there*, when we've only just now begun to live? Before, there had been the first Five Year Plan, and then the Second, and then the War. Why, only now could we breathe deeply, not so much breathe deeply as catch our breath in secret; and it wasn't 'thirty-seven anymore, they don't grab people indiscriminately now, the main thing is not to blab. . . .

She overcame it—the vow of unthinking silence imposed on her in the name of her life and her family—and after a sleepless night without consulting anyone (who would she have consulted?—it would have only multiplied the danger), I don't understand why, don't understand how, she called me from a phone booth.

Even if she didn't tell me everything, well, fifty percent was enough.

"Don't say my name," she said slightly plaintively.

Who are you, reading this now? How old are you? And why does it interest you—and it must interest you if you've gotten as far as this page. If you are of my generation and you lived through those years—no, not those: let it be earlier years—in the Soviet Union, in Russia, then you have your own memories, as bitter as mine. You, my reader and my contemporary, you cannot not have such memories. Anyone who didn't have them wouldn't have started reading this story, or if he started, wouldn't have gotten to this page. Or is it just that it's your job?

But if it's your job, it's not worth it. There's nothing here that the "organs" don't already know. Why, They "know all." Can it be They've forgotten and want to remember? But that's not Their business, memories—not others' memories, I mean, but their own. One's own memories: that is consciousness—excuse me—self-consciousness. Which is really conscience. For our two words, consciousness and conscience, some languages have only one. Some languages are too poor; others, too stingy.

And if you are not of my generation, but of my children's, grew up somewhere else, not in these cities? As a child, listened not to Dunayevsky and Tikhon Khrennikov but to boogie-woogie? Or rock-and-roll? Or "disco"? And you got as far as this page?

I've always wanted desperately to know what a woman of my generation, my race, a woman something like me, might have been doing on that January in 'forty-nine, in the city of New York.

And—see how terrible it is!—I can easily imagine how her telephone rang that morning, and a familiar voice said to her—Well, not necessarily "Don't say my name," but something like that, a warning. And the owner (male or female) of the voice met her somewhere in a supermarket on Forty-second Street—were there supermarkets back then?—and then she heard how They were asking about her there. There, it would be the Committee on Un-American Activities. Now we know what it was spawning in secret. Yes, she wasn't being threatened with Kolyma, or with the loss of her children; but still she had something to lose. And she, too, stood alone against the iron machine of the State.

For one and the same idiot wind blows around our little globe, our green spaceship with the light-blue sails.

Whoever you are, come with me, dear reader, since you've gotten as far as this page. Let's spend some time together in Leningrad. On those few streets that are the real Leningrad. And even if you lived in an alley in Porokhovye and know every crack in the old, prewar pavement—still for you, Leningrad won't be Porokhovye, but these ten or twelve streets. Much has changed in the last thirty years, even on these streets; but you'll remember them, all the same.

We'll go into the courtyard of a building on Dobrolyubov, number 19. A turn-of-the-century building, a profitable, well-made building. In the winter of 'thirty-seven–'thirty-eight, automobiles black and quiet as owls stood for a long time at its gates every night; and when they finally drove off, there was one passenger more inside. It was from this very building that They took away forever the rector of the University, Lazurkin, "a friend of Bukharin," they said and later whispered. As you came in off the street, what a main entrance hall: mirrors, loges for the doormen, a wide, baronial staircase. Down this staircase Lazurkin and the others were led away. It wasn't the Politkatorzhan building, of course not—do you remember that big building on the Neva, the most visible building on Petrograd?—which by then was absolutely empty. At Dobrolyubov 19, too, there were a lot of vacant apartments. Not for long, it's true; the apartments near that stairwell were obviously very nice. In my time Tributs, the commander of the Baltic fleet, lived there with his young wife of the moment; and there was the family of a general who had served in the Army of Occupation: a wife in silver-black fox, and well-bred, well-dressed children.

We don't live on that stair; our staircase leading from the courtyard is dark and smells of cabbage soup. We'll go past the fountain which I don't remember ever once flowing—its three dejected stone toads have dried out and turned black. A courtyard like a well: six-story walls look at each other out of large, sad windows. The courtyard, an asphalt desert, has not a blade of grass—the courtyard where intelligent Leningrad cats stroll about. Then "The Arch," long as a tunnel; and the street. The Avenue. It clamors damply with wind and trees; it has a wide, prerevolutionary sidewalk with an "other side." The "other side" has no houses: lawn, trees, lawn, and a little farther off, a nursery garden where even in the years just after the war you could buy autumn asters in pots on the Feast of Faith, Hope, and Charity. There, on the "other side," grandmothers used to take children for walks; a twenty-year-old student could ask a fellow student, "Don't you remember me? We're from the same building, we used to go for walks on the 'other side.' "

Now, while you and I are walking toward it, dear reader, there is slush and mud, not grass; and the trees are black on gray; and the air carries a sweetish, sticky smell that clings to your lips, from nearby Vatny Island, from GIPKh, the State Institute of Applied Chemistry. But it *is* air, humid, wet, trembling with cold drops of still-uncondensed steam; and besides GIPKh it smells of the real and the literary Neva. And now, now we'll go to the Neva, to the Builders' Bridge, still in its old place, which doesn't yet reach the former customs house that's now the Pushkin Institute. Below our feet, wet wooden boards; and below the boards and beyond the railing, to the right and left, the gray, tarnished, dark, leaden, gleaming, heavy water of the Neva, the tenderest and gentlest in the world. . . . Breathe, reader, breathe with me the snowless January morning of 'forty-nine, because we've already crossed the Builders' Bridge. Breathe with me the blessed city rawness, the loamy, warm west wind; wade through the tortured, chemical-blackened mud on the stones of the Palace Bridge. Look around. See the houses securely anchored here between the yellow paws of the Admiralty; and there, the long facade of the Winter Palace; and there, where in summer there are thick, green clumps of trees, is now a single spire, a needle without an eye. But the main thing is, breathe. Because very soon, in a few hundred more of my small steps, there will be nothing to breathe. One more breath. You can't smell GIPKh anymore—we've left it behind us—only dampness and the west wind.

She was waiting for me outside the commission store. She said, "Go away somewhere." And she burst into tears.

From that morning in front of the commission store until our arrest was eighty-five days. In the interval—on the fifteenth of February, my birthday—our friend was arrested. So "Glassful of Pearls" remained his Marseillaise. He never wrote another song.

We got ready. We burned our correspondence from the maternity hospital, and a thick Yugoslav book with pictures of all the members of Tito's clique. How we had acquired this powder keg is another story, which I'll tell someday. My husband's mother, who had been a member of the Bund and later of the Social Democratic Party, destroyed her letters from Karl Liebknecht. In the letters themselves there was nothing incriminating, only the German language and the address; they were addressed to Mr. and Mrs. Karl Radek. My mother-in-law had been married to Radek briefly, in a civil ceremony.

In those days she was a revolutionary, a Social Democrat; she had a party, a platform, a program. . . . What did we have now? Only tragic disagreement and anxiety.

"Lis'n," said Achilles. "What the Soviet government is worried about, I can't understand. Nobody has a real program now anyway. You can't just make up some slogan like 'Backward to Capitalism, A Bright Future for All Mankind'!"

But at this very moment schoolgirls (soon to be my companions), because they had belonged to the "Back to Lenin" Society and the Union of Friends of Freedom, were already in the camps. There were Zionists there, old ones and new ones. But there were no participants in the human-rights movement in the camps, because there was no such movement—its time had not yet come. In our peculiar undeclared social contract with the State, we silently acknowledged, on its part, rights and obligations, and on our own, only obligations.

On the eve of his arrest, Achilles held forth. "To whom did they give the right of residence inside Russia? I'm speaking from the point of view of people within the Pale of Settlement. Artisans and merchants of the first guild got the right. What are *we* supposed to do? You certainly can't be a merchant; but an artisan—It's time we studied some skill. If we had a skill, it would be possible to get out somehow. To Lodeinoye Pole, maybe. Or to

Vologda. Or there's a little town outside Odessa, used to be called Yelisavetgrad, then Zinovievsk, then Kirovograd. A friend of mine from school has been hiding out there ever since 'thirty-seven—made a splendid match in 'thirty-three and married someone in the Ukrainian government. *She* saved herself!"

But we didn't have any skills. Especially me. I didn't even know how to cook or take care of children—I'd grown up in the era of household help. As for cutting and sewing—forget it.

But deep down, where real desires stirred, or longings, there was no desire to leave. There was: What will be, will be. There was: Maybe it will blow over (this feeling never lasted, because right away some ominous sign would invariably occur). There was fear, always; and there were paroxysms of terror. And subconsciously there was curiosity. What was it like—*there?*

In 'forty-nine in the inner prison there was someone serving as a warden who—I almost said, everyone loved him. Well, I don't know how to put it. Let's say, everyone spoke highly of him. He had a pensive voice; he'd look around the women's cell and say reproachfully, "Why are you making so much noise? People are working, and you're bothering them."

When this warden finally took me out to the transport, I said, "No hard feelings."

He answered, "Nor you, either. We're just doing our job."

It was this same warden who, when he first led me along the trapeze rigging of the inner prison with its white nets beneath, sensed my curiosity and asked politely, "Have you visited us before?"—the way the hospitable guide at Tarkhany asks, "Have you visited our village before?" Not without pride in the village, which has been roofed with slate for the current jubilee.

I think he could have told me when, in what year, on what account these white circus nets were stretched from floor to floor. In the cells they said it was after Lazurkin, the rector of the University, threw himself down. Occasionally someone else was named, but always someone well known. It was as if we, unknown, doomed to a vegetable life and death, grew in stature by sharing their fate. What vanity will feed on!

And curiosity. Eve's daughters, all of us: both in the common cell of the Big House, and later, in the transit prisons, we kept asking with a terrible, insatiable curiosity, "What's it like—*there?*"

Prison we already knew all about. We were—strange to say—used to it. What frightened and attracted us was another dark hole: the camps.

Yes; and we heard about the camps, a different story every time. A middle-aged bookkeeper astonished us the most. "The camp—it's a kind of freedom," she said. She'd been in a camp in Vorkuta and had been sent here to confront a witness.

We feared the camps most of all. It seemed to us that if we could go on like this, without heavy work (we city-dwellers still hadn't heard the expression "in the warm"), we could manage even on prison cabbage soup, on fishbones.

And yet—we were curious. As long as you're already on the road to Hell, why not look around and try to see a little more? What for? Who knows.

The overseer of the camp in the Far East was Tarasov. He told us about some really terrible camps, where people were chained to wheelbarrows and slept like that, by the wheelbarrows. Was it true? Or did he exaggerate the awfulness? Or had he been ordered to spread these rumors so that people would feel grateful that they live so well, thank you; no leg-irons and wheelbarrows, don't even have to wear numbers. And so they would try to hang onto their good fortune.

Maybe, if there really were such camps, they told other stories, stories even more terrible, there. About the last, most hellish circles, about the clutches of Beelzebub himself. I don't know; I never met anyone from there. But one couldn't help being curious. Dante himself was curious, and he was a man, and even a political figure. . . .

I rode along Nevsky on the number one trolley, to the Yevropeiskaya. I had a "date" with my Elizabeth Arden. And whatever might be in store for me, I'd spend a few murmuring hours with her. So good. Sit with my eyes closed and feel her fragrant hands on my face, and her creams. And have a leisurely discussion. About crows' feet and frown lines. Quiet, warm, the radio singing, "Coming in on a Wing and a Prayer. . . ."

The door of the cosmetic salon was wide open and from inside came a cheerful metallic sound. Workmen were removing the radiators and partitions.

"Remodeling!" they answered me. "How do we know? Go ask. . . ."

Ask who? I asked the coat-check man, a veteran. He shrugged armless shoulders, looked closely at my face as if memorizing it, and said, "I don't know, I don't know, they don't tell us anything, we're little people. But there goes one of you. Ask her."

Coming toward me in an unfamiliar, dark-green coat, wearing a pained expression and rolling her eyes, was the "lean cow."

"You heard?" she asked in a tragic whisper.

I nodded.

"Come over here." She grabbed my hand and dragged me over to the stairs, whispering in my ear, "Yesterday They took her away. Right out of the salon. The woman in charge of that floor told me, she's a friend of mine. Right out of the salon. A good thing you and I weren't there! You'd already finished the course, you'd gotten everything; but I still had three sessions to go. Just think! But who can you trust? Why, you'd have thought that here, at least, in the Yevropeiskaya, they'd have checked on everybody. How did they foul up? Well, they'll get it now."

"Who?"

"What do you mean, who? The personnel department, the director—why, the whole management. And it's happening all over, all over. . . . They think: We've won the war, so now we can rest in peace on our laurels." That's how she put it: rest in peace.

The two of us squeezed into one section of the revolving door and popped out onto the wide asphalt step like corks.

A tall old man in a foreign coat, hatless, raised his eyebrows and sidled in the door. The lean cow sighed. "They keep coming, and coming. Then they turn out to be spies. Why do they let them in in the first place?"

And it had promised to be such a fine day!

The Feast of the Annunciation. "I'm setting a little bird free." In the bakeries there used to be buns shaped like larks. Little bunbirds with raisin eyes. Those larks you could never set free; but maybe I could buy a live bird? I walked through the Sitnoy Market and looked around. Cages, large and small, with small birds that had probably been saved especially for this day. Yes; but why should I buy a cage? Besides, they're expensive. My husband had by that time already lost his half-time appointment, and even his position at the publishing house was in jeopardy. After our friend's arrest it became clear that his turn would come—as clear as if he were standing in line.

My case wasn't so clear, even to me. In fact, friends with whom we'd held a council of war after Achilles Levinton's arrest just waved it away. "They'll never take you! You'll go on pounding that typewriter, typing for your Chinaman!" And that was what I feared most of all. Not the typewriter—the life. A life with two children in my husband's family. A life among people who "hadn't yet been touched." A life whose burdens weren't shared with anyone. The lines at the little window in the prison. The lines at the investigator's. The fear of saying, somewhere, something I shouldn't. The fear of not saying something I should. Fear of words, fear of silence, of action, of inaction. . . . I couldn't, didn't want to, make choices any longer; I wasn't capable of choice—which *is* life. I was incapable of life. I was ready for prison.

So on that day, the sixth of April, I didn't buy a little bird to set it free. I even thought: But does it need this freedom? The other birds will peck at it like a stranger. So I didn't buy one. I walked home through the Gosnardom Garden, past the Zoo, where I'd so often been with the children, past people with worn winter coats and lit-up spring faces; and I said to myself that they would remain and would be walking back and forth when I was gone, in a month, in a year, in ten years, forever. . . . A hobo, eyes blue with spring, came up to me and said firmly, "Gimme something. Whatever you got." And when I started to burrow in my purse, he clarified quickly, "Not coins—a ruble."

Memory misleads. I don't remember anymore how much half a liter cost then. I didn't want to leave the street, glittering with April, for the darkness under the Arch.

When the doorbell rang, the sound I'd been expecting for so many months, I didn't recognize it. And when a short little man in civilian clothes showed me a red State Security ID, I didn't recognize that either. He said politely that I would have to go with him to answer a few questions; and I concluded that They'd finally decided to *ask* me. I got dressed. The children came out into the foyer to see me off. My daughter, jumping up and down, said suspiciously, "Where is Mama going?"

"She'll come back, Mama will come back," answered the little man cheerfully.

I thought, How many times have you said that, knowing Mama won't come back. And even then, I didn't realize.

"Shall we call a taxi?" I suggested.

"I have a car." And he waved a hand as if to say, What else?

The car was waiting at the gate. Inside was a second man; he had the iron face of someone in a Soviet war movie. I greeted him cheerfully; he responded. The little man sat with the driver, and I sat next to the second man. It seemed strange to me: the little man was very pleased with himself about something and kept smirking; he tried to draw the second man into his good mood, but without success. The second man, infinitely more interesting, behaved as if it weren't a young woman he was sitting next to, but an empty space. I said something about the weather. He answered in a monosyllable without turning his head. For some reason, my ears began to ring. O God, they'll ask about Levinton, tell me what to say! Inspire me! I prayed and looked out the window at the Leningrad snow thawing under the April sun; but the noise got stronger.

We drove up not to the main entrance but to a huge gate on a side street—on Voinov Street—and the car honked, and slowly the gates parted, and slowly we went in. I saw a man turning an enormous wheel—for the gate. We'd seen something like it recently in an American film, *Ali Baba and the Forty Thieves,* slaves turning a wheel, straining; here it was a properly dressed soldier. Progress! But then even the little man stopped talking to me, suddenly became somehow distant. I wouldn't have been able to hear him, anyway, because of the roaring in my ears. I just kept looking—ahead and to the side. We got out, went in somewhere, a stairway, then a narrow corridor, not long. I looked, tried to memorize, so I could hold on to it, tell about it, describe it. But I didn't manage to memorize anything that way—not the walls, or the number of steps, or the length of the corridor. We came to a small door, and the Iron Man threw over his shoulder, "Wait here."

I sat down on a chair and opened a book by Galsworthy that I had with me, *Over the River.* For that I'd been prepared—that I'd have to wait. And the roaring in my ears calmed down. This had happened before: sit and wait with a book until the man in charge can see you. But I didn't seem to sit there long. The Iron

Man opened the door and nodded his head. I went in, sat down; I remember some sort of wooden balustrade in front of me, behind which the Iron Man was standing. He gave—no, presented me with—a piece of paper: a large sheet, thick, on which everything was printed; only my given name, patronymic, and surname were typed in. I saw the large black letters: ORDER FOR SEARCH AND ARREST.

As if someone had put a huge pillow over my head, the roaring exploded and was gone.

The roaring quieted, and I stepped onto the stage.

And my Elizabeth Arden?

I never saw her again. Our paths never crossed, not in the common cell, not in the transit prison, not in the camps. I would have liked to end this story with a meeting somewhere in the Far East, in Raichikhinsk or on Sredne-Belaya. But it didn't happen. And she never reappeared in the stories of the men and women who were my fellow passengers on the journey into the whirlwind. I remembered her—not without bitterness—whenever I looked in the mirror and saw the white wrinkles in my darkened skin, like fissures: "You have fery, fery dry skin."

But once in a while, for some reason, I dreamed of her. I couldn't understand it—she was so far from my thoughts. . . . Then I noticed. After the dream, invariably something good would happen—a letter would arrive, or they wouldn't make us go out to work, or something else. All kinds of wonderful things. I began trying to think of her before going to sleep—but no, I only dreamed about her when I wasn't trying. It would happen that I'd dream of her even when there was no reason to expect anything good—and she wouldn't fail me.

She appeared in my dreams for the last time on the twelfth of July, 1954. Already four women had left before their sentence was up, something that had never happened before to anyone imprisoned under Article Fifty-Eight. But nobody got excited. Four, but that was four isolated instances.

I was the fifth. Elizabeth Arden didn't mislead me. Only it didn't work right away. The telegram, "You and your husband released," came not that day but the next.

After that I never dreamed of her again.

1979, 1981   *Translated by Ann Harleman*

Kuzka's Mother

In 1951 the harvest was good. The summer was long and sunny, with brief, warm rains. The potatoes multiplied prodigiously: large, pink, almost twenty to a bunch. Huge clumps of them grew before your very eyes. We covered them hastily with their green leafy tops and kept walking, on and on; the potato field was endless. The drivers from the transportation brigade couldn't get the potatoes to the storage sheds fast enough. That year they didn't even sort them. There was no time, and anyway it didn't matter. One potato was as big as the next.

We went out before the sun was up and got back after moonrise. Our days off were canceled. All of us who were able to work—even the "marshmallows" who had jobs inside the zone— were sent out to the fields. One morning Nastya Gavrilyuk, our orderly, was sent out to the field; in her place they put one of the invalids, who didn't have to go out to work.

"Girls, what if Kuzka's Mother is assigned as our orderly?" Masha Lukina said on the way to work. "I heard they're going to make her an orderly somewhere. What if it's with us?"

"Oh, come on!" we objected. "There's no way she'd agree to that! Can you see her with tubs and buckets—"

"*Khiba*, can you believe somebody like that—one of the intelligentsia—being sent to us?" said Nastya, pursing her lips scornfully.

"Let them pick her, if they want," said Margarita Vladimirovna, who used to be a translator. "At least we wouldn't have to listen to any more squawking. All Gavrilyuchka knows how to do is howl . . ."

"Fine," answered Nastya. "Wait till you come home, and there's no water to wash with, no tea to drink. Then you'll know. You thought Nastya was a pain! You'll cry plenty when you're stuck with Kuzka's Mother . . ."

"Hey, girls, why cross a bridge before you come to it?" said

Nadya Petrova, the brigade leader. "Where did you get the idea they'll give us Kuzka's Mother? Maybe it won't be her at all."

But it *was* her they picked. That evening she appeared in our section with her bundle and the inevitable Kuzka.

Kuzka's Mother was what the camp called Lidiya Alekseyevna Vorontsova. Masha had given her the nickname, and it stuck. One of the people freed the winter before had presented her with a rust-colored cat; she'd named him Kuzya and wouldn't be parted from him day or night. The whole zone knew her. They treated her a little ironically, as they would someone feeble-minded. Everybody knew that she'd gone to the camp commandant the winter before and asked him for permission to get meat scraps for the cat from the kitchen. And apparently the commandant asked her what her name was, and when she told him he said, "Oh, that's right—Kuzka's Mother!"

She was tall and skinny, with a thin, sorrowful face and luxuriant, dry, black hair; she wore a tight black dress and an amber necklace. They said her husband was a well-known Leningrad conductor. In short, to imagine this woman scrubbing floors was simply impossible.

"Why, you couldn't lift an *empty* bucket," cried Masha when Lidiya Alekseyevna told Nadya shyly in a hesitant voice that she was to be our orderly. "And you know how much water has to be carried in for us? Well, girls, if we're stuck with her, that'll be the end of us, we'll be eaten up with scabs. . . . Her and her Kuzya—oh, my God! Pipe dreams with polka-dots!"

We all started hollering. We didn't have anything against Kuzya, but we didn't want *her* for an orderly. How in the world would she manage? Water was a problem for us: it had to be brought into the zone. And when we came in from work, we stripped naked and shoved our way up to the washtubs under the awning to wash. . . . Water refreshed us, washed away the dust and tiredness; water gave us pleasure—and the pleasures we had could be counted on the fingers of one hand.

"Maybe, Lidiya Alekseyevna," said Nadya Petrova tactfully. "Maybe you'd really like to just live with us. Why don't you? I'll fix it with the higher-ups. But being an orderly would probably be hard for you."

Lidiya Alekseyevna looked at her with timid, glistening black eyes and pressed the kitten to her chest. "Please . . . I'll try very hard. . . . You wouldn't have to. . . . I know how to do everything. . . . And Kuzya—he won't make a mess, he's trained. . . . I can't leave him; he's got nobody but me!"

"Don't you understand?" Margarita Vladimirovna lectured me the next day when we were coming home from work, tired, dragging our feet. "She lives on love. For a woman that's the only happiness in life: I'm needed! I'm so needed. And to live without that 'I'm needed'—she just can't do it. People aren't much interested in her—so she gives her love to a kitten. And let me tell you, *Plus je connais les hommes, plus j'aime les animaux*. Which means, The more I know people, the more I love animals."

"Is that really what you think, Margarita Vladimirovna? Come winter, you'll be busy every night with your drama group again."

"Me? Not on your life! Me get involved with that menagerie? All right; okay. Let's be patient with Lidiya Alekseyevna for a few days—you shouldn't hurt someone's feelings—and then we'll demand a real orderly. They can't let the whole brigade fall apart."

Lidiya Alekseyevna and Kuzya were waiting for us. The floors and table were scrubbed clean, the washtubs were full, the cots were neatly made up. "My dears, poor things, how tired you must be," she chattered, helping us take off our dust-laden jackets. "Wash now, girls, wash and eat. I'll bring your dinner here, they'll give it to me, they promised!"

"Girls!" An exultant voice from under the awning. "Warm water! She's even heated the water!"

"Well—intelligentsia," was all Masha Lukina said.

Intelligentsia was already hurrying off to the dining room for our dinner, with Kuzka bounding after her.

"This is great!" Nadya Petrova closed her eyes and crouched under a stream of warm water. "Oh, terrific—girls, she's not around, is she?—Hurrah for Kuzka's Mother! What is it you say, Masha? Pipe dreams with polka-dots?"

"How could you ever have doubted her?" Margarita Vladimirovna wondered. She had already forgotten everything she'd said to me on the road. "She's a Leningrader, after all, she lived through the blockade; so it's no wonder she—"

Someone poured a dipperful of water over her.

And only Nastenka Gavrilyuk, the former orderly, snorted and refused to wash. Think what a miracle: warm water!

And so we accepted the new orderly. We helped her carry heavy pots of soup, took off our shoes in the entryway, reserved for her the best place, the place of honor, in the corner next to the brigade leader; we even tried to bring her stolen potatoes from the field—only she always refused to take them. We got used to her hesitant voice, her timid smile. True, we didn't fall in love with Kuzka: he really was very mangy.

She changed. Gray appeared thickly in her dry hair, her face darkened, her hands got callused. Now she wore large men's shoes and a bright-orange cotton dress—the dress which for some reason they issued to all the invalids that summer. "What kind of color is that?" said Masha Lukina, baffled. "Like a nasturtium. Well, now none of the invalids can even think about escaping. In a dress like that they'd see you coming three kilometers away!"

I

Morning. The noises of getting ready for work. The "queen of the zone," the work supervisor, has already looked in twice. Masha, in a dress and work-jacket, about to jump down any second, sits on the bunk watching Valechka Afrosimova, who has a small mirror propped on her lap and is carefully fashioning her abundant hair into an enormous stylish twist that falls over her eyebrows.

"Don't you ever get tired of making yourself into a scarecrow?" says Masha interestedly.

Valechka presses her lips together and begins expertly stabbing pins into her hairdo.

"Will you look at her," Masha says loudly. "Roll call has already started by now, and we sit here and wait for her. . . ."

"Ah, leave her alone," interrupts Nastenka Gavrilyuk. "*Khiba,* Can't you see she's almost ready?"

"Don't I have the right to say anything? *Khiba, khiba* . . . shut up, Gavrilyuchka. I want to make a real person out of this doll!"

"Let's go, girls!" The bass voice of Nadya Petrova, the brigade leader. "Valya, hurry up!"

We dig potatoes. Masha is in the lead with three rows; Valechka does one. She's a little weak—delicate. Last year, when there were still men living in our zone, one old fellow who'd seen better days said to her, "You're a white dove among crows." Then this disinterested admirer of beauty sold his only jacket and sent her a half-kilo of butter. Now Valechka tries to keep on being a dove. She wears a homemade gauze hat to shield her face from the sun. Sometimes she steals a look at her hands: not getting calluses, is she? At that moment the voice of Masha rings out unexpectedly. "Girls, Afrosimova's afraid she's spoiled her manicure. What kind of worker is that? Pipe dreams with polka-dots!"

At midday they bring lunch. If they've managed to bring water at the same time, we wash "ladder-style," five people to one thin stream of water. You have to conserve water if it's to last through the long summer day. There aren't enough soup bowls to go around, either. We eat in pairs, taking turns; nobody thinks of washing the bowls.

Valechka has her own enamel bowl, which was at some point sent her from home, and an old but very clean napkin. The napkin is wrapped around a chunk of bread for her lunch; Valechka daintily bites off small pieces. Even at home, she never takes bread in her bare hand.

Masha lies on her stomach smoking and waiting her turn. She's bored.

"Afrosimova!" she cries. "Let's you and me lap it up together!"

"You're so crude, Masha!" sighs Valechka with meek displeasure.

"So what? So I'm not delicate enough for old men to send me butter. Come on, what do you say? Let's eat our soup together."

Valechka turns away.

"Or are you an Old Believer?" Her tormentor doesn't let up. "Girls, she's a real Old Believer!"

Nadya Petrova the Just, laughing, comes to the rescue of her silent comrade. "Sit here, Masha, eat with me."

It's an honor to eat with the brigade leader, and Masha leaves off her teasing. But not for long. Soon her voice resounds over the whole field. "Afrosimova! Hold your shovel right! It's not a teaspoon."

It isn't the first year we've lived together and we no longer care who wins. But our life is so uneventful that Masha's futile efforts to "make a person out of Valechka" amuse us and cheer us up.

The harvest was coming to an end. At first the days stayed dry and warm. We didn't see the mountains of the High Altai more than three times the entire summer—for some reason they're only visible before it rains. Meanwhile, they were predicting snow before the Feast of the Intercession, and very little time remained until the Feast of the Intercession. We got thinner and quieter and no longer asked the authorities for days off. We had to hurry to harvest everything before the "white flies" descended on us; otherwise we'd have to dig potatoes in the snow again, like last year. We dug and dug. . . . Our hands cracked and got black— a blackness water wouldn't remove. We had to clean it off in the field with the little green potato balls that looked like small plums. Even their taste reminded you a little of plums, only you had to swallow them without chewing; otherwise, instead of the sweet, half-forgotten taste of fruit, they left in your mouth a nauseating sourness.

Masha lit a small bonfire of potato leaves and cooked green potato balls. "Someday we'll look back on this—eating Altai plums," she declared. She worked easily, cheerfully, her movements unexpectedly graceful.

"What's happened to you, Marya?" old Auntie Anya Barabashkina said to her. "Do you think it's your own garden you're tending? Or do you plan to take these fruits to the bazaar?"

Auntie Anya had been a berry picker. At night she was sad: Now someone else picks berries in my place.

"Never mind, Auntie Anya," answered Masha. "When I go home, I'm going to start a garden right away. Right in the middle of the street. What else can I do? Have I gotten my qualifications here for nothing? I have to feed my children!"

She had three daughters in a children's home. The older two were twins; they were due to start school that year. Somehow Masha'd gotten it into her head that this would happen in her presence. All winter she wrote petitions to the public prosecutor, to the Supreme Soviet, even to Stalin himself. The first petitions had been refused; she was pinning her hopes on the letter to Stalin.

"He's got to see that I'm in prison unjustly, doesn't he?" she kept asking Margarita Vladimirovna, her black eyes flashing furiously.

Margarita would say, "Who knows! Maybe you'll be lucky." And we'd be silent.

In prison unjustly? Think of it, how amazing! Which of us *is* guilty? Lidiya Alekseyevna, perhaps—a traitor to the State? Or Margarita, who got ten years for having a sister abroad? Or Nadya Petrova? Nadya was locked up for two days by the Germans, along with the director of her infirmary. And for that she's already done ten years. Her child—she gave birth in the camp—is being raised by her mother-in-law.

For us there is no amnesty, no release order, no "pardon."

Sometimes—about once every two years—the order would come to the camp: Free any women who have children. Children under the age of seven. Of ten. There was even one order: Under the age of fourteen! And those women would go home.

But none of us went. Those sentenced under Article Fifty-Eight "didn't qualify."

No, Masha pinned her hopes on her letter in vain. An answer came at the end of harvest.

We no longer crowded under the awning: the evenings had grown cold. Lidiya Alekseyevna dragged the washtub inside the barracks. We washed any old way and immediately fell into bed. She served dinner quietly and cautiously woke those who'd managed to fall asleep. They chased her away, shouting, "Go to hell, you lie around here all day with your Kuzka, you don't know what rest means for someone who works!" Then they ate and fell asleep again—snoring, whistling, groaning, the sleep of people who are dead-tired.

One night I heard Valechka's whiny voice. "Masha, stop sighing, would you? I haven't slept in I don't know how many nights because of you. And the planks of your bunk creak. . . ."

As if in support of her words, the planks gave a terrible creak and Masha sat up. I could hear her whistling whisper: "You cold fish! Cold fish! Shut up! Hang onto your three planks, and keep quiet! I can't sleep; I can't sleep. Get it? It's all black inside. Get it?"

"Quiet!" someone howled in the darkness. The planks creaked despondently once more; then all was silent.

Something was happening to Masha. We all noticed it, once the harvest was finally over and the first snowstorm began to blow. For us, prisoners under convoy, a snowstorm meant, above all, rest—the full, deep rest we dreamed of for eight months of the year. They don't make us go out to work, they take roll by barracks, they bring us lunch. . . . In the morning, lying in bed, we all tell each other our dreams. Auntie Anya knows how to interpret them. You see a towel or a ribbon, it means a journey or a transfer; meat—a sickbed; a church—you'll be released; a clock—you'll be released, only you have to get a look at what time it says. But best of all is to see an old man in your dream. It means you'll be released for sure; he will guide you.

But somehow none of us saw old men in our dreams, not even Valya Afrosimova. And no one was released. There were still long years ahead of us—at least, we thought so then.

In winter we all took up needlework. Even Margarita Vladimirovna at one time took to her needle. "Hey, girls, there's going to be a general pardon!" Masha cried over her embroidery. But in the end she didn't finish it; she got involved in the drama group.

They didn't bring movies into the zone—we didn't have electricity. So the performances of the drama group met with great success, even though all the male roles were taken by women. And for that reason Margarita Vladimirovna, the leader of the drama group, was treated with respect even by the real criminals.

And so, when Lidiya Alekseyevna, out of breath, came into our barracks one morning and gasped out, "Snowstorm," a delighted scream answered her. Even Nadya Petrova herself cried out in her bass voice, "Hurrah!"

And only Masha said meanly, "What are you so happy about, you fools? Now how many days will we have to go without mail?"

Some of us fell silent. Others muttered something like "Big deal." We didn't expect many letters. Sticking out her lower lip, Nastya Gavrilyuk remarked: "Our Mariya has really gone nuts!"

"It happens," Margarita Vladimirovna, who was a longtime resident, said musingly. "In the third year, it happens; a person loses hope and, as you put it, goes nuts. Never mind, later the damn thing comes back again—this hope. What year are you, Masha?"

"Oh, get lost," answered Masha, and abruptly put her head down. The planks underneath her gave a groan.

The snowstorm lasted five days. And for all those days, Masha lay like that, showering those below with tobacco and ashes. We liked to gather "*chez* Margarita Vladimirovna," beneath Masha's bunk; sometimes we sang, sometimes we told stories. . . . Our brigade had several storytellers, each with her circle of listeners.

Valechka Afrosimova was a storyteller. Once I even heard the beginning of one of her stories. "Now I'll tell you the life story of Raphael," she cooed. "He was terribly in love with a certain interesting lady."

Masha never once broke into the conversation, never joined in the singing. Sometimes she'd lean down. "Give me a light, I'm out of matches." They'd hold out a lighted homemade cigarette; she'd light up, and when her own cigarette flared, crackling, we would see her dark face, her mournful eyes.

"You know, I'm afraid of her," Valechka informed Lidiya Alekseyevna in confidence.

Lidiya Alekseyevna tucked her legs under her timidly and hugged the restless Kuzka, who with the onset of winter wasn't behaving well at all.

"She's always thinking, nothing but thinking," whispered Nastya Gavrilyuk, and her eyes grew round.

"Oh," sighed Margarita Vladimirovna. "I have to tell you, *Plus je connais les hommes, plus j'aime les animaux!*"

"You mustn't think that!" Lidiya Alekseyevna was frightened. "Don't you think that!"

"Actually, I think it a lot, believe me. Well, goodbye; or my actors will be kept waiting."

"How will you get there? There's a snowstorm."

"Oh, that's no problem. It's not far to the dining hall." She took off her glasses, put her *bushlat* jacket over her head, and went out.

In winter we needed a second orderly, and Nastya Gavrilyuk returned to her duties. In the mornings her shrill cry again rang out. "Girls, up on your bunks, we're going to wash floors." When the snowstorm was over and we began going to work, she greeted us with wailing. "What's the matter with you? *Khiba*, watch where you're walking!"

Lidiya Alekseyevna was now night orderly; but under the command of the bossy Nastya she unprotestingly carried water, scrubbed floors, and removed traces of Kuzka's transgressions with special care.

She wasn't always successful. Coming into the barracks, we'd sniff the air suspiciously, and inevitably someone would say, "Girls, Kuzka's done it again!"

At that moment Kuzka would be prudently hiding under a bunk. Lidiya Alekseyevna, ashamed of her foster-child, would be ready to do the same. But it was when Masha came in that she would start to be really afraid.

Masha would burst into the barracks like a storm and ask, "Has the mail come?"

"Nothing for you again, Mariya Gavrilovna," Lidiya Alekseyevna would answer tremblingly.

Masha would throw her a look of hate and go out again, slamming the door as hard as she could. Sometimes we'd go after her. Striding widely, she'd go out to the *zapretnaya zona,* the forbidden zone, as we called the small clearing around the camp, fenced with barbed wire on both sides. Beyond the wire was freedom—the boundless expanse of the steppes. But she didn't look in that direction. She strode violently around the enclosure, head down, now and then pulling her *bushlat* tight across her chest. Sometimes the guards shouted at her from the observation posts, "Hey, *mora!* What are you pacing up and down for? Get back in the barracks!" *Mora* was what they called gypsies in the camps. The authorities all thought Masha was a gypsy.

She'd return to the barracks. And she'd start in, "When is this damn barnyard going to get cleaned up? You can't breathe in these barracks anymore."

No one would answer her. Then, furious, she'd go over to Lidiya Alekseyevna's bunk.

"You'd better get out of this barracks with your damn cat! People can't live like human beings on account of that cat!"

"Masha!" The brigade leader's bass would sound a warning.

"Well, isn't that the truth? Isn't it?"

Once Valechka got up her courage and came to Lidiya Alekseyevna's defense. "Masha, do you really think Lidiya Alekseyevna's to blame because you don't get letters from your children?"

Masha turned white and went toward her, holding our her hands like a blind person. . . . Valya let out a shriek and just as she was, in her dress, rushed out of the barracks. . . . We threw ourselves on Masha, grabbed hold of her, held her down. . . .

Valya spent the night in the infirmary and didn't come back to the barracks until the next morning when the brigade had already gone out to work. Suddenly we realized Kuzka had disappeared.

I had a fever, my head ached, and the "medical assistant" had given me an exemption (in winter our doctors were more lenient). I was lying in bed and through a haze of sleep I heard Lidiya Alekseyevna walking, heard her calling softly (so as not to wake me), "Kuzya, Kuzya. . . ."

Then Nastya Gavrilyuk said, "For sure, that crazy Mariya must have gotten rid of him!"

"What are you saying, Nastenka!"

"Well, where would he disappear to? *Khiba,* do you think he ran off all by himself?"

"My God, Lidiya Alekseyevna, did you really not understand, all this time?" Valechka's angelic little voice.

"No, why, how is. . . . It's freezing outside! An animal would die! Why? She's not an evil woman, Mariya Gavrilovna, not really—She couldn't! Kuzya! Kuzya! Kuzenka!"

But Kuzka was gone.

Everything became quiet. Lidiya Alekseyevna went out to look for her darling in the other barracks. It was a while before she returned—Nastya had already begun to wash the floors.

"You were right, girls," she said in a strange, subdued voice. "At roll call the work supervisor saw Mariya Gavrilovna carrying Kuzya out under her *bushlat.*"

"What a snake!" Valechka cooed.

We were silent. Then Lidiya Alekseyevna began to speak, stuttering and choking, "I'll leave you today, girls. Let's just wait until the brigade comes back, and I'll go. Because this kind of cruelty. . . . I wanted to live with you because—I wanted to live with young—I thought, I can be useful—I thought, a warm, human word to them—Taking care—But this kind of cruelty—If *we're* like that, what can we expect? What? I wanted, like a mother—"

I was sad. It was hard to imagine our barracks without Kuzka's Mother. I was sad for her, and sad for myself, for us; and anger rose in me against Masha. What had happened to her, had she truly become an animal?

After lunch red-haired Liza, the librarian, brought the mail: a

postcard for Margarita Vladimirovna and a letter for Masha Lukina. "You haven't found your Kuzka?" she asked. Clucking com-
passionately, she went out.

Lidiya Alekseyevna went over to the table, took Masha's envelope in her hand.

"Look. Finally there's a letter for Mariya Gavrilovna. Maybe if
it had come yesterday, nothing would have happened—and Kuzya
would—"

This time Masha didn't ask about the mail; but they didn't give
her time to take off her coat. "A letter for you, a letter!" cried
Auntie Anya, and Margarita Vladimirovna, and Nadya Petrova.

Masha flung herself away from the door. In her *bushlat,* her
felt boots, her tightly wound kerchief, she stood by the table and,
holding the letter very close to her eyes like someone unaccustomed to reading, she read it to herself, moving her lips. Then
she let out a howl, yelled, threw herself on the bench, let her head
fall on the table.

"What is it?" cried Nadya Petrova, who was changing her
clothes in the corner. "Margarita Vladimirovna, be so kind, read
what they write her."

"Dear Mama." In the silence that had fallen, Margarita Vladimirovna began to read. "We've already learned how to write.
Come home soon, dear Mama, we miss you very much."

"There's nothing, then!" Masha cried out heartrendingly,
raising a twisted face. "Nothing! No justice! No freedom! We'll
die here like dogs—on this godforsaken steppe. With a tag on our
foot. Like dogs! There's nothing. Nothing. Nothing."

"Masha," said Margarita Vladimirovna in a trembling voice.

"Why? Why should I? There's nothing! I write and write, I ask
for simple justice, and they send me a refusal—A refusal—And
the children are growing up—"

Lidiya Alekseyevna came up to her very quietly, carrying an
enamel mug in her outstretched hand. "Mariya Gavrilovna," she
called, and put her narrow, dark hand on her back. "Mariya
Gavrilovna. Drink this, it's sweet tea. . . . It'll make you
feel. . . ."

Masha's eyes flashed. With all her strength she shoved away
the outstretched hand. The mug rolled along the bench, rattling,
and a dark puddle spread across the floor.

II

Spring arrived in May.

This was how the supervisors would summon us to work: "Hey, hurry up, the cow's waiting!"

In fact, it was true. Every morning, without fail, a pale-red heifer was waited for us outside the zone. No one knew whose she was, or why she'd attached herself to our brigade. But by roll call she'd already be standing at the gate, quietly swishing her tail, and then she'd amble slowly into the field after us.

Every day Masha would suggest, "Let's put our new brigade worker on the list, so we can get a ration for her. Why not, after all? She works alongside us without a break, and she gets no ration. What kind of justice is that?"

Masha seemed to be herself again after the winter, as if she'd never cried out on that terrible evening, "Nothing left! Nothing!" Once again she laughed, joked, teased Afrosimova, wrote petitions—in short, everything was as before. And once, when we were coming back from work, she burst into song:

> My sweetheart has a little nose
> That's really very fine.
> Eight hens could perch on it,
> And a rooster'd make nine.

"Aha!" said Margarita Vladimirovna meaningfully. And we all burst out laughing.

"What's all that about?" asked Masha. "What's come over you, some kind of laughing fit?" But against her will she smiled.

We knew her sweetheart. Now we never sat in the field without water, because he was a water carrier. He was called Lyosha—a handsome, tall fellow, only in place of his left leg he had a piece of wood. When his white mare appeared on the road, we'd call to Masha, "Mariya! Here comes Peg-leg!" And Masha would run to meet him as fast as her legs would take her.

"Tsk! She moves like an unbroken filly," Auntie Anya would observe disapprovingly.

"*Khiba,* Auntie Anya, have you forgotten what it was to be young?" Nadya Petrova would say.

"I had some shame when I was young, that's for sure," Auntie Anya would grumble. "There she goes, running off! She'll go off and fool around with him, and the brigade will encourage her! No doubt she's even forgotten how to think!"

But nobody was on Auntie Anya's side. We all supported Masha's romance wholeheartedly and we were prepared to manage without her the whole time Lyosha was in the field. And he was in no hurry to leave.

Now Masha had a lot of work to do even in the zone—washing for Lyosha, mending for Lyosha, embroidering for Lyosha. Lyosha had already received a pillowcase with the legend "Good Morning, Lyosha!" and a towel with roosters on it, and, of course, a tobacco pouch. The tobacco pouch Masha didn't even try to embroider herself but commissioned from the camp's best needlewoman, Tomochka Kravchuk. It turned out to be magnificent: a light-brown pipe was embroidered in satin stitch surrounded by wavy light-blue lines, and another intricate legend which had cost her a lot: "May Your Troubles Go Up In Smoke."

Masha saved up sugar and bread to feed Mortar—as for some reason Lyosha's docile mare was called—and her foal. The foal was very young, smoky gray, with long, thin legs. Its mane and tail curled tightly. "Ringlets like you've never seen," Masha said, impressed. "Afrosimova must surely envy that!"

Admiring the foal, Masha would sit next to her sweetheart while he gently tugged on Mortar's reins, and they would go slowly across the field to the steady slap of water in the barrels. "Like being on a boat," Masha would laugh.

The foal would lag behind. Sometimes sleep would overtake him suddenly: he'd throw himself down into a furrow and doze for a few sweet minutes. Then abruptly his whole body would shudder and he'd burst into a frightened, piercing whinny. From somewhere in the distance his mother would answer him with a reassuring call; then he'd leap up and rush across the field to her.

Spring, spring. . . .

Around the zone, "administrative" geese strolled with their broods (our whole administration kept geese). The geese swayed proudly, conscious of their maternal glory; and yellow balls of fluff came tumbling after them. We'd follow them with our gaze. Then we'd go past the pig farm. On the first young grass squirmed a solid mass of pink-and-white piglets; and Nina Sviridova, who was from Moscow, the senior pigkeeper and the most beautiful girl in the zone, would be standing in the middle of them, illuminated by the sun, tall, golden-haired and erect, like Diana the Huntress. In front of the cow sheds, the calves pranced triumphantly, tails held high.

Spring, spring. . . .

And one fine day Lyosha brought Masha Lukina a tiny fox cub tucked into his winter hat. We all came running to look at him. He was almost gray and must have opened his eyes very recently—he blinked so wonderingly at the world revealed to him.

"I had to lie in wait for them quite a while," Lyosha told us in a satisfied voice. "There's a whole litter of them there. They crawl around in the sunshine, waiting for their mother. There was no way to get near them—they'd hide. So I creep up—Now you'll have some mending to do. Look, my clothes are all torn."

Masha was radiant. "Of course I will," she said. "You have no idea how happy you've made me."

She scratched the fox cub behind its ear. The cub opened its wide pink mouth, in which the teeth were just beginning to come through, and yelped, distrustful and angry.

"Well, a real pup! Girls, you know what? I'll give him to . . . Kuzka's mother! She'll be his mistress and she'll love it."

We stayed there the rest of the day, taking turns looking after Kuzka the Second and feeding him soup; he ate, looking around watchfully. It was Masha who carried him home, carefully wrapped in her old jacket, from which his long head protruded. Auntie Anya walked beside her and said sarcastically. "Well, now what? Your young man's a big help, that's plain! Now we've got a beast like this on our hands. Soon we'll have a cow!"

"You said it, my friend," answered Masha good-naturedly. "He's already dressed me from head to foot—he even bought me a comb and slippers!" But the radiance never left her face.

Lidiya Alekseyevna hadn't left us. Maybe Nadya Petrova talked her out of it—they had a long, serious talk on that memorable evening, after everything had calmed down in the barracks. Or maybe she just changed her mind. We didn't know. But she stayed on as our orderly, and our barracks became number one in the

157

zone for cleanliness. Now, in spring, we brought her flowers—picked furtively on the way to work. On our table, on our night-stands, even by the washtub there appeared fresh bouquets of bright-colored wildflowers, which for some reason we called tulips.

It seemed as if Lidiya Alekseyevna didn't even remember Kuzka. We were actually a little disappointed: she'd been so taken up with him, loved him so; and now it was as if he had never been. But she never spoke to Masha, as if she didn't notice her; didn't respond to either her veiled hints or her direct remarks. And it seemed to us that this made Masha anxious.

So now, as she approached Lidiya Alekseyevna with the fox cub in her arms, everyone listened closely. Each of us tried to look busy with her own affairs, while an unusual attentive silence filled the barracks.

Masha said, "Lidiya Alekseyevna, look, Lyosha brought me a little fox cub. And I want to give him to you. Lyosha says he'll only be ugly like this while he's little—"

"What do you mean, ugly!" answered Lydia Alekseyevna fiercely. "He's a fine animal. . . . Only, Mashenka, he's yours. . . . Naturally I'll look after him. . . ."

"No, you must take him. I want you. . . . Call him Kuzka."

We stopped listening after that. Peace had been declared.

Kuzka the Second became the darling of the zone. Even the supervisors would drop in at our barracks especially to see him. I can't say these visits gave us pleasure—we had to hastily conceal strictly forbidden needles, scissors, homemade knives. But Lidiya Alekseyevna showed them her new foster child with quiet maternal pride.

She washed him carefully, ignoring his indignant yelps, fed him milk that she bought from women on the sick list. She found a way to earn money: she drew cards in colored pencil and sold them for fifty kopeks apiece. Within a short time, these cards achieved great popularity; we enclosed them in letters home, and even non-prisoners bought them for their children. Fluffy, cunning kittens frolicked on them, flowers of unimagined color and beauty bloomed on them. . . . After a while, the star of the cards emerged, Kuzka himself—Kuzka in a little skirt and bonnet,

Kuzka in front of a bunch of bright-green grapes, Kuzka *au naturel,* sitting on his hind legs with his fluffy tail curled around his front paws.

He quickly grew bigger and smarter, and became more noticeably red. His tail got more and more luxuriant; he trailed it behind him like a train. We soon stopped leaving our shoes under our bunks: Kuzka began to stay awake at night and steal anything left lying around. He'd bury his loot right away, somewhere around the barracks. When we outwitted him, he immediately started going on raids to neighboring barracks, where at first they accepted him trustingly—the more so, as he managed to become famous for exterminating mice. But after a shoe belonging to Lida Selikhova, the brigade leader of the next barracks, disappeared forever, Lidiya Alekseyevna started locking our barracks for the night.

One night, for some reason, Yerofeyev—a middle-aged supervisor who now and then allowed himself a chat with the prisoners—came to our barracks. He sat for a long while watching Kuzka, who was stealing silently across the barracks, hiding from an invisible pursuer under the bunks, diligently covering his tracks with his tail.

"Mousing!" he said thoughtfully. Then he added, "You must tie him up at night now. Soon he'll know the road beyond the zone, he'll start to run off at night and steal chickens. He'll get in trouble for that. They'll kill him."

"But I lock him in," Lidiya Alekseyevna objected.

"What good is that! Somebody'll need to go outside during the night, and he'll scoot right out, you won't even see it happen."

And Kuzka just about lost his nighttime freedom. He got a dog collar; Lidiya Aleseyevna attached a short, thick rope to the collar that even Kuzka couldn't manage to bite through. And he began to whine inconsolably, complaining of injustice, of deepest mortification. We couldn't sleep. A distraught Lidiya Alekseyevna would untie him again, and he'd run away from her under the farthest bunk. But their estrangement never lasted long. Lidiya Alekseyevna would barely have lain down when he'd promptly jump on her bed to make up, lick her face all over, and fall asleep with his narrow, cunning muzzle on her neck.

He knew his own name and, like a puppy, could distinguish

Masha from the others: she occasionally brought in for him from the field a dead bird or a field mouse in an old mitten. . . . But it was live, hopping sparrows that interested him. He'd approach them stealthily on his stomach, trying to blend in with the ground, one eye closed. But the sparrows, alerted, would fly off anyway. It wasn't until July that Kuzka caught his first live prey.

We heard about his victory in the field from Lyosha. He brought the sensational news: "Kuzka strangled three of Petrenko's chickens. What a racket! It's curtains for him now. He knows the way to the chicken coops."

Kuzka was doomed.

Lidiya Alekseyevna didn't let him out of her sight, the supervisors watched him, the free women from beyond the zone chased him with sticks and stones; and still he got out again and again, returning toward nightfall from his raids, tired but satisfied. Then one evening he didn't come back.

Through the camp poured a piercing, mournful sound: the man on watch was pounding out Retreat on an iron rail. But Lidiya Alekseyevna kept on standing at the gate, waiting for Kuzka.

"Go to sleep!" Yerofeyev, who was on duty that night, said to her severely. "You know the rules, Vorontsova!"

"Citizen Chief, Kuzka's outside the zone—He's always come back by now—"

Yerofeyev scowled. "You!" he said with annoyance. "Didn't I tell you to tie him up! Now you'll see. He's done for now, your Kuzka. What kind of life is this for him? We all know what a fox is. A chicken-thief. Well, you go in and go to sleep, you know the rules. If he comes, I'll drag him in myself. But from now on I won't let you keep him untied."

Lidiya Alekseyevna didn't sleep that night, though it was Nastya's turn on duty. Masha didn't sleep either. In the stuffy darkness I could hear her passionate gypsy whisper. "Now don't you be sad, Lidiya Alekseyevna. Maybe it'll work out. What kind of beasts do you think they are, the people outside the zone? They know it's a tame fox, your own special. . . . What kind of people are they, would they really want to take away a prisoner's only joy on account of some chicken?"

"Masha, have a heart," Valechka moaned plaintively. "Let us sleep!"

"Never mind sleep! Now, Lidiya Alekseyevna, you listen to me. . . ."

I fell asleep. And at that very moment—or did it only seem that way?—Nadya Petrova was shaking my shoulder. "Time to get up!"

It was morning already. Outside the zone, the roosters were crowing at the top of their lungs. We dressed quietly. Today half the brigade would go out before reveille: the cabbage had to be watered.

"The cow probably hasn't even come to the gate yet," said Margarita Vladimirovna gloomily.

"Uh-oh, it's going to rain, isn't it?" yawned Auntie Anya. "What do your bones say, Lukina?"

No one answered her—Masha wasn't in the barracks. Nadya said quietly, "She and Lidiya Alekseyevna are out by the sentry post—Kuzka's crawled up to it. He's been hurt."

We rushed to the sentry post. Right at the gate, clutching the wire in her hands, stood Lidiya Alekseyevna, saying quietly in her hesitant voice, "Kuzka! Come, sweetheart, come on. Come! Come!"

From up above came the cry, "Hey, you! Kuzka's Mother! Get away from the *zapretka,* do you hear?"

Masha—I hadn't noticed her at first—grabbed Lidiya Alekseyevna and dragged her off to the side. There she knelt down, stretching out her skinny arms toward the *zapretka.*

"Oh, my God!" breathed someone, Auntie Anya perhaps.

And then I saw. In the *zapretka* lay Kuzka, a small red ball against the blackness of the ploughed earth. He was still alive. His sunken side heaved: he was breathing.

"Kuzka!" Lidiya Alekseyevna called.

He heard. He crawled on his belly, using all his strength, dragging his fluffy tail. Just as he reached the wire he fell over onto his side.

"Kuzya!"

A long spasm shook his narrow body. Then he stiffened, stretching out his paws.

"He's dead," sighed Masha.

"Lead the brigade out, Petrova," Yerofeyev commanded angrily.

"Because of a chicken!" cried Masha. "Someone's only joy—because of a chicken!"

We were counted, led out, lined up in formation. . . . I looked around. Lidiya Alekseyevna, in her ugly bright-orange invalid's dress, was still kneeling, her thin hands clasped together at her throat. And in the *zapretka,* between two rows of barbed wire, something brown lay pale and motionless on the black earth—something that had, not long ago, been Kuzka.

1981   *Translated by Ann Harleman*

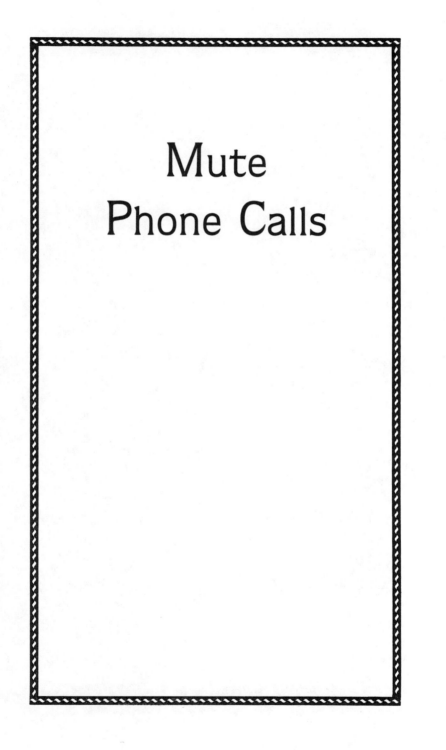

Mute
Phone Calls

THEY gave me one room in a two-bedroom apartment. I've been in this world for all of half a century, and this was the first room I'd had to myself.

This room was light, and completely bare. I'd been told that it was sunny, but now, in November, I couldn't quite believe it. From the big window I had a view of three birches covered with snow. Next summer they'll be green, and the tenants will supposedly plant ornamental bushes in the courtyard. That's what Veta Andreyevna said, the woman with whom I share the apartment.

I had to buy absolutely everything. I didn't want to drag into this place anything from my former life—not a bed sheet, not a frying pan. How much can you need when you're alone? There were almost a thousand rubles in my savings account, which represented my advance for a screenplay. I've never had so much money of my own. By May I should have the first draft; if it's accepted, I'll get four hundred more. So if I'm careful, I'll have enough for the year even if I buy things now.

I sat on my suitcase and made a list of what to buy first: a couch, a small table, an armchair, a kitchen table, two pots, a tea pot, a coffee pot, cups, two sheets, a blanket, a pillow . . . plates, spoons, forks . . . an ash tray. . . . It came to more than I'd expected. Lucky that there was a closet in my room. I added to the list: hangers.

Veta Andreyevna looked in:

"I'd like to give you a bookcase. I got myself a new glass case." She laughed. "I bought it!"

"Thanks a lot," I said. "But I don't need a bookcase. I haven't got any books yet."

"They'll accumulate!" she said with conviction. "What do you want me to do, throw it out? It's very small. It would fit right into this corner here, see?"

She dragged me to her room. It was bigger than mine. A gray rug on the floor, a light cover on the couch, matching curtains and a dressing table. I'd never in my life had a dressing table. A crimson carnation in a glass vase. A large plant in a flower pot. On the wall, an oil painting, a lilac face with an Elizabethan ruffled collar. The room looked consciously and deliberately created, nothing haphazard about it. One could work well here, or stretch out to read, or have a heart-to-heart talk. The lamps were placed just right. Pleased by my remarks, Veta Andreyevna said:

"I don't have a TV, but I do have a record player, see?" It was placed conveniently on the floor by the couch.

"I've got some pretty good records, so, if you like music. . . ."

I said that I didn't. She became anxious:

"Will it bother you if I. . . ."

"No, don't worry. I like to hear music from a distance. I just don't like to sit down to listen to it."

She nodded as if she understood, and then showed me the blond bookcase partly hidden behind the corner. She stroked its light surface and said:

"It's been a good friend to me, take it. . . . Might cheer you up."

So I took it. I must admit that in my room the bookcase looked less cheerful. Veta Andreyevna and I pushed it into my niche. She said she could also give me a cot and mattress that had been lying around the attic for over a year now. In this case, I didn't need to be persuaded: I knew I wasn't going to buy a couch right away. To thank her, I told her the story of the man who meant to write his memoirs "Forty Years on a Cot." She liked the story, laughed a lot and then asked:

"And then? Didn't the construction boom in co-ops affect him, too?"

"It did, but differently. He got himself a new family, a new apartment, and a double bed."

She nodded:

"That's the way it goes in the world. Now, let's go to the kitchen and have a cup of tea. You know, I think you and I could get by with one kitchen table. At least at first. And you can use my refrigerator. It's rented, we can pay by turns. My former neighbor and I. . . ."

Veta Andreyevna chattered. To be precise, she didn't chatter but tried to draw me into her circle of happy animation in which everything was so easy and comfortable, where all the colors matched. But I wasn't drawn in. I sat with her in the kitchen, drank her strong tea, ate her "Sadko" cookies, made female conversation about mohair sweaters—but never felt drawn in.

All this was a bit much: "Sadko," and the refrigerator, and the unspoken offer to live like one family. . . . I yearned to be alone, to hide myself away; instead, I was immediately offered attention, friendship, and I don't know what else.

When I finally managed to get out of the kitchen under the pretext that I had to go shopping to have things for that night ("What do you need? Sheets? A blanket? I'll give them to you!"), I felt tricked and disturbed. The thin facade behind which I used to hide began crumbling in all the usual places. I saw that this lone woman was happy, and the sight of happy people was too much for me. I plucked her out of my thoughts—I know how to do it now!—and began thinking about sheets and cups, about the fact that now I can buy one hundred grams of butter—being alone it will last me a long time. I haven't bought anything for myself, just for me, in such a long time that this thought cheered me up, made me feel younger. . . . The last time I bought fifty grams of butter and a hundred grams of cheese just for myself was in the store on the Kudrinka. I remembered exactly: the morning of June 22, 1941. In the courtyard of the house where I rented a room I heard a dark-haired girl shout to someone: "Didn't you hear the radio? Hurry home! There's war. . . ."

She pronounced the word "war" with added breath, almost in a whisper. It was frightening yet festive for her to say it that way, for the first time in her life. Everything is festive the first time around. Everything that's not yet commonplace is festive. And my day today is also a special holiday.

I took the bus to the Nevsky and the shops. My special day continued. In the Arcade, they were already selling Christmas toys. The New Year is coming inevitably. Veta will buy herself a tree. She works as an editor or, rather, as a senior editor for a large trade publisher and, apparently, earns enough to indulge herself sometimes. All editors received a raise recently. Today is a weekday but she's at home; she probably takes her work home, or it's her publisher's "library day." My shopping bag has become heavy—living by yourself you still need a lot of things!—and I still had a blanket to buy. I didn't see the kind I wanted in the Arcade, and I didn't know where else to go. I wandered along the Nevsky, my feet freezing—I never did order the warm inner soles from the shoemaker on the corner where I used to live. The shoemaker was young and swarthy; he wore remarkable sweaters, looked at women with agitated horse's eyes. Why do I think "was"? He is still sitting there on that corner, and his friends, squeeze into his tiny shop, or maybe non-friends, his connections. They too are swarthy, young, dressed in showy clothes. When an outsider drops in, they stop talking.

Maybe I should go back to my street? The street where I lived only yesterday. The street where all year round it smells of gas, or rubber, or rotten fish, or some mysterious chemicals. The street where. . . . Actually, I don't know just the street but the whole neighborhood. There are eight stores—two dry-goods stores (surely in one of them I could have bought a blanket, and if they'd been out of them, they'd have said: "Come back in a couple of days, we'll put one aside for you!"), one movie theater, a snack shop, a luncheonette, a takeout place, a bar and a café. I never went to that café—why is that?

Finally I bought a heavy cotton quilt, sensibly navy blue, and then took the bus home. I opened the door with my own key. I was afraid Veta Andreyevna might pop out any minute, say a few friendly words, start helping me spread my things around. But she didn't. I could see the light under her door and could hear the music. I made up my cot immediately, slipped under the covers, and started thinking about Veta Andreyevna. I thought how she was the person with whom I'd be spending a certain portion of my life from now on, whether I wanted it or not. Yesterday I'd known nothing of her existence, and now I'd have to live next door to her; she'll know what I'm like in the morning, she'll notice everything, all my habits, because she's the kind that notices; she's alert to the appearance of things. I bet she'll take notice, explain matters to herself, and maybe to others, too. She has some friends, of course, and some close women friends; she's very outgoing. I'm sure she has a Friend. Or do they call them something else these days? Once, I remember, two people came visiting my mother, a woman and a man. The woman, Paulina, visited us only rarely, but I still remember her. She said to my mother: "I'd like you to meet someone. This is my Friend." For many years mama kept telling us how she said it: "I'd like you to meet someone. My Frrriend! Yes, Frriend! MY FRRRIEND!"

Dozing, being a hundred years and a hundred versts away from my new room and from Veta Andreyevna, I could hear in the hallway her muffled:

"Oh, just once more, please. . . . That's all. . . . That's all. . . ."

And the other whisper:

"Of course, darling, but. . . ."

Then the door slammed. Heels tapped languidly along the hallway in an uneven, almost halting rhythm—probably into the kitchen.

If I don't manage to keep a certain distance, she'll certainly come knocking on my door at such moments. Women like to relive everything once more, in words.

I thought to myself: she has the right to do it. A lone woman always has the right, because she alone pays for it, and the highest price at that. She pays for everything: for a moment's tenderness, for a pitiful semblance of care (He asked: "How are you managing here without me?" He asked: "Have you had dinner tonight?"), for a kiss. She pays—with joyless sex, with constant worry, with recurrent shattered hopes, and sometimes with her love, as well.

In the game of love she's almost always the loser (if she's not indifferent). Anyway, can one win in this game? Marriage? In olden days they used to say, portentously and thoughtfully:

"Marriage . . . is a lottery."

I'd say, it's a lottery without winners.

But maybe I'm wrong in feeling sorry for Veta Andreyevna. She may be quite content. It looks as if she's happy. That's why her presence isn't too oppressive for me. As a rule, happy people aren't deaf, they don't hear only themselves, that's why others seek their company. Happy people are born that way. It doesn't mean that all's well for them or that everything turns out well. I once knew a happy woman who told me how she used to wait for her husband at night. "It's two o'clock in the morning, three o'clock—I can't sleep. I hear a car drive up. . . . The house door slams shut, then the elevator starts up. . . . I stop breathing! But the elevator goes by again. . . ." Her eyes shone, her cheeks glowed as she described the sleepless nights. Those nights over, she's again the same as before. No, you've got to be born happy.

The water starts running in the bathroom—Veta Andreyevna must be taking her evening bath. Too bad I didn't borrow a book from her. On the other hand, I forgot to add a table lamp to my shopping list. Veta Andreyevna has somewhat reddish eyelids—she's probably too vain to use glasses at work. She's not particularly good-looking: wide cheekbones, her head thrusts forward like a duck's, her upper teeth protrude somewhat. I don't like that physical type; there's something greedy in it, almost carnivorous about such a person. But she's fascinating to look at: her face is alive, and her protruding teeth, ready to snap up her catch, glisten like lump sugar. How old can she be? Thirty? Thirty-five?

I thought and thought about Veta Andreyevna, so as not to let my thoughts slip into their usual rut. It will soon be a year since I stopped sleeping. Sometimes I manage to fall asleep right away deeply and happily, but when I become more wakeful a clear thought or memory comes up. No sleep then! And here, in a new place, I don't even bother to fall asleep—the sound of the silence here is too unfamiliar: the elevator doors bang on various floors, the dry wallpaper crackles, pigeons coo somewhere, and under our windows the trolley tracks are being repaired. Carefully I step around my memory rut and think about Veta Andreyevna. The tracks are fixed, the elevator is silent, and only the pigeons, like owls, refuse to sleep and coo on. Fifty cubic meters of air in my room grow denser by the hour. Finally it occurs to me to open the little window: freezing air comes in, I wrap myself in the new blanket and fall asleep.

In the morning, sounds become tamer. But the pigeons' cooing follows me into the bathroom, the hallway, the kitchen. When Veta Andreyevna, pink from sleep, appears in her bright short robe, I ask her where these tireless birds hide out; she bursts out laughing:

"But that is the refrigerator! I don't even notice it!"

Two weeks have passed. I've more or less come to terms with my memories, and I've gotten a feel for the neighborhood. The best thing in this part of town is the churchyard where children are taken to play. And the Strelka is near; there, ages ago, I used to neck with someone who's now a professor. The professor was twenty-five years old then and I was seventeen. I was proud and also embarrassed that he was so old.

Nowadays nobody goes to the Strelka. Students prefer to go on outings or to sit in a café. The churchyard, though, is densely populated. Kindergarten children are taken for recess there. Other children stroll there with their grandmothers; I noticed one little fellow in particular who walked with his mother. She talked to him all the time in a tender voice. She is very elegant: a white felt hat, white boots, and her coat with white fur is so short that I ask myself—what will happen to her legs when the real frost sets in?

The real frost hasn't come yet, and there's little snow. The trees in the churchyard stand out black and clear. Fat, short-legged crows parade among the trees and call to each other, cawing hoarsely. The kindergarteners crunch through ice-covered puddles in their boots, while the other children who walk with their mothers watch them with envy (they're not allowed). The other day it was so warm that the schoolchildren were taken to the churchyard for physical exercises. I thought to myself, these are big, grown kids, fifth-graders. As it turned out, they were from the third grade.

If I hadn't been foolish, my youngest daughter (it would have certainly been a daughter) would now be precisely in third grade. I would be waking her in the morning, braiding her hair. Are braids still worn? No matter. I'd do morning exercises with her, I'd cook her cereal, fix her lunch—sausage, all children like sausage but for some reason don't get it. She'd come back from school, would toss her bookbag—no, a satchel, that's better for her posture—she'd throw her satchel on the chest, and I'd say to her: how often do I have to remind you . . . ?

What chest? There's no chest in my hallway. There's Veta's coat rack, and a mirror, and her box with boot-polishing stuff. Veta leans on this box when she polishes her cavalry-style boots and hums a tune like a carefree bootmaker out of Krylov's fables.

She's not consumed by cares. During the day she's in the publishing house. She comes back animated, tells me about her co-workers, her bosses, and her authors. I must admit that in her accounts, her co-workers, bosses, and authors—yes, even authors—turn out to be quite amusing, rather unlike each other.

Sometimes she brings back a blouse from her office or some gloves or a shopping bag: "Could you use this? The husband of my colleague brought it back from abroad. . . ." I don't need it. Then she calls pretty Tyusha, who, of course, wants it. Veta never goes shopping for clothes but still dresses quite attractively—she gets "outfitted at work," like everybody else these days.

Besides Tyusha, a rare specimen of a beautiful lady of leisure today, there's also "Mary's Lamb." "Mary's Lamb" is a young editor in the same publishing house who looks after Veta constantly, takes her out to lunch, to the Philharmonic, to the galleries. I don't even know her real name, just Mary's Lamb. Mary's Lamb has a husband, but for some reason, and to Veta's amazement, she has plenty of time for all kinds of cultural events. She has a loose gait, a weak voice, and a passion for shows.

Authors also show up, though they prefer to telephone. Particularly insistent is a Muscovite whose textbook is coming out in Veta's publishing house.

"He's so polite," sighs Veta. "He'll never say what he wants directly. 'How are you? How's Sergei Ivanovich [a boss in the publishing house]? I met your cousin Valya, who sends you her greetings. . . .' And it's all about the fact that he wants us to send him money right away. But we can't do it before February. I think he must have spent half his honorarium on calling us here."

Yesterday I heard the end of their conversation. He must've asked what he should say to cousin Valya.

"Tell my cousin Valya," said Veta dryly, "that we'll send you your check in February."

Once or twice a week, in the evening, I hear in the hallway the familiar "Well, my darling. . . ." Then a long silence, then the door slams, then Veta goes to the bathroom. They must have set this ritual long ago. I conduct myself as before: I try not to notice, not to ask anything. But I can't help knowing more about her than I want to. I know the rhythm of her moods, I know that not all her days are the same: when she hums I know that all's well, when she whistles—something isn't right. I know that she likes Tyusha, and that she allows Mary's Lamb to like her. She's always busy, or not at home. Still, she pulls me into her life, with her stories, her smiles, with the tea we take together in the kitchen. . . .

172

A kind of common household has evolved, because I've got more free time and I go grocery shopping. That's how I came to know the neighborhood. Here, the bakery is better than ours, the grocery store's the same, except for the poorer liquor selection. Saturday night they're out of vodka, and I hear grumbling: "Have you been to the corner store? None there either? And no *Kolenval?*"

Sometimes I treat Veta to dinner, and I experience cook's primordial pleasure when Veta, swallowing a spoonful of soup, squints and says thoughtfully:

"God, that's so good!"

She doesn't question me about anything. It's I who question her: about Mary's Lamb, about her boss who's been quite fierce lately, about a movie.

I don't go to the movies any more. In my old place, the movie house was right across the street. I could see the ads from my window, and I used to go to the matinee performances. To get to the movies here, you have to take the bus, buy your ticket in advance, wait for the beginning of the show. . . . Besides, since I have to write a script I'm afraid to look at anybody else's work. Maybe I don't go to the movies for the same reason that I don't read novels and don't want to know about Veta's friend who says when he leaves, "Well, darling. . . ."

How long will this last? Half a year? A year? The time must come when I'll be myself again. But then I wonder—me—what's that?

It wouldn't matter, except that my work won't budge. The script won't take shape, I'm dry inside: dry in my heart, I have dry thoughts. To work you need your juices running. I could type something over now, but there's nothing to type over.

Oh, how I envy poets! Out of all this dryness a poet could hew a poem just fine. But I can't. I keep humming to myself some ridiculous little songs we used to sing at home—like, "Plight, plight, where do we go tonight." This relaxes me.

My work is still stuck. I'm under a contract to hand in a script by May, based on the outline I wrote in my former life, when I was happy.

Nonsense! I wasn't happy. I was calm, or rather, my life was calm for many years, and I noticed life only occasionally, by small

173

inconveniences: if there was no money, or if they didn't print my story, or when the children weren't studying properly, or weren't doing what they were supposed to. . . . Then suddenly everything crashed. And now, here I'm ready to believe that it all was happiness.

"There's no happiness in this world—just calm and freedom."

I'm glad they didn't make a popular song out of those lines. Or *did* someone put them to music? As they did with "I loved you and love is still, may be. . . ." There's no trace left of these lines in the music. There's only: *mi-sol, sol-re, mi-sol-fa.* . . . I resent it when a composer forces his will onto me. He should simply write a melody "on the subject," the way they make movies, on certain subjects. Then I'd listen, I'd want to hear how his tunes echo the words that I know so well, as if I'd written them myself. But with this music, go ahead, try and sing along his notes, as he hears it: "so si-ince-erely, so te-enderly. . . ." Here, I'd lower my voice, certainly drop it, almost swallow it; but he pulls it up, this *sol* of his.

Still there is happiness. It exists. I remember it: when all of you is alive, your whole body, your whole soul, your whole mind; when every wind is fair, when the sun's sparks reflect and dance in the gray clouds.

I used to ask intelligent women: when did they feel most themselves? Invariably, the reply: "When I talk with close friends. . . ." "In intellectual exchange. . . ." "In creative work. . . ."

Maybe it's true for them. But for me—no! With all my strengths and weaknesses, my joys and sorrows, I used to be myself most—only in love. Can I finally admit it, now that it's all gone?

Look what an old woman I am, and I'm still thinking about happiness. There's something indecent about this. At this age one's supposed to quiet down, forget about oneself, dissolve into other people. In other words, tend to one's grandchildren. Or busy oneself with philanthropy.

And if there are no grandchildren? Let's say it's clear that just now you're really not needed, not indispensable, that there's no place and no person you could dissolve into? What then?

This must be that certain age when one's not supposed to be an extremist. One is supposed to be patient, calm, hold one's breath, maintain appearances. In the name of . . . actually, in the name of what?

In the name of the twelve years lived together? But they're all cancelled out by the last, the thirteenth year. In the name of not being alone? If someone had dropped in on us, he would have seen how two people sat at a table, silent, with nothing to say to each other. Isn't that loneliness? In the name of old age, not all that far away, when ailments set in, sickness, abandonment, when all we need is compassion?! That's more frightening than anything else.

That's how my thoughts turn, and my work stands still.

The plumber comes to our apartment. Everybody calls him Sparrow. I don't know if it's his last name or his nickname. Probably his nickname, it suits him well: not even a hundred and fifty centimeters tall, he moves unevenly, in hops and starts, although he's not young at all. He works diligently but clumsily—perhaps because he's rarely sober. Since I've been here he's come three times—he keeps struggling with the toilet tank.

Our tank is obstinate. Sparrow hopping along, gets on a stool, opens the tank, and begins raving about Veta Andreyevna.

"To look at her, she's simply a woman, nothing special. Not at all like our accountant. When *she* comes in," at that point he outlines the indescribable contours of the accountant with his hands, the stool sways, "her nose in the air, doesn't look at anyone, walks into the office, doesn't say hello. Of course, you must understand, she's an ac-count-ant! Don't you even think of approaching her. But now there is a real woman!" and a gesture toward Veta, a screech of the stool. "Cultured, intelligent; and has so many books; and when she walks along she's always thinking of something. When you meet her she always smiles, says hello. Nothing special to look at, but you take another look—you understand: she's got culture! But that accountant. . . ."

With his hands spread out as wide as they'll reach, he outlines her bust and belly.

It's clear that the marvelous figure of the accountant has been disturbing his intoxicated imagination. In his small sparrow's heart he bears a not-so-small grudge against her.

For a while, our tank slips into its normal state. Sparrow gets his usual fifth and flies off inspired, praising Veta, and me too, and all those who're really cultured, who aren't stuck-up.

"Say what you want," says Veta, "but I'm not taking on this

female's book. She doesn't need an editor, she needs the city clean-up crew. You shovel out all her stupid stuff, shovel it out, and then she puts up a fuss, objects that there are too few pages now! If you'd actually squeeze her work properly, you'd get this much, if you got anything at all."

"Why don't you say all this to your boss?"

"You think I haven't told him? He agrees, he nods. Then he calls me up, he talks in such an oily voice: 'Veta Andreyevna, you're our most experienced editor. . . .' But they haven't got me cornered yet. I hold the ace in my hand: Shibanova."

"Who's Shibanova?"

"Ah, the famous Shibanova, a professor, a doctor of science. I'll tell them, if that's the way they want it, I'll have to hand Shibanova's book over to some other editor. They're afraid, though, of getting into any conflict with her."

Veta calms down and cheers up. She's starting to wash the floor in the bathroom, putting a fighting spirit into singing the "Wil-helm Tell" overture. And I set off for the Zoo.

The Zoo is nearby—which is another advantage to our neigh-borhood.

It's a cold day, hardly anyone here; and in the animal houses it smells sharply of ammonia. The baby giraffe has grown almost as tall as its incredible mother. The unmoving elephants are think-ing their eternal elephant thoughts. Buddhists believe that the ele-phant alone among all animals remembers his previous lives and keeps thinking about them, for long stretches at a time. Probably, this huge thing likes to think of itself as a butterfly. A day of life— what lightness! Not blinking, the elegant Nile crocodile watches its Chinese cousin who lives in the opposite cage, and marvels at his slanted eyes.

The predators have news: jaguar babies were born. Two of them lie obediently by their mother, the third one bounces around the cage playing with a metal tray: he'd like to get a response from it, make the tray chase him back. The jaguar mother licks her nice cubs, her eyes filled with maternal feeling. A girl in overalls walks between the cages and the railing, fearlessly sticks her hand through the bars and strokes the lions. "Vasya!" she says tenderly. "Oh, my Vasya!" And the black-maned Vasya squints and rubs his round forehead against the little hand and licks it with his wide pink tongue. "Vasya, open your mouth!" Vasya obediently opens his jaws, and the girl throws in a piece of meat, as into the door of a stove. Teeth gnash. "Oh, my sweet Vasya!"

Men look at a brave girl as Vasya does, with fawning admiration.

I feel good in the Zoo. I walk around, thinking about nothing in particular, remembering nothing. Time comes to leave the Zoo. I must go to the post office. I get my letters there, general delivery.

A letter from Asya, from Novosibirsk.

She writes: "Come! You'll rest up here, gather strength for your work, see new people, new places."

Asya is sure to know what a person needs. She's a born organizer. Except that she doesn't understand that in Leningrad I'm farther away from my usual surroundings than in Novosibirsk. Walking down the street I don't run into any former acquaintances. Nobody knows my address, nobody has my number. I've disappeared, gotten lost somewhere. . . .

No, I won't go visit her. And I won't visit Marisha in Petrovsk, either. My daughters are good girls, especially Marisha; but they're just fine without me. Both have husbands, neither has children—they don't want to help overpopulate the planet. What would I do there? I'm a poor housekeeper, and I don't understand their professions. Asya is a physicist, Marisha a doctor. Both of them lack my humanistic genes.

I love my daughters, yet I don't really like their names. Long ago I thought I'd call my daughter Irochka. As preschoolers there was an Irochka among us; she was my first love. I loved seeing her talk, seeing her smile, showing not her teeth but just her tongue; I tried to imitate her smile, but nothing came of it. I even liked how she cried; except I wanted her to cry and complain to me, but she paid no attention to me. She was already eight, and I was only seven; she was entering school. I couldn't forget her. Eight years later she and I turned out to be in the same class: she was a dumpy, dull, unattractive girl. Her last name was Liapis, she lived on Olgiyevskaya Street. Liapis and "Olgiyevskaya" still sound to me not quite ordinary. Back then, I chose the name "Irochka."

But I don't have an Irochka. Marisha's father didn't like the name, and Asya had to be named after her grandmother.

Maybe, if I'd had an Irochka, my whole life would have turned out differently. In fact, though, I never chose anything myself—things were chosen for me, or people chose me, which, in general, is all the same. I never—almost never—left anyone; others left me. True, I think I never betrayed anyone, nor deceived anyone. But these are not really alternatives: to betray or be betrayed. Or is there an alternative after all?

It doesn't matter. If I knew how to choose, I would now have an Irochka, and I would have what I can't live without—rather than a pile of unnecessary memories. During the war I could have been a nurse, which I wanted to be, rather than a typist in Division Headquarters. And I wouldn't have gone so far from the front to give birth to Marisha, and Marisha's father wouldn't have gotten killed. . . .

Free choice, free choice. . . . I didn't choose freely, even this apartment I share with Veta; it was offered to me. I was never given a chance to look at the room before moving into this apartment. And now, I don't like to come home to this place where there are no letters waiting for me, no phone calls.

True, I chose to be alone. But that came out of fear. Because I was afraid to stay in my former world where everything seemed the same, but in fact was all changed; even things were changed. Things turned hostile: dishes dropped from my hands, chairs warped and came apart, the headrest on the sofa broke off.

Asya's father didn't like Marisha. Her looks irritated him. Marisha was an ugly duckling, not likely to become a swan. She was a serious little girl when we married. She wore glasses, had a bad overbite, didn't twitter, didn't want to hug, didn't play around. In my eyes she seemed touching in her complete trust of everyone and everything—but that did not reach him. When Asya was born, Marisha turned out to be in the way. The four of us lived in one room in a large and crowded apartment. We kept sending Marisha to our neighbors, or outdoors for fresh air, or to her classmates to do homework.

I always felt guilty about Marisha. Guilty that I married a man who didn't become her father, guilty that I bore Asya, guilty that I never had time for her. This sense of guilt deepened my love for her but took all the joy out of our relationship. And Marisha felt sorry for me. She wasn't a brilliant student, but she tried hard. She quickly wore out shoes, socks, dresses; in third grade she started patching and mending her things. Then she began losing library books. She was eager to enlighten others: if she enjoyed a book she'd hand it on to a girl friend and forget it.

"That's robbery!" Asya's father yelled at Marisha. "Not returning a library book amounts to stealing it."

Marisha shed her tears silently. She solemnly believed that grown-ups were right. After the third lost book she never registered again at the library. "Can I help it if I'm so absentminded?" she'd say. She started reading my grown-up books, and all went well as long as her friends weren't interested in them. Then, my books too started disappearing. I shouted at her, and Marisha cried bitterly:

"What can I do if I'm so absentminded? I couldn't ask your permission, you're never home. And later I forgot. . . ."

"Oh, don't cry, why are you crying?"

"I'm crying because you yelled at me. It's bad for your heart to get so upset."

She never took her stepfather's books—he kept them separate! As the years went by he began avoiding her, as if she were not a little girl but a clump of nettles.

That's how he dealt with everything that didn't please him: with neighbors, with my ailments (after Asya's birth I was sick quite often), with the newspapers of the early fifties, with what I told him was happening all around us. He started drinking, he drank more and more, weekdays and holidays, with friends and by himself. When Asya started school we all left him—for a man who promised to be a father to "the three girls."

He *was* that. He played with Asya, talked to Marisha about historical justice, read my first works pencil in hand. . . . It was a new life for us all: in the morning, at breakfast we'd get so involved talking that the children would be late for school. He made Marisha wear braces on her lower teeth to adjust her bite, and me—he made me write not "out of my head" but about things I knew.

I started writing as a child. I liked words for the way they string themselves together, play, ring. I liked melodic phrases, their singing, their rhythm. . . . "Write what you know well." But what was that? Who'd want to hear what I knew? The war, that day-to-day life in Headquarters. . . . Who needs the memories of a typist, and of one who doesn't observe what's around her but keeps retreating into herself, into her vague dreams? What else did I know? School, prewar university (three years!), the TsKB office where I worked as a typist, my family. . . .

The girls were growing up, they talked about what went on at school, had lots of unsolved problems. Can friendship exist between boys and girls? Can you live without compromise? And, most important, would you choose duty or love? I made a story around one of these questions, a fairly moralistic story (I hid the sermon between the lines).

He read it, praised it and said:

"Give it a try, send it out."

He mailed it to a youth magazine. They published it as a sketch in the section "On Moral Questions." At that time, magazines had just started such sections as "Open Talk," "For the Home, For the Family" . . . They took my second sketch too, and a third. Finally, I could quit my office work.

I was absorbed with writing, I thought I could give advice: I was the right age, I was well read, I had had children. . . . Letters to the editor told of people's experiences, usually had happy endings. Sometimes I would turn these letters into journalistic pieces and point out the moral. Or sometimes I'd be sent by the magazine to meet the authors of these letters, to see with my own eyes, and then add lyrical brush strokes to the stories.

He praised me, he always praised me. Then he'd say carefully:

"You seem hemmed in when you write, all tight. Let down these defenses. Write the way you tell me these stories. Don't be afraid, tell the truth."

"Do you think I am lying?"

I didn't understand then what truth he was after. My writing went well, my stories went by without making noise, or ripples. . . .

And then we read a story together—and I understood what he was trying to get me to do. This story was a description of a visit to a famous gardener. Its language seemed virgin: as if all objects were named now, at this moment, for the first time; all was pure and festive as on one of the first days of creation. The old gardener walked among his fruit trees, talking, using local speech, and his own expressions, which he'd repeat now and again. The author walked behind him. She saw not what was being pointed out to her, not what she wanted to see, and not what they hid from her—but what things were really like. Myself, I didn't know how to see things that way, or how to write that way.

Then I noticed other stories by this author, written with the same directness. By that time my book was out. I knew then that I'd never be able to write the way she wrote. Sure, I'll achieve something too, when I learn to drop my defenses, when I cut myself free from this literary corset. If I manage to cut it.

At night I'd tell him how difficult this experience was; I'd tell him everything. For the first time in my life I felt sure a man thought everything I did was important—not the results of my work, but the work itself. For the first time I was myself, day and night, in talk and in hugs, alone and with others. I didn't pretend to be different, to seem simpler, more naive, nicer; I didn't pretend to be cheerful when I was sad, or in a good mood when I was angry, or flip when I actually felt quite serious. I was myself. I didn't want to be anyone else.

Then it all came to an end.

The frost set in, sharpened by the winds. The winds change—sometimes a southeaster, sometimes a northeaster—but the freezing weather stays unchanged, the temperature doesn't rise above twenty. People in our neighborhood rush along at a run, they don't notice each other. The children in the churchyard march silently, their mouths tightly covered by scarves. The elegant Mama in her little white cap parades as before in her short coat, but refrains from talking to her child. Only the crows keep cawing, reluctantly though.

My work goes slowly, nothing seems to gel. I hope that after New Year's everything will get going. Everybody knows that it's easier to start a new life after New Year's or on a Monday.

Veta sees the New Year in at Mary's Lamb's place. Something is happening to her. For a while I haven't heard the familiar "Well, darling!" in the hallway. They must have quarreled. I can hear her running to the phone and her bright "Hello!" Then her voice drops, becomes forced, impersonal.

181

Coming home from work she asks: "Did anyone call?"

I list them: Vera Aleksandrovna called, then Tyusha, Sergei Ivanovich. . . . I know what it's like when no one has called. Her face dims. In the morning, when she drinks her coffee—a tablespoon of coffee to a cup of hot water—she frowns, then raises her eyebrows as if in a dialogue I can't hear. Then she goes off to work, dragging the briefcase that seems too much for her.

I returned her cot, bought a big mattress and put it on four blocks. She said:

"You're bent on being independent, aren't you?"

"Is returning a cot a symbol of independence?"

"The cot? No, it's just a sign. I, for one, don't yearn for independence. I've always had it, and I don't need it. Couldn't care less about it!"

Somehow this doesn't seem to be her vocabulary, "couldn't care less!"

I keep reading Veta's books. She's got English and French books, which I can't read, and also a bunch of different things from the twenties, what's left from her parents' library. I read Panteleimon Romanov, Nikiforov, Gumilevsky. Very readable; they set me on to new thoughts. Curious, why is this literature so dead and forgotten? I wonder why Veta, who knows various languages, never translates. At one point I asked her about that.

"I am, one could say, insanely proud!" she declared. "I don't wish to be below Lozinsky."

I looked at her in amazement. She laughed.

"Seriously?"

"In a sense I am serious. I know myself. I'm not creative. But as an editor I'm worth something. Even Sergei Ivanych understands this. By the way, I saw his wife yesterday. Quite imposing. By size and plumage, I'd say it's a male."

Veta laughs, her eyes sparkle. Then she's silent, and again her face grows dim, shrivels, freezes. To hell with Mister "Well, darling!"

"Tyusha called, said she'd stop by. Your Shabunina called, or whatever her name is. . . . I think that's all."

"Nobody else?"

"Someone else called, but it was a wrong number. . . . No,

really, a wrong number. I answered and he said immediately: 'Oh, wrong number again!' "

Her face melts before me, the glaze slides off her eyes, her cheeks, lips.

"Wrong number. . . . He wasn't the first to hang up?"

"I think I hung up first." I'm beginning to gather that all this is quite important.

"He was taught long ago"—says she, smiling uncontrollably. "He was taught that a man mustn't hang up first. They trained him to perfection."

"Veta, are you getting married?"

"Married? What for? I'm thirty-five, I was never married—and none the worse off for that. I think—it makes sense. No responsibilities, except for what I take on myself of course. Rights only. True, not many rights, but at least—at least I'm free."

"But you said that you couldn't care less for independence!"

"What don't we say when the mood's right! Sure, sometimes I too want a husband, a child, everything normal people have. But then, you see how other people live. . . . No, I'm better making my own way!"

She laughs:

"You know something? I've never seen a man shave."

Finally I saw the one who always said to Veta "Well, darling." It was the day after New Year's. Veta asked me very solemnly to the kitchen, to come toast the New Year with them: "With me and Aleksandr Ivanovich!"

They had cognac Veta had bought well ahead of time, and a bottle of a Hungarian "sparkling," obviously brought by Aleksandr Ivanovich. Aleksandr Ivanovich had a self-satisfied face, cunning eyes, and a sharply sloping forehead. He talked ingratiatingly and softly, moved deftly and cautiously around our small kitchen. He looked like a big, splendid feline who keeps prettying himself up.

The refrigerator was gurgling and groaning. Aleksandr Ivanovich frowned:

"You're a writer. Could you explain, please, why we in our country sell refrigerators with this kind of music? I'd like to expose these shoddy producers!"

"Such refrigerators are no longer made," said Veta soothingly, squinting in the sunlight.

He pulled the shade, Veta smiled in gratitude, and he continued:

"I'm asking our writer. How come, comrade writer?"

"Well, I wouldn't call myself a writer."

"Still, you're in this. . . . Or don't you deal with this stuff— refrigerators and similar mundane things?"

"To tell the truth, no."

"I can appreciate that. Of course, it's not a good subject, life's incongruities, the prose of life. And what are your subjects, if I may ask? What do you write about?"

"About people," I said haltingly, and reached out for the bread.

He immediately moved the bread closer, the butter too, put some food on my plate and said:

"About people, I understand that. But what, exactly? About love, probably?"

"Oh, about love too. Do you think love so unimportant?"

"No, why should I?" He didn't want to argue with me. "As I understand it, for a woman it must be quite important."

"Love, love . . ." said Veta. "Let's talk about something more cheerful."

"Shall we bring Raikin in here so you'll have some fun?" asked Aleksandr Ivanovich.

Veta laughed at his joke. Displeased, he almost shut his eyes.

"She laughs like a small child. Here, writer, go ahead and describe this: a woman of thirty-five who's still a child."

"I don't get it; do you think that's good or bad?" asked Veta.

"I haven't figured it out myself. Will you write about her? About us both, for example? Or won't they print that?"

"Would you like them to print it?"

"Well, still . . ." said he. "I would be curious to see how we look . . . as characters."

"You didn't like him," Veta concluded.

"For God's sake, Veta, why do you say that?"

"I can see, I can see it, I'm not blind. I think it's how you measure people."

"How do I?"

"You seem to have one measure for all people. And I have different ones. It's more fun that way. Aleksandr Ivanovich and I meet only for pleasure. In this case everything is simple—he's married, has grown children, his own life, his own troubles. . . . I'm not his daily bread, he gets along without me splendidly, as I do without him. So? I don't want to be his bread! It's more interesting this way."

"You may be right. In general, you have a man's point of view in these things."

"For God's sake! The whole point is not to lose your head. You probably think that I must be bored with him? Don't you?"

"Well, maybe. . . ."

"See, you're wrong. He's bored with me."

I had nothing to say to that.

It seems I've begun writing. Whatever I see and hear snags something in me. I'm not yet at the typewriter, but something is already knocking in me, remembering, selecting. For example, it's clear my hero will have an uncle. I know quite a bit about that uncle: I see his easy and careful moves, hear his tenor voice, know that he's annoyed as he narrows his eyes slightly. Also, I know these eyes: Not large, greenish, sharp, they reflect no soul, they just observe.

Aleksandr Ivanovich will not read the script, and in the movie—if there is a movie—he won't recognize himself. Soon he'll acquire other people's traits, words, friends. Once I start banging on my typewriter everything will help my work—each meeting, each conversation, each landscape.

The neighborhood air has changed: the winds have died down, the days are freezing. I've finally started to talk with the elegant Mama in the churchyard. She is a saleswoman, that's why she's so well dressed. She seems to like me, offered to get me woolen tights. Salespeople are a corporation, a fairly powerful one, busy supplying themselves with things. They have their own hierarchy, their own code of behavior, their own view of life. I'd like to write about it some day, although I doubt that I'll be able to: to do it you'd have to be that other short-story writer.

In general, I'm beginning to see, to hear. For a year, for a whole year I didn't see anything, heard only myself. I kept making the rounds of my friends, like a Chekhovian "aunt." Mostly I wanted to talk about myself, pour out my feelings, cry, and hear in response: "But you've invented all this, none of this is true, he loves you, adores you, it's all a mistake." Yet nobody said this to me— maybe because I didn't tell them anything, didn't pour out anything, didn't cry.

Tears came later. Short, quick, hurried tears that instead of relief just gave me a headache. A strange habit appeared—biting my upper lip: I saw myself do it in the mirror. "Friends in need" showed up. That was most unpleasant.

I don't like friends who hurry to gather for a wake. Where do they hide out when you feel fine? Why don't they want to share your joys? I can assure you, it's much easier to feel for another person's troubles than to rejoice in another's happiness. Such commiseration smells of perspiration from a sense of duty well fulfilled.

Now I'm alone. The wave of commiserators has receded, taking with them their voluptuous curiosity, their sympathy-filled phone calls, visits, letters. I'm alone. And I'm beginning to see, hear, notice the weather. Sometimes I even feel cheerful.

Veta called from the office:

"Shibanova is supposed to come see me at home. Remember, she's one of my authors. But we're having our regular meeting here in the office; in fact, it's a special one. That is, it's an extra board meeting. So please ask her to wait for me."

Shibanova turned out to be elderly, fat, and good-looking. There are women who stay good-looking forever. We took a long time adjusting ourselves to each other; her pretty black eyes kept prying into me to make out who I was, what I did, what I amounted to. Finally she figured out that I was a humanist and was glad of it.

"Humanists think they are the only intellectuals, as in the old days!" she said, barely separating her teeth and breathing fast with her whole chest. "But in our view, in the mathematicians' view, they're uncultured people. The language of the contemporary intellectuals is the mathematicians' language. Half of the globe's population speaks that language. Just imagine their presumption, their self-importance: ignorant of the universal language, yet they consider themselves intellectuals!"

It was hard to argue against that, especially because deep down I often thought so myself. But I felt offended for my profession and wound myself up:

"And what if mankind is going down the wrong road? Had the humanities not been constantly obstructed, had they not been held in suspicion, had the churches of all eras and all peoples not stunted them, hen man might now be flying without a flying machine!"

"Levitation!" said Shibonova, translating my nebulous talk into the sphere of clear formulas.

"And the language of music? That's a language too. . . ."

"Semiotics!"

I was indignant.

"What did the development of your mathematics lead to? If the goal of progress is to make man better, then you achieved quite the contrary. The means of mass annihilation. . . ."

"Ah! All right, fine, . . ." said Shibanova and settled into her chair more comfortably. "Go ahead, go ahead, I like such arguments."

"Well, no!" said I, cooling off. "What arguments? But why this 'universal language'? Two hundred years ago there wasn't any such language, and two hundred years hence there won't be any either."

"What about now?"

"What about it? That's not enough reason to celebrate one's superiority."

Shibanova was clever. She laughed.

"Just celebrating my own Saint Fool's day!" she said gaily.

The doorbell rang.

"Here's Veta!" said I.

It wasn't Veta, though, it was Aleksandr Ivanovich. He stepped in, took off his hat and looked at me in surprise.

"And where's . . . ?"

"She's delayed at work. They had some special meeting. Do come in and wait for her."

"No, thanks!" said he, squinting in displeasure. "I'm in a hurry. I was just passing by."

Shibanova came out into the hallway and looked at the visitor carefully. When I shut the door after him she asked:

"An author, too?"

"Think so. I don't know."

"He's somehow. . . . You know, when I was little I saw a picture, 'The Evil Relative of Vas'ka the Cat.' A lynx or a tiger, I don't remember. Looks like him."

I was amazed at her insight.

I had a good time with Shibanova. That was soon after New Year's. But on New Year's Eve I remembered my former lives just like an elephant. That was not a happy night. Summing up.

A letter from Marisha came, in answer to the tights I'd sent her.

I wasn't able to save Marisha, I missed my chance. I was too busy with myself, my work, my small successes. There were always a lot of young people in the house, young men—one and all in love with Asya. It never occurred to me that Timofei kept coming to see Marisha, not Asya. When it happened it was already too late. They married and moved to Petrovsk, because Marisha suddenly decided to move. Timofei didn't care where he lived. Each year he switched institutes, attended lectures sporadically during the first semester, then dropped the routine. He probably had some talent, everybody said so. You had to hand it to him, he passed each entrance exam brilliantly. He studied at the University, then at the Polytechnical Institute, then at the Drama School. . . . Nobody had ever looked after him; he came from a small provincial town. In Leningrad he earned his keep by doing various city jobs: fed animals in the Zoo, sold newspapers at a newsstand, delivered mail, hammered crates together. He didn't need much. He didn't drink.

Marisha now works as a surgeon in the Petrovsk hospital and he—I don't know what he does. "Timofei made me the desk at which I am writing you this letter," Marisha proudly informed me. He's got clever hands: he makes things look elegant, even if they're not very solid.

That's how they live. It seems they're happy. For how long? Who knows? The town of Petrovsk isn't exactly a gem among Russian cities: it's a mining town where everything lies under black coal dust, where the climate is particularly bad for you, where in alcohol consumption the population firmly holds first place in the entire country.

Marisha believes that intellectuals must spread out over the whole country, though she would never admit that such idealistic thoughts led her to choose Petrovsk. Instead, she starts to explain how in Leningrad they had trouble finding an apartment, or how useful it is for a young specialist to work in the provinces, and I don't know what else. Marisha has such a lofty sense of duty that she's afraid to cramp others with it. And so she's exacting of herself but indulgent of others. That explains Timofei.

I asked him once: "Don't you feel awkward, being supported by a woman?"

"She likes it!" he answered in his simplicity.

He doesn't need much. Winter and summer he wears jeans and an old jacket, eats little, doesn't drink at all. He's always good to talk to. He takes his time to talk to you about what you do; that's why he's well liked. Also, he's not a sponger—in fact, he earns enough to keep himself going, as they say. He's a strange guy, a rather harmless one. But how could I have guessed that this strange guy'd become my daughter's husband?

Marisha believes that he's trying to find himself.

Mary's Lamb caught the flu, so I got dragged to the Philharmonic by Veta.

"Shostakovich's Fifth and Ravel's *Bolero*," she said in a tone that didn't allow for objections. "We'll sit at the very top, won't walk around at intermission. You won't run into any of your former friends."

She never asks me about anything but understands it all. She knows that I don't want to meet friends.

All in all, it's remarkable: since I moved, I haven't met anyone, not a soul. It's a big city—you might not run into someone for years.

I dressed the way Natasha Rostova did for her first ball. It was already February and I was still wearing pants and sweaters. Luckily the winter was cold. I discovered that I had gotten too thin for all my dresses. The suit I bought last year now hung on me as on a coat hanger.

Veta is in high spirits.

"Nobody would ever guess your age! God, how I dreamed of being tall and thin! And instead. . . ."

She spreads out her arms. Her arms are a bit short. In general, she is, as a hunter would put it, "a bit short on the muzzle and a bad tracker," her upper teeth come down too far over her lower ones, and her arms are just a bit short. Still, she's fascinating to watch: her face is alive, her body keeps dancing.

"I love Mravinsky," she confides to me mysteriously while we ride the bus. "I like him best in this *Bolero*. He gives me a real high."

"Oh, you certainly have no need for a high."

"Don't say that!" She dims for a moment. "Sometimes I do, very much. Before, I used to be like a self-tuning engine, but now I can't live without outside stimulants. You, for instance, are one."

"Me-e???"

"Of course. Don't be surprised. You have a very strong aura. Don't you know it?"

Veta's scientific terminology—there's a good reason for her being with a trade-book publisher!—lends her words a certain solidity. I'm beginning to think about my "aura."

I'm not at all strong. I can't make anything of myself, I can't say "no" to anything, I don't know how to be patient. My aura might work, but not for long; it's "on" for only a short while— that's why, probably, I haven't saved anything, not even friends, not even Marisha. I don't know the strength of this aura, what force it has. If I can influence people, the influence isn't bad and isn't good—it has an accelerating effect. When there were still people around me, their ties to each other defined themselves rather quickly: they got married, fell in love, divorced. . . . That interested me. I preferred being a confidante to being a performer.

In the end, the very end, I became a performer in one of the most banal dramas. Not used to acting, I behaved, probably, not in the best way.

Good God, did this really happen to me?

We were a bit late for the beginning of the concert—thanks to my dressing, of course! We left our coats with a hatcheck girl who greeted Veta cordially, then went upstairs to the highest seats where I hadn't been since I was a student. I'd heard Shostakovich's Fifth Symphony there for the first time. Now, as we took a couple of free seats in back, I heard the first bars and started to remember: not what happened to me in the last two years, but something different, something terribly important, which was slipping away either in the music or in myself.

We had a Lena in our class—tall, thin, swaying. She had a long, beautiful neck. She never missed a performance of the Fifth Symphony. She used to say: "I have my own conception of this piece." At that time this word "conception" was fashionable (I never heard it from my daughters). Lena had conceptions about everything. Now Lena is fat; she no longer sways but lumbers along, and she doesn't come here any more. Once every few years I see her in the street, in the theater or in the trolley: we have nothing to say to each other. But there was a time when we were passionate friends and understood each other at the slightest hint.

In 1941 I wrote her from the front that I remembered her conception of the Fifth Symphony, and that I agreed with her entirely. I remembered how she explained that the victorious fanfares were not the main point, but the weak receding voice was, the ta-ta-ta-ta-tam, ta-ta-ta-ta-tam.

After the war, Asya's father and I listened to the Fifth. We sat in the seventh row; we had season tickets. The booming of the brass instruments deafened me; I sat waiting to hear the thin complaining ta-ta-ta-ta-tam. Asya's father didn't like music; he kept coming here because it was *done,* and I missed Lena with her excitement and her conceptions. I missed all that was gone from my life; I missed men and women, words and gestures, books and performances. I'd like to preserve everything, everything. But a person cannot contain all, only lose and lose and lose.

Finally, the thin complaint came, but I suddenly realized that now I didn't want to listen to it. I looked at Veta: she was silently prompting them, dictating to the flute. Her face was tense, wrinkled, her shoulders raised, she worked with the players, with the conductor, the composer. She didn't care at all that people might glance at her, didn't care what they thought. Marisha is timid, she observes herself, doesn't let herself relax. And Asya—Asya simply doesn't have the time to think about it, she's too anxious to live in this world. I'll never understand how Asya's father and I came to have such a daughter.

Asya doesn't criticize me, doesn't give me any advice, doesn't ask me to visit her. She just writes whatever occurs to her, funny and serious things all mixed—always clever, always happy, always fully convinced that I'll care about it all. But I'd like to know—does she write to her stepfather? They always got along well. He didn't like it when she got married: he'd hoped for a more brilliant husband for As'ka. But Asya knew quite well what she needed.

After she left, the house didn't collapse. It began crumbling after Marisha married. We weren't prepared to stay on together alone.

At that point I started our dialogue. I talked, listened to his evasive replies, poured out a pile of proof of my unassailable correctness. In fact, though, the dialogue had ceased long before that.

I shouldn't have come to this concert.

The Fifth Symphony was over and I had heard none of it. During the resounding applause I told Veta that I'd like to leave. She woke up, looked at me carefully to see if I had suddenly gotten ill, and then shook her head emphatically:

"Don't even think of it! We'll now take our proper seats and we'll see everything from there. *Bolero* comes next!"

I gave in. We changed our seats, passed some girls, then sat down close to the railing. From up there I could see slowly emerging out of the rows—gray heads, bald heads, gray heads. . . . My place is there too, down below; somebody's else decision brought me up here, among the young people.

Then the gray and bald heads swam back, the full lights lit the stage, and Mravinsky walked on amidst applause. He came to a stop on a dais, put one arm behind his back, like a skater who's still holding back on his tempo. *Bolero* began.

I looked down. I was watching the gray head of irregular shape with a small bald spot and thought: why is he alone? I was ready to see him here, ready to see next to him another head, blond, hair combed smoothly into two halves and into a bun in the back. But he was alone. Maybe she can't make up her mind to leave her husband?

Mravinsky took his arm from behind his back. *Bolero* resounded. Veta's face was happy. I noticed a spot on my skirt, not a large one but noticeable—why hadn't I seen it earlier? I had a broken nail on my index finger and began carefully peeling off the nail polish. Then I worked on the other ones. By the time *Bolero* ended I had no polish left on my nails.

He started walking along the aisle, let women go first. I saw his lowered head and slow steps. For the first time I watched him going away—going away and I didn't know where. I did not want to catch up, throw my arms around him; I watched him go, dumb, perplexed; I felt as if my own feet were going away from me somewhere, as in a drunken dream.

"Let's go on foot," I say to Veta as we come out onto the street.

"Fine idea!" she says, and takes my arm firmly. I lean on her arm, on her, although she's smaller than I. She seems so firm, so reliable.

"I saw my ex-husband in the audience below," I tell her.

Veta squeezes my arm closer.

"You're not angry that I dragged you here?" she asks me.

"Oh, no! That's over. Everything passes, Veta, even hurt. Although hurt stays longer than anything else, even in good-natured people."

We walk on in silence. Then I say:

"Aleksandr Ivanovich doesn't go to the Philharmonic, does he?"

Veta smiles.

"He prefers the operetta. In general, I've never . . . never had an affair with a man who'd go to the Philharmonic with me. That's my fate. Or perhaps I just don't like that kind of person. He'd be too much like me. And Aleksandr Ivanovich isn't like me. And I'm not like him. Still, I'm attached to him."

Veta becomes thoughtful about her attachment, and I wonder— what would Marisha say if she had seen us today, me and her former stepfather?

"Attachment!" says Veta. "How badly things are arranged: on one side the attachment grows, on the other it weakens, and both sides feel it."

"The hardest thing," say I, "is to break such ties. They are already weakened, and yet one is still quite entangled in them. You have to break them. Once they're broken, what's left will disintegrate—with time, as other friendships develop, and circumstances change."

"The hardest thing," says Veta, "is to be attached to a very different person, who thinks about everything in a very different way. I once read in Saint-Exupéry: 'Love is—not when you look at each other but when you both look in the same direction.' And what if you do look at each other? Or when you look at the other, and the other looks at the door?"

She laughs.

"Why is everybody so afraid of being alone?" I say. "For a month it's hard, or for a year, well—for two. And then you're used to it. Once you have played out your role as a mother and wife, you can start living by yourself, as an individual. Work—is life, and nature—is life, and even these city streets—"

"Spring'll be here soon!" Veta sighs. "You can't see it yet, but you feel it in the air. . . . I remember, during the winter of the blockade Mother kept saying: soon spring will come. I believed her, I always believed Mother, but in the bottom of my heart I doubted it."

"You were in Leningrad during the blockade?"

For a while we walk on in silence, and then Veta begins telling me about the blockade, about her mother who died fifteen years ago: I feel a kind of affection for her. I found out a long time ago: when you imagine a grown-up as a child, you feel closer. Should we do it more often? Veta says:

"That war will be felt through many generations, for a long time, even by people born after the war. Without the war their parents might have had a different life, would have been healthier and happier. The children, too."

"Marisha would have been different," I agree. And I describe Marisha to her.

She says:

"You're lucky. You are the mistress of your life. You chose everything yourself."

"Quite the contrary," say I. "Circumstances determined everything for me. Circumstances and other people did."

"That doesn't matter," says Veta. "You were at the front, you had children, you have work. . . . You're lucky."

"And to me—you seem lucky. No matter how your life turns out—you're happy, naturally happy, from your character."

"I'm not happy, I'm cheerful!" says Veta. "But that's not enough. I'd like to make people around me happy. Especially one person. And he has no use for it."

"I think he does!"

"That's not what I'm talking about. Women usually complain that men don't commit themselves completely. That's all right, I can accept that. What I mind, though, is that he needs so little from me. Don't laugh. I understand that I'm not a gold mine, I'm an ordinary woman. . . ."

"I'm not laughing. If a flower became aware, it would complain about the bee that wouldn't take all of its nectar."

"How beautifully you put it!" says Veta. "Well, so be it: flower, nectar. . . . But that doesn't make it easier. . . ."

We walk into the main lobby, take the elevator, and Veta says:

"Since people don't understand each other, they don't believe each other. You expect the other person to deceive you, to trick you. . . . Even if you're not suspicious or cunning by nature. . . ."

"If people don't believe each other, then there's no deception!" I say. "Deception comes when people believe. When one person believes."

Veta opens our door and we hear the telephone.

"Hello!" says Veta. "Hello! Yes?"

She's silent for a while, then she hangs up.

"He's checking!" she says. "He's checking if I'm home. . . . What shall I do, tell me? Please, tell me what to do!"

"If it's too hard for you . . ." I begin.

"No, it isn't. And maybe it is. I know I've got to put an end to it. Fight fire with fire."

And she begins to tell me about her life, her motley life, her pitiful woman's life. About the boy she was in love with in tenth grade, and he loved her girl friend. About how her mother died, and she had to switch to evening sessions in the Institute, and start earning money. . . . And about her first "grown-up" affair with a married man that ended badly, like in a magazine story, with pregnancy, abortion. . . .

"Know what?" says Veta. "He left his wife, later. He married a girl with a face like a pig's and was very pleased with her. You should see her!"

And then, Aleksandr Ivanovich again. And again. Once, some time ago, he too was "her author."

"I'm attached to him," says Veta. "You know, I have . . . as people say, a soft spot for him. I'm always afraid of hurting him. He's so big, but I keep thinking that he's easily hurt. Funny, isn't it? I don't even think that he's a very good person. Judging by everything, he's not a very good person—the way he talks about others, himself, or our relationship. He says to me: 'Don't be so complicated.' He says to me: 'If only you could bear a child!' But I can't, after that abortion. He's bored with me, I feel that. He said it himself: 'Women become boring, don't you see!' As for my attachment, it's not that bad. The main thing is—to root it out!"

Her life envelops me, I feel her anxiety. I feel sorry for her and I no longer think of myself.

Next morning I go to the Zoo. The jaguar cubs are grown, and may soon be taken from their mother. A bright cold sun is out— the gullible predators trust it: they're warming themselves in the sun. And the birds are fooled, too: pelicans with their ugly beaks begin to fight, cranes are starting to dance.

Spring is coming, spring is coming. . . .

Last year I never noticed the spring.

"Give me time!" he said. "We can't decide everything so fast. Give me time!"

I agreed, retreated, stopped talking—and everything started all over. Because he couldn't just quit his job, and it was there that he met her every day. This kept on and on. And it wouldn't have ended had I not left.

Is it better for him to be with her? He didn't look too happy to me. But maybe I saw only what I wanted to see?

When I came home I saw Veta washing the hallway floor, whistling a tune from *Bolero*.

"Veta! Why're you doing this? It's my turn."

"I need physical exercise, I'm getting fat," she says seriously, looking up at me with her reddened face. "And, for the rest, a new life is starting today."

"Aleksandr Ivanovich?"

"Right. He didn't even object. I said to him: 'We'll never see each other again, chance brought us together. . . .' And he says: 'I agree with you.' That's how it happens nowadays: 'No fuss, no muss. . . .' Come on, it's okay to walk on!"

She tosses a rag over to me, and I carefully step on it to reach my doorsill. She says:

"At least I'll no longer wonder: Poor dear, how's he doing without me? This is a poisonous thought, don't you agree? It grows out of conceit. He'll be fine without me, as always, and even better without me! Please go to the kitchen, I've put on the kettle."

I finished my script and went to Moscow to show it to the studio people.

I knew it wasn't quite the "first version" yet, but I wasn't too worried. The deadline was still far off. I wanted to find out, though, if I was on the right track. This was my first script. I felt that some parts had come out quite well: for example, I was pleased with how I showed the hero's thoughts in a number of scenes, without a heavy inner monologue.

And they criticized me for this "new approach!"

Director Alekseyev seemed very interested in my sketch at first, anxious to bring it out on the screen. Now he said (though trying to be polite):

"Can't you see, Valentina Petrovna, that a hero must act? Do you understand what it is—to act?"

"I think I do."

"It means: to perform actions. Your hero's actions, though, end somewhere in the first quarter of the script, or even sooner. After page fifteen, he just thinks; ruminates, and ruminates."

"Right. I thought it would be very interesting to show how a person thinks, the process of thinking."

"What about the audience, though? Believe me, the audience simply won't get what's happening on the screen. How will we show the transition from thought to reality? Sorry, but what you have here is a kind of mysticism: dreams and reality! There was something like it in a film by Kurosawa. . . ."

Alekseyev then told me what that film was about. He described it very well and even acted out whole sections of it. I was fascinated.

"There, in his film, it made sense," Alekseyev said. "It advanced the action, it advanced the story. But in your screenplay the effect is reversed: all this stuff simply slows everything down, obscures it. . . . This is supposed to be a motion picture! And another thing: that hero of yours. Excuse me for saying so, but your hero isn't a hero at all. It's quite puzzling why your heroine falls in love with him."

"Do people have to love for a reason?"

"All right, it does happen that you can love for no good reason. But then, this has to be explained. At the very first directors' meeting they'll tell us. . . . And then, here you write: the girl walks slowly along the path. . . . She must run, run! This is a movie! And why don't you have any funny scenes?"

"Do I have to have them? In the sketch. . . ."

"Valentina Petrovna, you and I agreed: we'll take the basic plot from your sketch. But the rest must be added. I don't know how to film psychological stories. I like humor. There were some excellent moments in your sketch. For example, when the hero visits his girl friend's mother. . . . You can make that a very funny. . . . You have to create it, though!"

He was probably right. He knew how films were made, and I didn't. But I was afraid if my hero starts running back and forth instead of thinking, or fighting and riding a wild horse—that he'd become quite a different person, one I didn't know.

"Your uncle came out quite well," Alekseyev said suddenly. "Somehow, true to life. One can feel him."

I decided that this director really understood some things.

"Maybe we should make him the main hero?" he thought out loud. "Don't reject anything offhand, Valentina Petrovna," he added hurriedly when he saw my expression. "Think about my suggestion. Of course, make him younger, but you must keep him. . . . Who is he? A former pilot? Let him stay a pilot. . . . I think you should work with another author, someone who's experienced."

Still, this was all quite interesting. I liked talking to Alekseyev, watching him. Even better, I liked walking along the studio corridors: white doors, plates with names familiar since my childhood, white doors with signs that sounded strange: "The Magician from Alpukhara," "Golden Rain" . . . white doors like book covers of amazing, as-yet-unread books. Happily bustling corridors where everybody knows everybody, beautiful girls, men with good Russian faces, languid boys, guys with bangs, sporty young men. And an occasional "himself": Smoktunovsky himself, Romm himself, Peter Finch himself. A kind of working holiday was going on behind the white doors and quite openly in the corridors, too. I enjoy these first encounters most, the initial expectation of gladness, when you look at everything as a trusting guest. With time, you learn that there is a deception in this, that much is only show, and still you know that there's a kind of truth in it all, in this happiness, in the hope, in the expectation and even in the showing off. There's truth in holidays, and in working days. Ah, how glad I was that I hadn't lost the knack of feeling happy! I could have said about myself: I am happy, and therefore I am!

The failure of my "pre–first version" didn't put me off too much. The corridors, the white doors, and the enticing holiday feeling meant incomparably more than an initial failure. Nobody can do it just like that—write it, hand it in, have it accepted. . . . You might be able to do it if you wrote a sketch; even then you couldn't be sure, though.

The day after the Philharmonic concert, I sat down to write my screenplay. No special inspiration, no back-tingling, no inimitable words coming out of the depths of pre-dawn dreams. No. Just— the time had come. And I sat at my typewriter for two weeks. The uncle who resembled Aleksandr Ivanovich was a great help. Next to him, other figures began settling in: not yet people, only figures who still talked as I do. I realized they talked too much, and too much alike. Again, I did not trust myself, I would remember, then immediately correct my memory to make it look like "real literature." But what I had to do was not invent anything, just remember, remember—to remember what happened to the people I had in my sketch, and what happened to me and my friends. Then it would turn out better.

On my way to Moscow I already knew quite well how important that was. But Alekseyev said nothing about that. I was puzzled. And also, why collaborate with another writer? I never had a co-author.

After he mentioned the co-author, he took me to meet his teacher, a famous director whose name I had known since I was little. This man was not familiar with the characters in my sketch, but he knew much more about them than I did. When he asked gently, "It looks like your boy had no friends at all?" I realized that he was right, that this fact was terribly important and if it weren't true the whole story would be quite different. He kept commenting. "It's frightening where loneliness takes you when you don't know how to be alone." "He becomes a pigeon fancier, skips school because of these pigeons. . . . You know it's a real passion, these pigeons; not just a hobby, but true passion. Pigeons are live creatures. Maybe he isn't shallow but has a deep, inner life? Where there is passion there's a secret."

He began telling me all sorts of incidents from his life. The more he talked, the more I wanted to get down to work, right now, on the spot. The question of a co-author was put aside till after I came back with my first version.

In the train, going back to Leningrad I thought of the old director, of the white doors, of my hero the pigeon fancier—and my life seemed again to be full, no longer meaningless. Strange, I now felt that life did not need to wind down at my age, that I could start anew! Veta once told me a French saying: "God tempers the wind to the shorn lamb." Maybe so! If I hadn't had this work, this trip. . . .

The call from the Moscow studio came when our divorce was in full swing. I was leaving the apartment I had had for two years, a splendid, separate apartment with a garbage chute I had so liked at first. I was leaving the apartment that in the last year had become so somber that even the light bulbs seemed only half-lit. It was then that for some reason my work started going well: a small book of stories came out, even a review of it appeared, and then, on top of it, the call from the studio came: "We'd like you to write a screenplay based on your sketch. . . ."

Shorn lamb, shorn lamb. . . . I might have been much happier had all been fine at home. At another time, there would have been so much talk about my sudden luck. But here it passed unnoticed. It meant only one thing: that I could now work without pressure this year, even if the screenplay didn't come to anything.

With each day I moved further from my former life; with each book I read, each page I wrote, each new encounter, each conversation. "One has to go to bed with one's sorrow," said one woman in the Urals, whom I met on an assignment for a large magazine. How many nights I've already slept with my sorrow. . . .

The train coach was half empty. Some people were dozing, others read lazily. . . . After Bologoye, when the lights went on, I too pushed my seat back and dozed off. I had a dream, a strange dream. In that dream I was quite little and I was running up and down the hallway of the our huge apartment, knocking on all our neighbors' doors. It was a communal apartment; and there were some neighbors I liked, others I didn't. A wedding was going on, and I had to call everybody together. In one room the tenants seemed to change quite often: as I remembered, first there was a single man whom they called the Student, then an old couple, Evgenii Ivanovich and Anna Gavrilovna, then a noisy family, the Chernoivanovs. In my dream they all lived there together, and that wasn't surprising at all, and they were all cheerful, and glad to see me. . . . I was supposed not to miss any of them, and I could feel my palms getting sweaty from the weight of responsibility.

That's the shape my thoughts took of my new life and the holiday. I had grown up in an era of communal apartments and live-in maids. Each apartment was a noisy world, socially colorful, emotionally saturated, ethnically various. We children had a good time there. In the hallway we became friends, started our quarrels, learned life's many secrets; in the hallway we kissed when we got older. At the bottom of my consciousness our anthill apartment stayed alive and stormy. It rises up in my memories and dreams with all its smells and squabbles, with the wood piles, and the chests where the maids bedded down. On my trips now I often dream that I'm on my way home, that I'm returning to my father's place, to that communal apartment.

In fact, though, I was returning to my new home, the apartment where Veta lived and where I felt I was a tenant in just one corner of it, or only a guest. "My room," my first room in my life, refused to become mine: nothing happened in it except for my loneliness. The phone was in the hallway, my conversations with Veta happened either in the kitchen or in her room. If Marisha or Asya were to visit me, my room would immediately fill with life, with a live spirit, and also with memories. But will the two of them ever just come and visit me?

When I got home, Veta had guests, Mary's Lamb and Kolenka. Kolenka is Mary's Lamb's younger brother who's been watching Veta with a devoted look for some time. He's a designer, works in an institute, and isn't married. Mary's Lamb started bringing him along after Aleksandr Ivanovich disappeared. I took a liking to him: he seemed nice, soft, unobtrusive.

Veta called me over and I stopped in for a minute. Mary's Lamb talked about a show she'd seen recently.

"You know, actors aren't used to paying attention to the text," she complained in her weakened, limp voice. "This play has such good dialogue, but these miserable fellows stand in the way of our hearing it. The director stresses physical action, and so the actors play with some silly scarves, or with some long walking sticks. . . . As if it is their task to deflect the audience's attention at all costs from what is being said."

"Their task," said Kolenka knowingly, "is to make the audience watch at least. Nowadays, no amount of money will induce the spectator to listen! You know why? The culture of the spoken word is gone. Actors don't know how to enunciate, they don't know how to coordinate their words. Spectators today are just spectators, not listeners."

"Blame the spectator!" blurted out Veta. "Don't you see, the director wants to express himself, and the spectator must take the blame."

She was angry though, not at the director, but at her guests, particularly at poor Kolenka. It was clear to all three of us. She was angry at me, too, or rather, just irritated by my presence. I went back to my room, went to bed and heard how in the hallway clever Mary's Lamb was going on about some plays. She loves performances. As I understand, she spends all of her salary on ballet, theater, and the Philharmonic. Her husband is chief engineer at a big factory and apparently pays very little attention to her. Kolenka also likes shows, and the three of them go everywhere together.

Some persistent sound kept me from falling asleep. In the few nights I was away in a hotel, I had already grown unaccustomed to our apartment. Now I listened closely: the refrigerator gurgled, the electric meter chirped like a cricket, water dripped from a leaky faucet. I got up and went to the kitchen—the faucet must have bothered me most. The faucet was tight, but the water kept dripping from a joint in the pipe. I brought a rag and a basin from the bathroom, wrapped the rag around the pipe as tightly as I could, and then noticed Veta standing in the door. She, too, was awakened by the dripping sound.

"We'll have to call the Sparrow tomorrow," she said. "I'll see the janitor first thing in the morning and I'll ask him to send the Sparrow over."

"How did you manage while I was gone, Veta?" I asked.

She stood there, holding her small chin in both hands.

"It doesn't help!" she said dully.

"What doesn't help?"

"Nothing helps. You can't just root it out. Why did I do it? Kolenka . . . just talks and talks. . . . But I don't listen to him. I don't want to listen to him, I don't want to see him."

"But don't you feel close to him?" I asked. "He even likes the Philharmonic."

"Close!" she said sharply. "I know ahead of time what he'll say. He says what Mary's Lamb says, or what I would say. Of course, he's close. But you feel strange going to bed with him—he's like a brother! As if that's important—close or not close!"

She went to her room.

In the morning we put on the table our usual tip for the Sparrow—for his bottle—and began waiting for him.

Instead of the Sparrow, though, there came an unfamiliar, dark-haired fellow. He went to work right away, asked no questions, and in five minutes had the pipe fixed. We watched his movements with delight but also with caution: we weren't used to seeing technology respond so obediently to a plumber.

"That's it!" said the dark-haired fellow. "Won't drip anymore."

He looked at me. I handed him the tip. He raised his eyebrows and asked:

"Why so much? One ruble is enough."

"For you, for a bottle!"

"But I don't drink."

He put the change on the kitchen table. Stunned, Veta asked:

"Will you come again instead of the Sparrow?"

"Doubt it!" said he. "I'm on vacation, but I agreed to help out while they're short on men."

"And where's Sparrow?"

"He died!" he said cheerfully. "Kicked the bucket. You know, it's curious how he died: he was on the trolley, talking to someone, then suddenly slumped to one side! What a way to die! Buried him day before yesterday."

He left without explaining whether he liked such a death or not.

"So our Sparrow's dead!" said Veta. "Died, and we didn't even know it."

She bustled around the kitchen for a while; she seemed preoccupied with something.

"That's how it happens," she said. "Bang, and you're down! And that's that! Poor Sparrow."

She went off to work, and I sat at my typewriter. A minute later the phone rang, but nobody answered even though I said "hello" several times. And I was glad for Veta.

When she came home, I told her about this call.

"You think it was him?" she asked. Her lips quivered.

"Who else? Maybe Kolya?"

"Kolya would have told you, he would have left a clear message for me. But don't talk to me about him. I don't like thinking about him. I told him not to call me anymore. He objected, got angry. . . . Oh, how much he talks!"

"Veta, why don't you call Aleksandr Ivanovich?"

"You can't do that to him," she said, melting into a tender smile. "You can't . . . impose your will on him. You have to wait."

I went back to my typewriter. Veta appeared on the threshold.

"Shibanova will come soon, with half a liter. Let's drink to poor Sparrow. I made an apple pie."

When Shibanova came, she smelled the pie from the hallway and asked:

"What are you celebrating, a birthday or a namesday?"

"A wake!" said Veta seriously. "We'll remember a good man."

Half a liter for three—that's style, a prewar portion. Too much for me, though. I thought I'd sit down and listen to Shibanova. But I got carried away: I began talking about the studio, about my screenplay. Shibanova listened intently, then said:

"So you couldn't do without love in your screenplay. As a writer you. . . ."

"I wouldn't call myself a writer!"

"Of course, you are. Now tell me: why do our writers, even the good ones, pay so much attention to this . . . spring chase? Today, love plays such an insignificant role in our lives. Well, I understand, in the nineteenth century, people had more time for it—the writers did, the readers. Especially the writers. But now? Try to find a man now—not a young fellow but a real man—who would have the time for all these outpourings of the heart. Do you know what place love affairs occupy in a man's life? Fifth. Yes, yes, don't be surprised. First place—for a grown man—is taken up by work, second—his family, third—friends . . ."

"Fourth, you'd say, drinking?"

"For some, maybe. Or whatever, hunting, fishing, various hobbies. And only fifth—so-called love. That's a matter of statistics. Our writers should take note of this. What's your opinion, Veta?"

"You're probably right," agreed Veta. "But the world's population isn't just men, there're women too."

"Of course, women. . . ." Shibanova thought for a while. "For them love takes on, sad to say, an exaggerated significance. But not for all of them! The trouble is, I'm sure, that too few women work creatively."

"So you think the crux is creative work?" said I. "What about poets? Artists? You think that in their lives. . . ."

"I have no creative work," interrupted Veta, "and I don't assign love an exaggerated significance. Good God! If people would only be more straightforward, how much easier it would be for them! We live such a short time, and we make things complicated, very complicated. . . ."

"Well, I knew all along that you were smart!" said Shibanova.

The phone rang. Veta went out to answer. Shibanova glanced at me quickly and said:

"Your husband and I were on a panel yesterday. . . ."

"I don't have a husband," said I. Shibanova floated off somewhere to the side of me, a resonant silence set in, and Veta's tender voice was heard: "Yes, hello . . . hello. . . ."

"I don't presume to give you advice. . . ." Shibanova continued resolutely. "I don't know what happened between you. But he didn't look well. You shouldn't have left him by himself."

"You see," said I, "I'm one of those women who do assign love an exaggerated significance."

"Ah, a woman's pride?" asked Shibanova with some degree of distaste. "Why the hell can't you be real friends with your husbands, you beautiful women with a woman's pride? You could be my daughter, that's why I can talk this way!"

She probably confused me with Veta—I seemed quite unsuited to be her daughter. Had we not had so much vodka, I wouldn't have let this talk come about. But I was pliable now, and glad to

be told how to live, glad that someone was concerned about me.
I said:

"He hasn't been alone for some time, your pity for him is mis-
placed. He's happy!"

"He doesn't look it!" Shibanova said.

Could it be that she didn't leave her husband?

Veta came in, her face radiant.

In the churchyard the settled snow was dark, the paths dry, the
aspen trunks sparkled with a mysterious greenish light. We
haven't had such a sunny March in many years. Or I may not
have noticed it before. The secret green luminescence surprised
me more than anything. There's no haze yet, the buds are just
barely, barely swollen, and a green comes out in the phosphores-
cence of the trunks; there's a green in the air itself. In my room,
too, there's greenery—my rosemary plant is growing with such
tender, weak little leaves. Veta gave it to me. "It'll do better in
your place, your room is sunny."

A sunny room! Only a Leningrader can understand the luck of
it. My room is not just sunny, it's a kind of repository of sun.
The houses across from me are submerged in a deep winter, but
on our window sills we could grow cucumbers. After a night's
sleep, I wake up and, first thing, look at the sky. The sky is clear.
I was damn lucky to get this room. I get down to work. I don't
want a co-author, I want to do it myself. Veta brought home
scripts in various languages for me. In the evening she translates
for me directly from the page. My taste is old-fashioned: I like
neo-realistic scripts, which are not at all fashionable now. Veta
prefers documentaries, unambiguous stories about real events.
And when I tell her that that's not the truth anyway, that it's only
one of many possible views, she objects and argues and doesn't
agree. Then she says:

"You have to write a contemporary piece, even if you have
to fight your own taste. After all, you're trying to write it for
contemporary people."

Contemporary people, contemporary people. . . . What about
me, am I not contemporary? Does remembering the thirties make
me less of a full citizen of the sixties? I don't like people to be
unemotional, and our notorious alienation seems more a pose to

me than a way of expressing a new truth. What the hell—I like sentimentality in art, in its original meaning; not drippy triteness. Originally, sentimentality did not exclude humor. Sometimes it's fashionable to demonstrate feelings, sometimes to hide them—but we musn't pretend that we are robots interested only in what can be calculated, measured, and weighed.

Veta and I spent many evenings arguing about such things. Kolenka has disappeared from our horizon, apparently forever. Shibanova has gone on a trip. Mary's Lamb feels offended on her brother's behalf. So Veta and I are alone. Plus the phone. Quite often our phone emits mute phone calls. Veta says: "If only he'd identify himself! His pride is so childish!" She smiles. She's waiting.

Bad examples are catching. Once, at midday, I dialed my old number and heard a voice that long ago represented security and peace. I hung up quickly, like a prankster. The phone rang back immediately.

"Don't hang up," said that voice. "Listen, let's talk like grown-ups."

"How did you find out my number?"

"That's beside the point. I . . ."

"Shibanova gave it to you?"

"Yeah, I guess. That's not the point, though. I'm calling to say good-bye."

"We said good-bye a long time ago."

"I'm leaving town, going to Novosibirsk, to Asya."

"Is Asya sick?"

"No, why? She's fine. I'm being sent there, to stay a while."

"That's good!" said I. A resentment against Asya welled up in me: she made arrangements with him behind my back. Just as I suspected, she kept in touch with him, discusses with him what I do, and criticizes my behavior or condescends to forgive it.

"How's your work going?" he asked. "What are you writing now?"

Maybe he'd really like to find out about my work. Some time ago I used to hide my skinny pages from him, but he used to find them, read them, and then talk about them.

"I'm writing a lot," said I, "all kinds of stuff."

He said nothing for a while, and then:

"I'm leaving tomorrow."

"Good luck."

"Would you like to come, too?"

"To doctor your wounds?" I asked. "I'm not very good at that."
My own voice grated in my throat. *Can I have said these words?*

He called me by my name.

My name got lost a long time ago; I had nicknames, diminu-
tives, incredibly stupid-sounding ones for unaccustomed ears. I
had a name some time back, when we still used to go out together,
when he would say my name with a kind of awe, deliberately
enunciating each consonant.

This name of mine floated up from an earlier, former time. And
that woman I once was answered in me, that woman of whom so
little was left. . . . How many rough rings have grown around me
since then; like on an old tree.

I hung up. The phone didn't ring again. I went to the post office
and picked up a letter, not from Asya but from Marisha.

Marisha wrote:

"You must go visit Asya. I'm not getting involved, and I don't
want to pronounce judgment, but I know one thing: you and Dad
are my favorite people. You're both unhappy. That musn't be. I
cry over your cheerful letters. Even Asya is troubled by it. Really.
You think that grown children aren't bothered by their parents'
divorce, but that isn't so. It destroys all that's stable, the whole
world. Don't you know this? Oh, Ma, forgive me, but I won't
erase this, I want you to know. . . ."

Neither she nor Asya saw us last year. She writes: I don't want
to pronounce judgment. But she does, she blames me. She wasn't
with us that last year, doesn't understand that if he's unhappy,
it's not because of me. This means, that the other one didn't move
in with him, couldn't make up her mind, wants to keep both him
and her husband.

At the end of her letter Marisha struck the decisive blow:

"You'll be going to see Asya anyway, since she's having a baby
in six months."

"I'm expecting a baby," said Veta.

That was at the end of our conversation, which started with
my solemn announcement:

208

"Aleksandr Ivanovich called and asked you to call him back. He'll be in his office."

She went to the phone without taking her coat off or putting down her briefcase. With briefcase in hand she talked.

"It's me," she said. "Don't call me any more. No, I'm not angry. Yes, you guessed. Thanks. Take care."

"He thinks that I'm a whore," she told me. "Let him think so. Let him think at least something, just so he thinks again. Let him think in the morning and at night. I don't need anything any more. Let me never find out about it, but let him think. Then I'll be able to survive."

"What's the matter with you, Veta?"

"Nothing. The usual: there once lived a woman who thought she was having a good time and that all was well. She thought: 'Oh, how clever I am, how smart, how cool.' But, as it turns out, not that cool. That's all there is to it."

She ran her tongue along her lips, and they stayed dry.

"But, Veta, he called!"

"I'm pregnant," said Veta, "by Kolenka."

"This is my last chance. If I don't give birth now, I'll never have a child. The doctor told me so. Since that first time I haven't been pregnant again.

"Now there'll be someone in this world who'll need me like bread. For about fifteen years I'll be needed. And then—I'll be an old woman.

"Light and easy—I can't bear this lightness any more, the price for it is too high. All right, it'll be hard for me, very hard—thank God. You know, I once read in an Indian book: 'I don't want to be sugar, I want to eat sugar myself.' So there—I'm fed up with being sugar. I've made my choice.

"If I had told Kolenka then, he'd have probably, like a man of honor. . . . But I wouldn't dream of it. You know, though, that as a man he suits me very well. I think that's why I got pregnant. After all, we women don't get full pleasure very often, but with him—no trouble. Still. . . .

"All right, forget it. I'll think about the baby now, I'll look after myself, I'll gather the dowry for her. Now I have to have a quiet life if I want the baby to turn out well. I'd like to have a girl.

"Good God, what's there to be afraid of? So many women have children just like that, and it's all right, they raise them by themselves and manage fine. Do you know when I realized that I loved Sasha, that is, Aleksandr Ivanovich? When I had to choose, when I realized . . . well, when I realized that there'll be a baby. At that moment I knew that I was giving him up.

"I'd like him to keep calling, though, and for me to keep saying no to him. You understand, I'd be . . . not happy, of course, but . . .

"But he won't give me the chance to say no again. I know him.

"Listen, won't the baby be good since I got it at such a high price? Don't think that I'm superstitious, I've dropped all superstitions a long time ago. But in this case, I think, some things have to fall together. Justice? Balance? Maybe there'll be something of Sasha in this child. It could happen. So people say.

"I'll be all right, it won't be too hard for me. My publisher's nice to me, Sergei Ivanovich, too. . . . I'll take my work home, do it here, they'll agree to that.

"I love this man. I'd be happy to darn his socks, stand in line for him, wash his underwear. I could do all that. But one thing I can no longer be: his sugar.

"Will you teach me how to take care of the baby? At least in the beginning?

"For some reason I think it'll be a daughter. I'm a bit afraid of boys, I never even had a boy for a cousin. Or would I love a boy even more?

"Tell me, giving birth so late—won't that be bad for the baby?"

I split in two, in a strange way. I thought about the babies to be born from my daughter, and from Veta whom I hadn't known until recently and who was now close to me. At night I dreamt that I was giving birth, I felt the baby move in me. In my dream I dreaded delivering, as I always dreaded it, and I remembered that I was no longer at home, and I thought I had to get back home. In my dream, home was always my parents' home, that communal apartment.

During the day I worked. It seemed that work had never resisted me so much. My characters wanted to talk only about what I was thinking about, forgetting their own cares, which were no less important. I wanted to compose good tales with happy endings. Something new was taking shape in me, in my innermost self. How could I have thought that I was dry to the bone! To put it in a nutshell, I was getting ready for grandmotherhood.

After an icy, sunny March came a grayish, soft April. Several times Veta and I went to the Hermitage Museum—for the baby to grow beautiful. She carried it easily, without morning sickness or dizziness. She felt embarrassed that it was so easy.

"Is this normal?" she'd ask. "I've often heard how women suffer during pregnancy. I don't have any spots."

"It's too early for that."

"When will I feel the baby move? At four and a half months? What a long wait!"

Asya wrote:

"Don't be mad that I wrote Marisha first. It just happened that way. We're waiting for you, we are. . . ."

I answered that they shouldn't expect me yet because I was deep in my work. I loved her, and I knew that I'd love the little one, but I couldn't get over her treachery: how could she make plans behind my back!

My own state, which made it hard for me to breathe, was abating. Maybe because I knew that Leningrad was now empty, that everything had been transferred to Novosibirsk. Even in my thoughts this state wasn't called "husband" or "former husband" or anything else. It was darkness and suffocation, and it was now receding—it wasn't gone entirely but it had loosened its grip.

This darkness sometimes came back at night. But now I knew how to fight it. Simply, when I slept on my left side my heart began to ache and my breath tightened—exactly the feeling I had all during my last married year. Now, barely waking, I knew to turn on my right side, and everything passed, and children came into my sleep, some smiles and gurgles and little fingers all spread out. . . . When I woke up I knew that my alienation was over, that I wasn't alone, that I was needed, and that I needed a lot—people, cares, work. I then realized that alienation comes in grief, and old age. My old age receded.

One morning Veta came running into my room, all excited:

"Guess what! I've got milk already!"

She threw open her robe, pressed her fingers against her small breast, round and golden like a little melon, and on her dark nipple shone almost transparent drops.

"Is this supposed to happen? Is it?"

I reassured her. I told her this was a sign that she'd have plenty of milk for the baby. I invented this on the spot.

"Oh God, what would I do without you!" she sighed.

She's got so many friends, and still she says: "What would I do without you!"

Her friends don't know it yet. Outwardly nothing has changed. As before, she brings home from work some clothes for Tyusha, and they chatter for a long time, tell each other where one can get a fur coat restored, or where one might find some marvelous pearl clips. . . . As before, she talks with Mary's Lamb about art, flirts with her authors by phone. She's getting ready for the elections to the local trade union committee, even takes part in pre-election intrigues. As before, she asks when she comes home from work:

"Did anybody call?"

Once in a while, when mute phone calls come, she cries, and then smiles through her tears:

"So he does think of me. It's him, isn't it? Who else!"

Mary's Lamb forgave her about Kolenka, especially because he seems to have consoled himself rather quickly. She says in her limp voice:

"Right from the start I knew that you and he wouldn't stay together for long. I'm even grateful to you—Kolenka will now begin to believe that women are capable of dropping him. That will do him good."

Only Shibanova with her sharp eye caught something. Suddenly she said:

"Veta, somehow you have an expression of a pregnant woman, as if you were listening to something within yourself."

"That's right," said Veta.

Shibanova was astounded:

"Really? I didn't actually mean it. Ah, wonderful, how clever! And what'll you do, get married, or do it yourself?"

"Myself," said Veta.

"Right," decided Shibanova. "Men are just good enough for that. Why should one put up with them all one's life!"

And she laughed heartily.

"I didn't know you were such a feminist," I said when Veta left the room. "You tried so hard to talk me into. . . ."

"That was a different question," she said. "I believe that a woman has to be a friend, and not just a female. Females can never forgive completely, but a friend can and must."

"That's all that women do: forgive," said I.

"Those are—women. But I'm talking about females. Females never forgive all the way. Twenty years might pass, and a female will still reproach a man. Are you that way?"

"A man who's betrayed you once will betray you again, don't you know that?"

"And you, have you never been unfaithful to your husband?" she asked, curious.

"No."

The way she asked, I felt embarrassed to admit it.

"Well, well!" she said. "You're pretty rigorous."

"He and I trusted each other," said I. I had no idea why I tried to explain it to her, except that I wanted to talk about myself. "Now I don't trust him. That's all. That's the end. I don't need him any more. Before, I thought that I couldn't live without him. Now I've built up my own life, my own world, by myself. There's no room for him in it."

"Well, well!" said Shibanova.

"Valentina Petrovna," said Veta to me one day as we sat in the kitchen chatting. "You say that you're through with your husband. Is that possible? Somehow, I believe that nothing ever comes to an end. It just keeps going on and on. As long as man is alive nothing's ever finished." She was thinking about Aleksandr Ivanovich. Without a hitch she said:

"Know what's good? That I don't have to choose a name for the baby. I can name it Sasha, whether it's a boy or a girl."

Veta and I had a big program planned for Saturday: a walk, the Hermitage, then a movie. We were about to leave when someone brought a telegram.

"It's for you!" said Veta. "From Novosibirsk."

"Daddy is sick/Heart attack/Come at once/Asya."

"Write down the time," I heard. "Here put it down, the time. . . ."

"I don't want to go!" said I. "Veta, I don't want to!"

"I don't want to!" I repeat as I sit in the plane. "Once again others have decided for me. I don't want to! I've almost recovered, calmed down, freed myself, built a world for myself in which I don't worry constantly, don't agonize. I don't want to! Why am I taking this trip? He didn't call me, my daughters decided everything for me, for us. I don't want to! What's past is gone, it never returns. . . . Why am I taking this trip? I don't want to!"

I'm looking down at the enormous geographic map spread out below us. Throughout this country—a clear day. Our height—ten thousand kilometers; our speed—eight hundred kilometers per hour. A few more hours and I'll see him. As long as we're alive nothing's ever finished.

If only he lives! I'll nurse him well, until he's healthy, and then, let come what may, if only he lives. What nonsense: grudges, keeping score, hurt pride—that's all imagined. If only he lives. All this was my love for him, it never ended, my one and only last love, my love that needs to know only that he's alive. Wherever, with whomever, but—alive!

Hang on, I say to him, *hang on, dear! A hundred kilometers more, another hundred. . . . I'll look after you, you'll pull through. Let it be the way you want it, or nothing, but live.*

As long as we're alive—nothing is ever finished.

1969   *Translated by Helen Reeve*

Umbria's Tender Haze

QUITE a long time ago a very old teacher told us a story:
"I was then teaching at an elementary school. One day, the supervisor dropped in on my class. I began trembling: this was only my second year teaching. We were reading, I don't remember what, and came across the word 'miracle.' I started asking: 'Children, what's a miracle, who can explain?'

"Nobody said a word, only one hand went up. That was Puzaitsev, the worst student I had. What'd gotten into his head? He raised his hand way up, everybody watching, and the supervisor was looking at him too. Couldn't do anything, I had to say:

" 'Well, Puzaitsev, tell us, what is a miracle?'

"He stood up, happy, grinning from ear to ear.

" 'Miracle? . . . Cigarettes!'

"I almost dropped through the floor. The point was—there was that supervisor! Actually, in those days there were cigarettes called 'Miracle.' Even after the Revolution."

In our daily life not many miracles happen. Or maybe we don't recognize them, at least not right away. Our days are so short, and the minutes so long; the measure of time is not constant, it vacillates greatly. As for us, it's only with God's help that we might be able to recognize some connections between events, where they intersect and become clearer as they painfully cut into our own flesh. Literature is briefer than life and its causes are more closely tied to consequences, its chain is shorter, easier to review. And we, learning life from literature, accept on faith her imaginary, distinct time. Still we think that literature mirrors something out there, forgetting what lies beyond the mirror; we accept for real the mirrored two-dimensionality, and we believe in the exactness of dimensions as we swallow the line: "three years passed. . . ."

Looking back, we remember miracles we have experienced;

sometimes we even call them miracles, and we may even understand that the greatest miracle is that we are still alive to this day.

These miracles, though, exist in a different time and are stretched out so that their outline grows faint, yet at times they light up brightly for an elusive instant, immeasurable on our scales.

And still. . . .

We had only one reason for stopping in Perugia: to visit the Collegio del Cambio to see the rooms Perugino and his pupils had painted. People rarely stay long in Perugia. She lies off the main tourist circuit. Like mushroom pickers, tourists divide into two major groups; some dash forward at near cosmic speed, barely take the time to bend down and pick a mushroom, or to stop at a chapel praised by all the Michelins. Others begin to pace over one spot, turn up a treasure spot of mushrooms and won't leave before they look under every single dry leaf. We are of the second sort, we had trouble tearing ourselves away from Florence to get to Perugia.

Collegio del Cambio had no tourists, Perugino not being fashionable, and his pupils not either. I myself overheard a French woman in the Prado say casually as she stepped away from Rafael: "but still, he's got some pretty faces!"

However, we didn't just happen to go there—we drove there in order to see these paintings. Perugino's, of course. "Perugino's Bianca" in *Nevsky Avenue* imbedded itself in our memory in childhood. Even more, though, we wanted to see Jan Niccola di Paolo. A very fine student of Perugino, he must have been too good, too obedient, and so never acquired much fame, people say. Here in Collegio del Cambio, he painted the second room, the chapel of Saint John the Baptist.

For four hundred years, hardly anyone in Europe thought of him, until Aleksandr Blok stopped in Perugia—a tormented Blok, haunted by the demons of Petersburg. He was struck by the narrow eyes of Giotto's and Cimabue's madonnas. He saw their partly closed eyelids and, lurking behind them, something demonic. Blok knew what demons tormented artists; he brought his own with him, but each time he gave them a different name. Here in Italy, he lay in wait for them, searching in dark faces, or in curtains behind which he suspected an artist lurking.

Poor Jan Niccola! Blok, it seems, found him more demonic than any, somehow Gabriel-like. Blok's "Annunciation" is about Jan Niccola's two frescoes. They're not large, half the size of the main one, "Christ's Baptism," which is in the center. On one of them is an archangel still in flight, then comes the large "Baptism," then the third one shows Mary with a prayerbook, in three-quarter profile, a quiet face, fine lines, somewhat reminiscent of Perugino. . . .

But here it is:

> The dark-faced angel with his brazen branch
> Says: 'Hail! You are full of beauty!'
> She trembles at the ardent words,
> Two heavy braids fall down her shoulders. . . .
>   And further on:
> He sings, he whispers—closer, closer,
> Above her arch his rushing wings. . . .
> And she, no power left, drops lower
> Her darkened gaze, her troubled eyes. . . .

In the chapel we found a tall floor lamp with a long moveable arm. We aimed the light here and there, wanting to understand, to see this demonic alarm.

Blok once asked: "Why are the garments so red on the dark-faced angel who emerges out of the deeply golden background before the dark-faced Maria in the frescoes by Jan Niccola Manni?"

They are really not so very red, but rather a pink lilac. And actually, both of them are not dark-faced. Were the pictures maybe cleaned, spruced up? This picture shows an Italian fullness of body and healthy flesh. And there is the sign: "Ave, gratiae plena," the famous Latin words so well known to us through Bach's "Ave Maria." There is no alarm here. A wind may have come in with the angel into this peaceful abode, but it seemed not to have touched her calm face. There is no sign of a storm or of noise of wings; there is only a quiet amazement.

Why look for demons here? As Patsyuk put it once upon a time: you don't have far to go if the devil's at your back.

The Prince had visited Perugia about a year and a half before we did.

Even today princes exist; they can come into this world just about anyplace, and invisible fairies will sit by their cradles. The princes live among us, dress like ordinary folk—some in jeans, others even in three-piece suits. Still, people invariably recognize them.

Our Prince was a prince among poets. He wrote poems in a Baltic language we couldn't understand, but those who could said that his poems were real. He was a happy prince, knew neither want nor care, because his father was an uncrowned Soviet king. His friends loved him, weren't even envious of him. How could they envy him if he got everything by chance of birth and never valued any of it? Women loved him and stayed friends with him even after they parted ways. And he loved them back, even when he left them; he loved his friends too, and poetry, and not just his own poems but poems of others as well.

What's more—we can't omit mentioning it, although it's a less charming trait—he loved to drink, with his friends, and also without them; mostly vodka, but wine too. Before dinner and after dinner. On workdays and holidays. Since he always remained a Prince even then, he was drunk happily, never had a big hangover the next morning.

The country he was born in—as were you and I!—everybody except the officials loved princes. The officials too would love them—aren't they human?—but they're not supposed to. What's more, their own princes are growing up. No one would mind that, as long as they stuck to the open, beaten track—going into science, or into diplomacy. Then, it'd be enough for parents to watch over them from a distance, give them a bit of a push when they need it, or hold them back some, not let them go too far. They know quite well what social class they belong to: among themselves they think of themselves as aristocrats. As things stand, there are families who've been feeding at the government trough for four generations.

Sure, it's all right if they go into diplomacy or physics. But what about lyric poetry? From there, it's not far to turning into a dissident. Take, for example, Ivan Ivanych's son. . . .

Our Prince's father died early and of natural causes; his mother neglected to keep an eye on him. And so it went: from poems to folklore, to identifying with the masses, to religion, to studying history, to joining the liberation movement. . . . Then came the strange sound of one's own poetry in foreign translations. . . . The end of the sixties was stifling, deadly stifling. For several years he tried to live with it, but then he left, became a. . . .

That's precisely the point: he didn't become anybody, because he was born a real prince. He stayed true to himself: wrote poems, picked up women friends who in Russian are called "little visitors," and in American—"girl friends." Sometimes he fell madly in love with somebody else's girl friend if he met her in a European capital. He received many invitations—a prince is always popular. He would arrive, read his poems, answer questions, drink with friends, then also without friends, go home—and sit down to write.

On the way from Assisi to Milan he stopped in Perugia. He had an assignment: would he please go to the Collegio del Cambio and then describe for her the "Annunciation" in his most precise prose, down to the tiniest detail, but please, not in verse, that has been done before. The assignment came by letter; the letter arrived right before he left for Europe and made him extremely happy. The woman who wrote him lived on the other side of America, had no plans to go to Europe. She was writing her dissertation about the "Italian Verses," either from an art history angle, or as a linguistic study of alternations of liquid vowels. Anyway, she would like to be able to visualize. . . . It made him happy that she needed from him at least this much.

True, he did not realize that coming from Assisi he would have to change trains. He did not think it would be so hot and that one could not open any windows at night: mosquitoes were hidden in all the cracks, and at night they feasted on him as they feast on the princes in Georgia. In town, rich Bavarians strolled around, or the inevitable American teenagers, carrying multicolored little houses on their backs—"all my stuff is with me!"; also some Swedes—what could a Catholic Hecuba mean to them? And nowhere even the slightest wind, not in the narrow streets, not up above, not below. He was glad to be leaving. Milan's heat did not frighten him, there the streets are wide.

It was early morning, around eight. Will the museum be open? Going by the train schedule, he had an hour to himself: half an hour for getting there and back, and half an hour in the museum. Like that Englishman who sailed from London to Petersburg to look at the wrought-iron fence surrounding the Summer Garden: he sailed in with his boat, took one look, and sailed off the same day home to England.

In Perugia there were wide streets through which the morning breezes flowed, light but clear. Even in the bus one could feel a breeze. He had to watch his money, he didn't know if he'd get paid by Milan right away or in two months—no taxis for now. The bus went up the hill in wide loops, let people off who'd sing out their *arrivederci* like in the opera, taking their time. Actually, to look at two frescoes you needed only fifteen, or just ten minutes. The less you look, the more you can write.

He bought a ticket from a sleepy-looking, bored girl and went immediately to the second room, past all the Peruginos. He was already familiar with the outlay of the Collegio. Blok's poems slid along his memory, snagging here and there. Ah, here are the frescoes: the Angel, the large Crucifixion, Mary. Blok's verses; which he didn't like. It was hard to keep liking Blok. On the other hand, he did not dismiss Blok. In general, he was against deviation. He simply did not need Blok any longer, but later— who knows? Some Leningrad poets—actually just one!—would shudder: "She's beautiful and young. Trrrbl!" Well, so what? He'd never take such liberties. But Brodsky takes even greater ones. He and Brodsky respected each other.

The curly-haired Angel was not quite touching down. He remembered seeing the first angel in his life when he was about four. He saw him in a box that arrived after grandmother died: huge, curly-haired, the head probably made of cardboard, his wings golden like the curls, and his clothes snowy white, cotton, with specks of something that glistened. . . . Catholics sometimes have their angels dressed in blue, or red, or lilac. That's something Blok couldn't go along with. In his memory also the angels were probably in Russian quilted coats. . . . This Angel's legs are very sturdy, legs of a runner. One leg, at an angle, is bare.

He looked the Angel over carefully, glanced at his watch—lots of time!—and went over to the *annunciata*. She was big, had strong shoulders, like Lyubov Dmitriyevna. That was strange: Blok himself was tall, but he liked big women. Delmas was also built that way, a Carmen and a half. And Nadezhda Pavlovich too. Whenever there was a Blok jubilee you'd see elephant-sized women emerge to commemorate him. . . . Mary's face was small, hard to make out. Only a tip of her bare foot at the bottom of her dress, the fabric not heavy, hugging a bent knee. At her back the sash, red, winding, snaking along in curves—was it the wind from the angel's wings that stirred it up? That's all there is of the storm. Red color: yes, the dress is red; and the cape, or shawl, is dark blue, properly so; then there's gold, slightly dulled, that's in the wreath. They say that Manni—where, by the way, did Blok pick up that "Manni?" All postcards have "di Paolo"—Manni was so glad when he received the order that he even kissed somebody's hand. But where did I hear that, do you suppose? All right, he may've done it. . . . Then Blok traveled here, now me. . . . Her face; fine lines, a Perugino bend of the head, eyes lowered. . . .

He pulled out a small yellow notepad and made a note about the red sash. In the first draft it said: "If Mother should now walk in, I'm ruined." How does anything begin? How does it start? Maybe as in Fet: "and passionate kisses, and tears." No, dreams and longing. No, no dreams here, it's something else . . . visions? Since childhood, visions and dreams.

He looked at the big figure again: navy blue, red, gold. Well, she knows about that. Actually, what does he need to do? Write down thoughts about the picture? But no thoughts came. He glanced at his watch. It's amazing how time drags on when you don't know what to do with it. He walked over into the first room, looked with pleasure at the red-cheeked balding Perugino who immortalized himself along with the saints, the wise men, and the sibyls. The red lay plentiful on the master's face—on his cheekbones, his nose, above the eyebrows. His blood vessels. Must have liked his Umbrian wine. One will have to have a taste of that wine. Actually, the sun won't be over the yardarm for quite a while yet, but at the railway junction, at the counter. . . .

He went back to the chapel to have a last look at this genuine, unsophisticated Annuciation, and began writing in his mind: "You might do well to take for your subject the discrepancy between a painter's and a writer's ways of expressing themselves. Gumilev looks at a greengrocer's sign. . . . Or would that be unsuitable for a dissertation?" She won't tear the envelope open, she'll use her scissors, and she will take her time reading his letter, at leisure. . . .

That's it, time is almost up. He was watching the inclined head, looking closely, but couldn't see anything new in it. A face without mystery. At the same time, he had an inkling that he'd caught onto something, maybe in the face, or he may have caught an idea and then let it slip away. Her sash? No, not the sash, not the Gabriel game—although it was precisely that game that his stern friend, Seryozha Solovyov, criticized Blok for. Where is my stern friend now? We're all dispersed, not a time to be stern. What a sweet term: Childhood friend. Since childhood—these visions and dreams, Umbria's tender darkness . . . no, haze. . . .

He stopped at the door, came back. The verse lines are about an Umbrian woman, a model. An artist's model. A model. Of course, that's the way it happened: the first four lines all came at once, as if from gratitude:

> Since childhood—these visions and dreams,
> Umbria's tender haze.
> On fences roses flaring,
> Fine bells are ringing.

He was exceptionally happy. Not a revelation, of course—someone else may have noticed this a long time ago—but he'll write to her precisely: "Don't search here either for blasphemy or for the Gabriel theme; rather this is everyday life soaring high, as it happens with Blok, taken to the nth degree." He gazed at this simple face with pleasure, and it even seemed to him that when he stood somewhat turned away and looked hard, he could catch a corner of her glance. Not so, she's hiding. Maybe you really were a dreamer of a little girl growing up here in Perugia? Now that I understand you, will you let me go?

Two people came in, a man and a woman, tall, blond. Scandinavians? He stepped back to let them pass. They began to aim the lamp in various directions, exchanging remarks in a quiet voice he couldn't understand. Time to go. He felt cheerful. Inadvertently his eyes met the gaze of the Scandinavian who gave him a smile and asked something, clearly taking him for one of his own. He responded by saying something polite in English, then glanced for the last time at the figure, which was barely illuminated. It was time.

Yet, again he didn't leave, for he seemed to hear, only seemed to—because there were no words, no audible words—he rather thought that he heard: you had better look carefully, gazing at the face that under his eyes kept disintegrating, like a word one repeats endlessly; it was losing meaning, evoked nothing at all. The Scandinavians left, he could not hear them any more. Now I can leave too, he told himself in words, or maybe again repeated only what he thought he was hearing. He himself did not know which.

In Perugino's room he glanced at his watch and gasped. He'd missed his train. The next one would arrive in two hours. Two hours. He might be late for his lecture.

The good mood stayed with him. He was amused at himself for falling into reverie before a second-rate master. Still, he kept thinking of the artist, when he finally reached the bar. The wine was good, wasn't diluted, was full bodied. No reason to hurry off. He went to the station in a happy state, not too happy, just right. There he found an unusual commotion, something'd happened, some explosion, not far. Who did it? How, when, why? Some shouted "*brigate rosse,*" others shouted "*fascisti.*" Not many people were there, but enough to represent a gathering. The cashier leaned out of his little window, exclaimed something, burst into tears and disappeared. The crowd boiled up again. They explained to the Prince what happened—in words, gestures, sounds, shouts, definitions. He could not understand right away what it was all about, and no one really knew exactly. . . .

That was the morning of the explosion at the Bologna station. News of it came like wartime reporting: sixty-six killed, two hundred and three wounded. August, summer vacations. Umbria'a tender haze. The Reds? The Blacks? It turned out to be the Blacks, the neo-Fascists. What's the difference? What did it matter to people who had packed their suitcases that morning, who had said good-bye for a while, had made arrangements, maybe even looked in the horoscope. But what horoscope or magician could give you an answer if the question is put incorrectly? In former times there existed men of destiny; but nowadays that's not enough, they've turned themselves into destiny. Reds–blacks,

blacks–reds . . . the colors of roulette, the colors of destiny, the colors of the times. . . .

He decided that there wouldn't be any lecture, felt free to relax, to think about his letter, which, maybe, he didn't need to write— he might just take a trip to the other side of America. Of course, only if he got a check from Milan. And what if he did not get to lecture? Nowadays, what do the the Italians care about our po- etry? In poetry *they* are older, as human beings—*we* are. Isn't that so? Does a poet have an age?

The lecture did take place, and was well received. He even told the story about Jan Niccola di Paolo and Blok, although he suspected that there was not much interest in Blok.

He had a girl friend in Milan. He was spending the night with her. In the middle of the night she woke him up:

"You were shouting," she said.

"Stones," he mumbled still half asleep. "They're piling up on me, can't breathe. . ."

"I'll open the window," she said. "It won't help much, but let's try it anyhow."

It barely made any difference. He could have fallen asleep had she not asked what he had been dreaming about. He tried to be conscientious and remember it, but his dream disappeared, it was gone altogether. She remarked that he was too impressionable, and before he went to sleep he probably thought of. . . .

"I wasn't thinking anything," he said and laughed.

"No, I didn't mean just before you fell asleep. What were you thinking about last night?"

"About Blok," he said truthfully.

"Listen, it is true that Blok worked in the Cheka?"

"No," he said, "that wasn't the Cheka but the Extraordinary Commission, at the time of the Provisional Government. Inves- tigating the Tsarist ministers."

"What's the difference?"

She had a child's clear forehead.

"Tomorrow I'll explain it to you," he promised. "First thing tomorrow morning."

In the plane, between the serving of drinks and food, he asked himself: What about me, could I have served in that Extraordinary Commission? No, I couldn't have—he thought, stirred by a tinge of self-satisfaction. But what if Over There everything turned topsy-turvy again, and the present ones were put to judgment? He saw before him that flabby face he'd known so well since childhood, distorted into a grimace of a crying old man, and he almost vomited. No, he could not. He could not judge them, he had no faith in the justice of human justice. . . . And if they put these on trial, the Reds or the Blacks who blew up the railroad station? In his memory stuck a woman's face in the newspaper, her mouth wide open shouting; he could hear the crashing and the shout. . . . Good Lord, no—I know I'm sparing myself, quite so, myself, but no, I could not. Yes, one could put it beautifully: "I cannot bear the sight of human degradation," while the people to be tried are put on view in disgrace. Well, what did these Napoleons, these Nechayevs think, in fact? Even so, I would have cried, he thought drunkenly. Cried not with them, but about them, about myself. A pathetic creature, that's me. But Blok could. Blok. *All that is transient and that is frail* . . . He was pure. Pure people can do it.

He fell asleep. In his dream he saw a boy in a photograph, silvery straw-colored hair, in a navy blue summer suit, and he felt immediately—or recalled—how the shorts had pinched him as he walked. And he seemed to be merging with the photograph while he was still a spectator; he saw both the boy and the big young woman in a long, dark-red dress, they both fitted in the frame, yet the distance between them was insurmountable and eternal, and the smiling boy was asking:

"Was it You who saved me? Surely I would've gone to the railroad station to have a drink at the counter. Was it You who saved me?"

He knew he had fallen asleep, but the dream had such charm that he made an effort—and did not awaken. He saw both the boy and the figure in red, and noticed the dark blue cape was the same color as the boy's suit. The boy held in his hand a gladiolus, white, the kind that grew in their garden. At this point the boy began to grow, and the figure too, and they became a canvas, and they were a picture from which he backed up further and further, away into eternity. . . . And the dream grew over with verses, like grass.

He did not try to write the letter, he took that trip to the other side of America after all, as he explained to his friends, to report about everything in person.

"A miracle?" she'd asked pensively. "You—the lush—you think you were worth a miracle?"

1983   *Translated by Helen Reeve*

Notes

A Long, Long Summer

Page
1 Frida Vigdorova (1915–1965): Journalist, novelist, and educator much admired by Ruth Zernova, especially for her lively interest in encouraging children to develop as individuals.

7 "No field work required": During summer break, students were sent to do agricultural work either on a *kolkhoz* (*kollektivnoye khozaistvo,* collective farm) or in the Virgin Lands (new settlements in Siberia).

10 Volga and Moskvich: The two most popular makes of car in the Soviet Union at the time of this story.

12 N.I.I.: *Nauchno-issledovatelski Institut* (National Research Institute).

13 "the Nevsky region, and . . . Vasilievsky Island": Parts of metropolitan Leningrad.

15 Natasha Rostova: The heroine of Tolstoy's *War and Peace.*

17 *Vanka-vstanka:* "Little Ivan Stand-up," a round-bottomed doll, weighted at the base, that recovers automatically whenever it is pushed over.

18 "five meters . . . fifteen winds": Note the word play in the switch from meters [*metrov*] to winds [*vetrov*].

Witches

Page
25 "Honored Artist of the Republic": *Zasluzhenny artist respubliki,* a rank of distinction in the arts in the Soviet Union.
Siverskaya: A small town not far from Leningrad.
Yevpatoriya: A spa in the Crimea.

27 Dachnoye: A section of Leningrad in the extreme southwest of the city.
Khrushchoby: A play on the words *trushchoby* (slums) and Khrushchev, refers to the large, poorly built apartment buildings erected in large numbers under Khrushchev.
"Nest of Gentlefolk": A reference to *Nest of Gentlefolk* (1859) by Turgenev.

Bacalao

Page
36 "*novio*": fiancé (Spanish).
chulo: jester, punster, or sly person (Sp.).

229

"Cid Campeador": El Cid Campeador, an eleventh-century nobleman Roderigo Díaz de Vivar. The legend of *El Cid,* the invincible warrior, became an important symbol in the struggle between Christians and Moslems in the twelveth century.

Foro: Lordship, or Court (Sp.).

39 *alpargatos:* canvas shoes with soles made of rope (Sp.).

42 Frederico García Lorca (1899–1936): A famous Spanish poet, dramatist, folklorist, and musician.

45 "Biurocrato": An imitation of the Russian pronunciation of "bureaucrat."

46 *feiner Kerl:* splendid fellow (German).

frecher Junge: brazen lad (Ger.).

Édouard Daladier (1884–1970): French Radical Socialist politician who signed the Munich pact in 1938, but declared war on Germany in 1939.

Sudeten: Before 1938, a region of Czechoslovakia bordering on Poland and Saxony, but annexed by Germany. This annexation was recognized by France and England in the Munich Pact ("Peace in our time").

50 Consalo of Cordoba: Consalvo de Córdoba, or Fernández de Córdoba, Gonzalo (1453–1515), Spanish general, called the "Great Captain." Fought in civil wars and in the conquest of Granada.

51 "Tovarich": A Spanish mispronunciation of the Russian *tovarishch.*

53 Argeles: A town in southern France.

The Bronze Bull

Page

57 The Peter and Paul Fortress is in Leningrad, on a small island in the delta of the Neva River. The sandy strip between the fortress walls and the river is a favorite bathing spot for Leningraders.

60 The House of Books: *Dom knigi,* a distinctive building on Nevsky Avenue, taken over after the Revolution from the Singer Sewing Company.

62 "Junker Schmidt": The main character in the satiric poem "Yunker Shmit" (1854) by Kozma Prutkov. The uncultured director knows only the Revolutionary hero Lieutenant Schmidt.

65 Siverskaya and Komarovo: Places north of Leningrad along the Bay of Finland, surrounded by woods where Leningraders like to go mushroom picking.

66 "in these two hundred and fifty years": Reference to the city's history.

72 "my mother to the Soviet Union in 1936": A reference to the evacuation of some Spanish resistance fighters to the Soviet Union at the end of the Spanish Civil War.

Velichko: Suggests *veliki* (great, large) as in *Pyotr Veliki* (Peter the Great).

Scorpion Berries

Page

75 Natasha Troshchenko: A friend of the author.

77 *Babushka:* Grandmother.

78 *Dedushka:* Grandfather.

79 *Sidorenchikha:* The suffix *chikha* has a common, derogatory connotation.
Katka: Short and strongly derogatory diminutive for *Yekaterina* (Catherine).

80 "They called me Anna at my birth . . ." An echo of Anna Akhmatova's poem *Epicheskie motivy* (Epic Motifs) (1913–1916).

81 *Borka:* Diminutive for Boris, not derogatory but signifying that he is very young.

83 Taras Bulba: The main character in Gogol's *Taras Bulba* (1835), a ruthless Cossack who executes his young, handsome son Andrey for treason.

89 *Tyotya:* Aunt.

90 *Katechka, Katenka:* Affectionate diminutive forms of *Yekaterina.*

Elizabeth Arden

Page

101 "dormitary": Mispronunciation of "dormitory," suggesting uneducated speech.

103 NEP: New Economic Policy, a brief period of economic freedom instituted by Lenin in 1921.

105 "rootless cosmopolites": A term used in a campaign to "expose" Jewish writers and critics; the real surnames of those using Russian pseudonyms were revealed.
NKVD: Narodny kommissariat vnutrennykh del, the People's Commissariat for Internal Affairs; first known as the Cheka, this body later became the NKVD, the MGB and MVD, and finally the KGB.
Lion Feuchtwanger (1884–1958): German anti-fascist, pacifist writer whose works were translated into Russian in the thirties.

106 "Covers the heavens with mist": From Pushkin's poem *"Zimni vecher"* (Winter Evening) (1825).

108 "Look what those bandits Marx and Engels have done": A saying from the novel *The Golden Calf* (1931) by Ilya Ilf (1897–1937) and Yevgeny Petrov (1903–1942).
Valentin A. Serov (1865–1911): Painter, known for his historical paintings and portraits.

110 *Natsbol: Natsiyonalnoe bolshinstvo* (national majority); *natsmen,* for *Natsionalnoe menshinstvo* (national minority).
consejeros: A term used by the Spanish for Soviet military advisors.
"Lev Kopelev": Lev Z. Kopelev (1912–), author, scholar of German literature, dissident, expelled from the Communist party in 1968 and from the Writers' Union in 1977. He now lives in Köln, Germany. This is a reference to his *Khranit vechno* (To Be Preserved Forever) (1975).

111 Aleksandr N. Afinogenov (1904–1941): Playwright, author of *Strakh* (Fear) (1931).

112 Semyon Ya. Nadson (1862–1887): Poet popular in the late nineteenth century (many of his poems were set to music).

"Small Series": *Malaya Seriya* of The Poet's Library (*Biblioteka poeta*), a distinguished Academy of Sciences publication.

Vladimir Zhabotinsky (1880–1940): Famous Russian Zionist, known as a journalist, writer, and translator.

"Cut-glass Tumblers": A song by Timofeyev-Yeropkin, popular during the NEP era.

113 Galich: Pseudonym of Aleksandr Ginsburg (1918–1977), a poet who sang the songs (generally political) that he composed, accompanying himself on the guitar; he became famous in the sixties.

114 "To Sech": The toast offered by the Cossacks in Gogol's *Taras Bulba*. It is the name of a Dniepr Cossack settlement of the twelfth and thirteenth centuries.

115 "recalled the wonderful moment": From the first line of Pushkin's poem "K . . ." (To . . .) (1825).

"passportization": The internal-passport policy. All city dwellers were required to carry proof that they were authorized to live in their city. This policy was abandoned after the Revolution, but was reinstituted in 1932. Permission to remain in the city was often denied; many people were "resettled" in the north or east. Leningrad's population was greatly reduced.

Freilakhs: A Jewish folk dance, now called the *sem sorok* (seven forty).

"hero cities": A distinction conferred on four cities—Leningrad, Stalingrad, Odessa, and Sevastopol at the end of World War II; Moscow was later added to the list.

116 Nikolai A. Nekrasov (1821–1877): Poet, prose writer, journalist. Some of his poems became popular as songs, among them songs about the plight of poor peasants and abused women.

"our illustrious Chekists": The members of the organization known originally as the Cheka, which is now known as the *KGB*. See the note to page 105.

Lenka Panteleyev: A real figure and popular hero of postrevolutionary Leningrad.

L.G.U.: *Leningradsky gosudarstvenny universitet* (Leningrad State University).

117 *Gosplan: Gosudarstvenny planovy komitet* (State Planning Commission), established in 1921.

persona brata: [His] brother's person, a play on *persona grata.*

118 Nikolai Ostrovsky (1904–1936): An uninspiring writer, ardent Communist, and author of the largely autobiographical book, *How the Steel Was Tempered* (1932–1934), subsequent editions of which were "fixed" to conform fully with all the rules of Socialist realism; used by the Communist party for the education of the young.

Viktor Kravchenko (1905–1966): Soviet official, defected to the West in the forties, author of *I Chose Freedom*, published in the United States in 1946.

Konstantin (Kostya) Simonov (1915–1979): Well-known writer, poet, and playwright; a favorite of Stalin; an officer of the Writers' Union during the forties and fifties; and editor of both *Novy Mir* and *Literaturnaya Gazeta*. "Veselovsky's parrots": Followers of Aleksandr Veselovsky (1838–1906), who pioneered a historical-comparative, anthropological approach to folklore and literature.

119 Aleksandr A. Fadeyev (1901–1956): Novelist, president of *RAPP* and later occupied various high positions in the Writers' Union; when he committed suicide, many believed it was because he had played a part in the arrest of writers for political reasons during the forties.

Rappovists: Members of *RAPP* (*Rossiyskaya assotsiatsiya proletarskikh pisatelei* (Russian Association of Proletarian Writers), disbanded in 1932; in 1934 the Writers' Union was created.

Formalists: Adherents of *formalism*, a literary trend in the 'teens, twenties, and thirties that rejected sociological, political, and philosophical criteria in criticism. They were condemned by the Soviet government.

Luga: A small city about one hundred kilometers from Leningrad.

Nikolai Zabolotsky (1903–1958): Accomplished "experimental" poet, who spent the years 1938 to 1946 in the camps.

Alexei I. Nedogonov (1914–1948): A minor yet politically "correct" poet.

120 Sarah Leander and Willi Birgel: German film actors of the thirties and forties.

"Arsenal": A British football (soccer) team.

121 "By the ribcage": Allusion to a passage from a poem by Pasternak, "*K drugu*" (To a Friend) (1931).

Article Fifty-Eight of the Criminal Code prohibited various kinds of political or group activity; its violation was cause for arrest and imprisonment.

122 *Julio Jurenito*: A 1922 novel by Ilya Ehrenburg (1891–1967), regarded as the author's masterpiece. Chapter 11, "The Teacher's prophecy concerning the destinies of the tribes of Judah," alludes to the word "no" as the Jews' favorite word and ends with a reference to "the spade in the thousand-year-old hand" that "digs graves" but also "turns the earth of the fields."

123 Olga F. Berggolts (1910–1975): A popular poet. She wrote about the siege of Leningrad.

Anton S. Makarenko (1888–1939): An educator, writer, and founder of reform schools.

"now she gets fifty rubles for him": Single mothers received fifty rubles a month from the government.

124 "Haze rye": *Derzhoko vysat*—a garbled version (with the first syllables exchanged) of *vysoko derzhat*, the first two words of the Communist slogans "*Vysoko derzhat znamya kommunizma*" (Raise high the banner of Communism) and "*Vysoko derzhat chest sovetskogo cheloveka*" (Raise high the honor of the Soviet individual).

Mikhail Kuzmin (1875–1936): Poet and prose writer associated with the Symbolist and Acmeist movements and the first openly homosexual literary figure in Russia.

125 *stukach* (knocker) and *nasedka* (setting hen): Slang terms for informer, or stool pigeon.

"era of Word and Deed": Beginning with Ivan the Terrible, the secret police, when making an arrest, used the phrase "word and deed."

tikhar (the quiet one): Another slang term for informer.

127 "workers": Undercover informers for the Ministry of State Security.

128 "organs": The Ministry of State Security, often called "our organs of security."

132 Kolyma: A peninsula in the northeastern USSR where the most terrible of the prison camps were located.

Porokhovye: A district on the outskirts of Leningrad.

"black and quiet as owls": An allusion to a poem by Blok.

The Politkatorzhan building, in the Petrograd district of Leningrad, was originally built to house revolutionaries who had spent time in Tsarist prisons or in penal servitude (*katorga*).

134 Karl Liebknecht (1871–1919): A German Social Democrat and a founder of the Communist Party of Germany who was arrested and killed along with Rosa Luxemburg on 15 January 1919.

Achilles parodies the Communist slogan "Onward to the Victory of Communism—a Bright Future for All Mankind."

Lodeinoye Pole: A small town near Leningrad.

135 Vologda: A town in northern Russia; both are places where one might be able to live unrecognized.

Tarkhany, now Lermontovo: The birthplace of the poet Mikhail Lermontov (1814–1841).

137 "I'm setting a little bird free": A line from Pushkin's poem "*Ptichka*" (Little Bird) (1823).

138 Gosnardom: *Gosudarstvenny narodny dom,* the State National Home.

140 "The roaring quieted, and I stepped onto the stage": First line in Pasternak's poem "Hamlet."

Raichikhinsk, Sredne-Belaya: Prison camps in the Far East.

"journey into the whirlwind": An allusion to Yevgeniya Ginsburg's (1904–1977) memoir *Krutoy marshrut* (Into the Whirlwind), which deals with life in the prison camps.

Kuzka's Mother

Page

143 "marshmallows": At the top of the work hierarchy among prisoners in the camps was the work supervisor; next came white-collar workers ("marshmallows")—bookkeepers and clerks and the like, who worked indoors—then ordinary workers who worked in "brigades" in the fields.

"inside the zone": The camp proper. The camp was divided into two sectors—the inner *zona*, surrounded by barbed wire, and the outer *zapretka* (forbidden zone, or no-man's land), also surrounded by barbed wire.

Khiba: really, look here (Ukrainian). Throughout the story, Nastya keeps speaking in Ukrainian.

147 Old Believers: A seventeenth-century Russian Orthodox sect who refused to accept reforms in church ritual and were widely persecuted for their conservatism.

149 Article Fifty-Eight of the Soviet Criminal Code, which covers political offenses. See the note to page 121.

Mute Phone Calls

Page

167 Nevsky Avenue: The elegant main street of Leningrad. This is also an allusion to Gogol's *Nevsky Avenue* (1834), a story that plays on the imaginary and real in an eerie setting in Petersburg.

169 *"versts"*: A verst is a unit of measurement equal to about two-thirds of a mile.

170 The Strelka: A point on the Vasilievsky Island, a borough of Leningrad.

171 I. A. Krylov (1769–1844): A famous writer of fables.

173 *Kolenval:* A brand of cheap vodka.

174 "There's no happiness . . .": The fifth line of Pushkin's famous "Pora, moy drug, pora! . . ." (It's time, my friend, it's time! . . .) (1834).

177 Novosibirsk: A city in western Siberia.
    Petrovsk, now Prokopiyevsk: A town east of Moscow, in the Urals.

182 M. L. Lozinsky (1886–1955): A well-known translator.

184 Raikin: A popular comedian.

Umbria's Tender Haze

Page

215 "Umbria's tender haze": The second line of Aleksandr A. Blok's (1880–1921) famous poem *"Blagoveshchenye"* (Annunciation) (1910) in the cycle of poems *"Italyanskie stikhi"* (Italian Verses) (1909–1914).

218 *Nevsky Avenue:* See the note to page 167.

219 "The dark-faced angel . . .": The two stanzas quoted are the fifth and sixth from "Annunciation."

220 "the country he was born in": An echo of Pushkin's lines in *Eugene Onegin* in which he alludes to his banishment from St. Petersburg (here Leningrad).

222 Iosif A. Brodsky (1940–): Poet and critic, born and raised in Leningrad, arrested in the 1960s for "parasitism," expelled in 1972, emigrated to the United States, lives in New York. He won the Nobel Prize in Literature in 1987.
    Lyubov Dmitriyevna: Blok's wife.
    L. A. Delmas: An opera singer; inspired Blok's "Carmen" cycle of poems.

223 Nadezhda A. Pavlovich: Poet, follower of Blok, author of reminiscences about him.
    Afanasy A. Fet (1820–1892): Famous lyric poet.

N. S. Gumilev (1886–1921, executed): Acmeist poet and critic, married for several years to Anna Akhmatova.

224 Sergei M. (Seryozha) Solovyov (1885–1942): Poet, theologian, nephew of well-known philosopher Vladimir Solovyov, second cousin to Blok.
"Since childhood—these visions and dreams . . .": First line of "Annunciation."

226 Provisional Government: Established in March 1917, overthrown in November 1917 by the Bolsheviks.

227 "Over There": The USSR. The phrase "that flabby face" refers to Brezhnev.
S. G. Nechayev (1846–1882): Leader of a radical group, a disciple of the anarchist Bakunin, organizer of the "Society of National Retribution," tried for murder, died in prison.
"All that is transient, and that is frail . . .": First line from Blok's poem "Ravenna" in the cycle "Italian Verses."